THE ACHIEVEMENT GAP IN READING

In this volume prominent scholars, experts in their respective fields and highly skilled in the research they conduct, address educational and reading research from varied perspectives and address what it will take to close the achievement gap—with specific attention to reading. The achievement gap is redefined as a level at which all groups can compete economically in our society and have the literacy tools and habits needed for a good life.

Bringing valuable theoretical frameworks and in-depth analytical approaches to interpretation of data, the contributors examine factors that contribute to student achievement inside the school but which are also heavily influenced by out-of-school factors—such as poverty and economics, ethnicity and culture, family and community stratifications, and approaches to measurement of achievement. These out-of-school factors present possibilities for new policies and practice. The overarching theme is that achievement gaps in reading are complex and that multiple perspectives are necessary to address the problem. The breadth and depth of perspectives and content in this volume and its conceptualization of the achievement gap are a significant contribution to the field.

Rosalind Horowitz is Professor, Discourse and Literacy Studies, Departments of Interdisciplinary Learning and Teaching and Educational Psychology, College of Education and Human Development, The University of Texas—San Antonio, USA.

S. Jay Samuels is Professor Emeritus, Department of Educational Psychology, College of Education and Human Development, The University of Minnesota—Twin Cities, USA.

THE ACHIEVEMENT GAP IN READING

Complex Causes, Persistent Issues, Possible Solutions

Edited by
Rosalind Horowitz
S. Jay Samuels

Routledge
Taylor & Francis Group

NEW YORK AND LONDON

First published 2017
by Routledge
711 Third Avenue, New York, NY 10017

and by Routledge
2 Park Square, Milton Park, Abingdon, Oxon, OX14 4RN

Routledge is an imprint of the Taylor & Francis Group, an informa business

Library of Congress Cataloguing in Publication Data
A catalog record for this book has been requested

ISBN: 978-1-138-01878-5 (hbk)
ISBN: 978-1-138-01879-2 (pbk)
ISBN: 978-1-315-77952-2 (ebk)

Typeset in Bembo
by diacriTech, Chennai

Dedication

In Memory of My Beloved Brother
Searle Seymour Horowitz
(1947–1987)
Who Believed in the Creation of Social Justice for All
Rosalind Horowitz

And

In Honor of Those Who Overcame and
Who Continue to Overcome Obstacles in Achievement
Rosalind Horowitz and S. Jay Samuels

CONTENTS

PREFACE

This book is designed to discuss why we have been ineffective in closing the achievement gap in reading. It describes the complex causes and persistent issues such as the lack of opportunity for many groups, but offers hope for change. It offers suggestions for how we might proceed in practice and policy. It argues that all students be given the opportunity to reach a level of reading proficiency and achievement that allows for continued advancement in schooling, and for students to enter and grow in the work world and lead a good and thoughtful life in the 21st century. This book is unique in that it is the first full-length volume to address the achievement gap with attention specifically to reading and reading research. The book proceeds as follows: We, first, provide research that addresses poverty and the populations most subject to poverty in the United States—Latino/a American, African American, and Native American groups. Second, authors address ways of closing the gap that characterize economics, language and discourse development, and motivational, social, and cultural factors—factors outside the school and inside the school. This book addresses national and international assessments and measures of reading proficiency and summer reading achievement loss, and provides a historical review of federal policy intended to close gaps. Third, some of the perspectives presented have been included in journals, books, and national or international reports, but they have not been assembled in one single source. By bringing these approaches together in one volume, we provide a unified analysis for implementing policy changes that hold promise for advancing reading achievement. This will also bring what is an extremely complex problem to greater clarity. The last chapter provides a synthesis of commonalities but also contradictions across chapters. It must be recognized that reading is the foundation of learning and thinking. It is vital to all subject areas offered in schools, and to the human development of consciousness about life—and of reasoning. It is also vital to the future and survival of a democracy.

INTENDED AUDIENCE

There are several audiences for this volume. It is essential reading for graduate students, who may include literacy coaches, teachers of reading, principals, supervisors, curriculum leadership, and school district administrators, researchers, and policy makers at the state and federal level. This book also might very well be used in a graduate course specifically designed to address the gaps in reading achievement or other achievements in schools across the United States. In addition, teachers in elementary and secondary classrooms—including across disciplines—have heard over the years about the achievement gap, and a book on this topic could clarify and update their knowledge about what may be some of the precursors of achievement gaps and how we might go about raising achievement in reading, which also will bear on achievement in other disciplines offered in schools.

ABOUT THE EDITORS

Each editor brings unique strengths to this project from assignments associated with national education research-oriented groups, as well as work with urban schools and ethnic and cross-cultural populations.

Rosalind Horowitz has been a professor for 36 years at The University of Texas—San Antonio, Hispanic-Serving Institution (HSI), one of the nation's leading Hispanic-Serving Institutions (HSI) where more than half of the students are first generation to pursue higher education. Horowitz was selected by the National Academy of Education as a Spencer Fellow, one of five, from 200 international applicants. She received the *Distinguished Alumni Award* from The University of Minnesota, from among 50,000 graduates, as part of their Centennial Celebration *Inspiring Minds for a Century, 1905–2005*. Horowitz served as Research Coordinator, Office of the Dean, College of Education and Human Development at the University of Minnesota and as Research Coordinator for the College of Social and Behavioral Sciences, at The University of Texas at San Antonio. She was selected as a Visiting Scholar by the University of Iowa for research in Russia and the Ukraine; has served as a Visiting Professor at The University of Toronto, Ontario Institute for Studies in Education (OISE) in Applied Psychology and Human Development; served as a contributor to the Shalom Hartman Institute of Text Study, Jerusalem, Israel; and has been an invited lecturer in a number of countries throughout the world, most recently Mexico and Latin America. Horowitz' research has addressed how speech is central to the development of the reading, writing and the literate mind; the role of dialogue in the understanding of academic and argumentation texts; and world-wide assessments and comparisons of adolescent literacy. Horowitz was recently honored by the American Educational Research Association for her volume *Talking Texts: How speech and writing interact in school learning* published by Routledge/Taylor & Francis.

S. Jay Samuels served as a faculty member at The University of Minnesota Twin Cities campus for over 40 years and is knowledgeable about Native American populations and the Hmong, an Asian American group in Minnesota and their difficulties in reading achievement. Samuels has contributed to numerous national reading research efforts. He was one of eight scientists selected from 300 nominees to serve on *The National Reading Panel* to address the *No Child Left Behind Legislation* and summarize scientific evidence related to reading achievement. Samuels received the *Wm. S. Gray Citation of Merit* from the International Reading Association (IRA), the highest research award given by IRA (now LRA). He is most known for the LaBerge and Samuels Theory of Automaticity, which as of this writing has received over 4,000 citations, and for his method of repeated reading in the development of fluency, which has been used throughout the world to increase comprehension. Samuels coedited, with Alan Farstrup, several volumes of *What Research Has to Say about Reading*. He is also known for his research on reading comprehension, sustained and selective attention in reading and the role of pictures in reading comprehension. Horowitz coedited *Comprehending Oral and Written Language* with Samuels; this work has been selected by Brill Publishers, the United Kingdom, for publication for posterity.

Each editor has served on editorial boards of prestigious psychological, cultural, linguistic, and literacy research journals. Each has won outstanding teaching awards at their respective institutions.

Their collaboration over the years has strengthened the research of each and contributed to the ideas expressed in this volume for equal and just opportunity for all Americans.

ACKNOWLEDGMENTS

We honor and thank our contributors to this volume, many of whom have devoted a half a century, a lifetime, to the pursuit of equity, the creation of opportunity, and excellence in student achievement in the reading act and literacy education of our nation.

In particular, Edmund Gordon dedicated 65 years to how to best create access, opportunities, and achievement for *all* human beings in our schools. He has served in a number of prestigious roles in education research organizations including as a member and leader of proceedings of The National Academy of Education.

Alan Farstrup, who contributed to the history of educational reform in this volume, passed on during the final production stages of the book. His faithful leadership and dedication to education and research through his work as Executive Director of the International Reading Association brought reading teachers and administrators together to inaugurate change and will be remembered. Terrance Paul, who spent many years studying parent–child interaction, also passed on. His contributions to the study of dialogue and the mechanics of data collection through new technology will make a difference in future family discourse research.

Faculty of The University of Minnesota—Twin Cities passionately pursued the study of educational reform, educational psychology, and reading and writing in literacy development. They, too, influenced our intellectual pursuits, including Gene L. Piché, Michael Graves, William Bart, and Albert Yonas, and we warmly remember Darrell R. Lewis and Theodore E. Kellogg and their work in the international economics of education and higher education respectively.

Students at The University of Texas—San Antonio gave time, without hesitation and with joy, to the production of this book, intuitively aware of the importance of our efforts. We thank Traci Kelley for her exceptional editorial work and organizational skills that made a world of difference in the production of this volume. Others who contributed to the details of this work were Gabrielle Cortez, Loren Torres-Cruz, Lisa Griffith, Jennifer Hooper, Kelly Hoy, Melba Ochoa, and Mingxia Zhi.

Colleagues at The University of Texas—San Antonio also treasured and have advanced the theme of this volume. These include Dewey Davis, whose memory is an inspiration, and who was a dear colleague and fervent in his fight for excellence, as well as faculty in the Department of Interdisciplinary Learning and Teaching, Department of Educational Psychology, and in the Department of Bicultural-Bilingual Studies.

Nancy Nelson, The University of North Texas, encouraged thinking about the meaning of literacy in terms beyond standards to the humane and the unique, creative expression of individuals through the local and global.

Ghassem Shalchi, a loyal friend, offered support and trust in this work. His interest always gave strength and energy to the project.

Naomi Silverman, our editor at Routledge/Taylor and Francis, was extraordinary. She showed unyielding faith. The consummate editor, with years of expertise, she understood the complexities of the project, offered astute editorial advise, and was an exceptional editor and human being who knew just what to suggest and when. This project reached fruition because of her support and recognition of the importance of this endeavor for the advancement of excellence in American education.

LIST OF CONTRIBUTORS

Richard L. Allington
Professor and Past President, Literacy Research Association
Department of Theory & Practice in Teacher Education
College of Education, Health, and Human Sciences
The University of Tennessee
Knoxville, Tennessee USA

Kim Atwill
Senior Researcher
Griffin Center for Inspired Instruction
Vancouver, Washington USA

David C. Berliner
Past President, American Educational Research Association
Regents' Professor Emeritus
Mary Lou Foulton Teachers College
Arizona State University
Tempe, Arizona USA

Jay S. Blanchard
Professor Emeritus
Educational Psychology
Division of Educational Leadership and Innovation
College of Education
Arizona State University
Tempe, Arizona USA

Sam David
Doctoral student, Language, Literature and Culture
Teacher, at New York City Department of Education
Vanderbilt University
Nashville, Tennessee USA

Keenan Fagan
Doctoral Student, Learning, Teaching, and Diversity
Research Fellow, Peabody College
College of Education and Human Development
Vanderbilt University
Nashville, Tennessee USA

Alan Farstrup
Former Executive Director of the International Reading Association
Newark, Delaware USA

Jill Gilkerson
Director, Child Language Research
LENA Research Foundation
Boulder, Colorado USA

Mark Gonzales
Assistant Professor
Project PROPEL
Peabody College
College of Education and Human Development
Nashville, Tennessee USA

Edmund W. Gordon
John M. Musser Professor of Psychology Emeritus
Yale University
New Haven, Connecticut USA
and
Richard March Hoe Professor of Psychology and Education Emeritus
Teachers College, Columbia University
New York, New York USA

John T. Guthrie
Professor Emeritus
College of Education
University of Maryland
College Park, Maryland USA

Michael Harwell
Department of Educational Psychology
College of Education and Human Development
The University of Minnesota—Twin Cities
Minneapolis and St. Paul, Minnesota, USA

Paola C. Heincke
Senior Research Project Manager
Educational Testing Service
Princeton, New Jersey USA

Rosalind Horowitz
Professor
Discourse and Literacy Studies
Departments of Interdisciplinary Learning and Teaching
and Educational Psychology
College of Education and Human Development
The University of Texas—San Antonio
San Antonio, Texas USA

Robert Jiménez
Professor
Department of Teaching and Learning
Peabody College
College of Education and Human Development
Vanderbilt University
Nashville, Tennessee USA

Richard Long
Executive Director
Learning First Alliance
Alexandria, Virginia USA

Anne McGill-Franzen
Professor and Director, Reading Center
Department of Theory & Practice in Teacher Education
College of Education, Health, and Human Sciences
The University of Tennessee
Knoxville, Tennessee USA

Angela McRae
STEM Coordinator
Catholic University of America
Washington, DC USA

Mark Pacheco
Assistant Professor of Bilingual/Bicultural Education
College of Education
Illinois State University
Normal, Illinois USA

Terrance D. Paul
Chairman
LENA Research Foundation
Boulder, Colorado USA

Lisa Pray
Associate Professor of the Practice
Peabody College
Department of Teaching and Learning
College of Education and Human Development
Nashville, Tennessee USA

Victoria J. Risko
Professor Emerita and
Past President, International Reading Association
Department of Teaching and Learning
Vanderbilt University
Nashville, Tennessee USA

S. Jay Samuels
Professor Emeritus
Department of Educational Psychology
College of Education and Human Development
The University of Minnesota—Twin Cities
Minneapolis, Minnesota USA

1

THE ACHIEVEMENT GAP IN READING

Unique Historical and Future Perspectives

Rosalind Horowitz and S. Jay Samuels

In this introductory chapter we identify what is unique about this volume in relation to other research and discussions of the achievement gap in reading in schools across the United States. Other books take a broader perspective trying to address all subject areas of schooling in which there has been a gap in achievement, without presenting in detail discrepancies in achievement by students in one content field over another—or in the case of beginning versus more advanced literacy required for content fields in the academic or work world. This extremely broad perspective prevents the discussion from bringing a change to practice. For example, among the Hmong community in Minnesota there are students who are successful in mathematics and are able to orally read, showing they have no reading problems. But on tests on reading comprehension, they show below satisfactory performance. As second-language learners, they may show vocabulary limitations that in turn restrict their reading but not their mathematics performance.

In this introduction, we call attention to specific contributions in Parts I through IV of this volume, characterizing race and ethnic group demographics and economics that contribute to reading achievement or its limitations; approaches to the achievement gap in reading based on quality of life and health; and the complexities of conceptualizing and assessing, quantitatively and qualitatively, reading achievements related to academic growth. Finally, we discuss the book's suggestions for solutions to achievement gaps, prepared by each of the contributors, by way of what we term *spotlight recommendations*. We isolate the historical efforts in the United States that have proven ineffective or made a long-term difference and those we argue are likely, with time and patience, to continue to make a difference in furthering student reading performances and, in turn, academic achievements.

We will also in this introduction present the following principles based on our review of the literature at-large and the contributions in this volume:

1. The problem of the achievement gap is far more complex than some scholarly articles and federal efforts, including *No Child Left Behind* (NCLB) legislation, or the media have led researchers, teachers, and the public to believe. There is *not one* achievement gap but multiple gaps. Also, in the area of reading, there is *not* one achievement gap.

   While we refer to the achievement gap, as many of the contributors to this volume do, the reader of this book should keep in mind, as one moves through the chapters, that there are multiple disparities and gaps. Further, the achievement gaps that exist in reading cannot be resolved by one solution but will require multiple perspectives and multiple groups and individuals who collaboratively tackle what must be recognized, at the very onset, as very complex problems. This book is intended to move us in the direction of better understanding the "achievement gap in reading" and alternative solutions that will benefit not simply single schools, but large numbers of schools and school districts across America, thereby producing vision and change at a truly national level.

2. There are differences *within* and *across* groups of African Americans, Latinos, Native Americans, and Asian Americans that warrant research and unique understandings, if there are to be solutions for improving reading in America. This is often overlooked. In many research reports and articles a given group is treated as homogeneous rather than defined precisely bypsychological-motivational, social-cultural, and socio-economic terms that will advance knowledge and, in turn, inform solutions. The federal government, for instance, uses the term *Hispanic* to include multiple groups—Mexican American, Latin American, Cuban, Puerto Rican, those from Spain, and other Spanish-speaking locations worldwide, yet there is much psychological, cultural, and linguistic variation across and within these groups that contribute to learning beliefs and habits, reading performances, and reading outcomes from text sources. Finally, the geographic spaces within which these groups reside, or move, the cultures of the schools that they attend, those social groups with whom they come in daily contact, and the intergenerational beliefs transmitted about reading as an activity may be contributors to achievement, or gaps, in reading. Several years ago, Ralph Tyler pointed out, in a face-to-face interview, that not only families and schools, but the school *neighborhood* in which learners reside has a tremendous influence on cultural groups and the schooling individuals receive within these groups (Horowitz, 1995).

3. The oral language experiences and linguistic opportunities students have are significant precursors to as well as contributing factors during reading processes. There is evidence that there are differences in the forms and functions of language and discourse exposure that children have from different cultural, social, ethnic, racial or economic groups. This can be language exposure from sheer

everyday talk in the home with parents, siblings, and extended family members, with peer groups, or interaction with/about text sources. There are commu- nication opportunities available in the home, through media resources—cell phones, computer chats, text messaging—and resources in libraries or book- stores that are accessible for book reading or reading with a mouse and com- puter technology. In many regards, the United States is a rich nation given its use of technology, but these technologies are not available to all. They are present within some neighborhoods and economic groups but not others.

4.   The life experiences of students today are increasingly different from those of the past few decades. There are rapid changes in low-performing populations due to family restructuring and family mobility. This variance in health and activity outside of school interfaces with variations in school cultures and institutional requirements. Not all students come prepared to learn within the institutional setting nor do all students receive equal intellectual nour- ishment once they enter our nation's schools. Precursors to learning—and reading—such as physical and psychological health, use of selective attention, facility in listening comprehension, self-discipline, consistent school atten- dance, elements of good character, and work habits associated with learning in schools need our study and support as these develop within families and community settings.

5.   Our definition of "reading" has broadened exponentially. We are adding critical, analytical, interpretive, multi-source, and multi-modal thinking pro- cesses to our study of decoding, word recognition, and literal reading. We are engaged in a reading that incorporates continuous, extended discourses, and non-continuous discourse elements such as graphs, charts, and tables, moving beyond books to iPhones and computer processing, and the understanding of complex language such as argumentation and persuasion, in more than one language and world region. There are also differences in reading styles—that reflect different thinking styles, e.g., fast (intuitive and emotional) and slow (more deliberate and logical)—that are needed by the learner in different con- tent fields (Kahneman, 2011; Newkirk, 2012). We expect that our students will perform a range of applied reading tasks as well, yet to be explicitly defined in the research, that will be needed for varied facets of 21st-century life.

6.   Educational reform has included comprehensive, broad-based federal initia- tives. As Vinovskis (2009) and other distinguished federal policy analysts con- vey, not enough attention has been given by the federal or state governments to effectively communicate these broad initiatives to ensure policy reform, adequate implementation into school-level practices, and rigorous evaluation. McDonnell and Weatherford (2016) use the *Common Core Standards* (2010) as an example to argue that education researchers need to pay as much attention to policy implementations as other phases of research. Moreover, shifts in federal initiatives are rampant and consequently prevent innovative initiatives from taking hold and being useful (see Long & Farstrup, 2017, in this volume).

7. On the other hand, in addition to these broad-based plans for reform, we have numerous special cases of schools and school districts in the United States that have been successful in raising test scores and academic achievement. Baskin Elementary in San Antonio, Texas, eliminated the achievement gap in passing rates for African Americans and Latinos within four years. In Houston, Peck Elementary passing rates for Latino students were raised within four years. The KIPP Academy in the Bronx, New York performed highly in reading in grades 5 through 9 serving Latino and African Americans. But little is known about what commonalities extend across such single groups and the individual school district success stories highlighted in the media that might inform a national policy (Daly & Finnigan, 2016).

All of these themes are captured within the chapters that follow with suggestions for resolution.

This Book, Persistent Problems, and Their Historical Background

For almost a half of a century, the federal government has tried valiantly to close what has been referred to as the achievement gap. The "gap" that we are referring to represents the differences in academic achievement that exist among groups such as Latino/a Americans, African Americans, Native Americans, Asian Americans—and European Americans. In addition, the gap has referred to the significantly increasing, very startling economic inequality and poverty that plagues and persists in American educational opportunities—and achievements. The achievement gap has also referred to the gap that exists for children where the language and discourse of the home is other than the English and discourses required for schooling and academic accomplishments. Despite the best efforts of the federal government to close the gap over so many years, the goal has remained elusive (Hoynes, Page & Stevens, 2006).

One effort to close the gap has been the *No Child Left Behind* (NCLB) legislation and related endeavors. NCLB spurred much commentary about the achievement gap, but a look at its history shows this effort did not represent solutions to a new problem, nor was it the first time the government had attempted to close what has been summarized under the one concept of an achievement gap. There are multiple strings of governmental reports and initiatives that, simply put, failed in bringing about significant change for those desperately in need of a better education and life in a complex world.

Nearly 35 years ago, in 1983, *A Nation at Risk* awakened and alerted us to the lack of achievement of students in United States schools. Turning to research in the field of reading, *The National Reading Panel*, in 2000, summarized scientific research on the teaching of reading with the specific intent that this research would help guide the nation in improving the reading performance of *all* children—whatever their race, culture, and income level. In 2005, the National

Assessment of Educational Progress (NAEP) tests revealed that only about six percent of English language learners in the United States were proficient in reading at the fourth, eighth, and twelfth grades. Robert Balfanz and colleagues (2007) presented alarming data indicating that over half of the population in urban schools did not graduate from high school. Further, ninth grade suspensions increased the likelihood of a student not graduating high school (Balfnaz et al., 2007). However, the *Every Student Succeeds Act* (ESSA) website in 2016 argued that there are not only fewer dropouts than ever, but there more students graduating from high school, and they are going on to enter and complete higher education, more so than ever before! President Barack Obama advertised ESSA on the same website, "With this bill [ESSA], we reaffirm that fundamental ideal—that every child, regardless of race, income, background, the zip code where they live, deserves the chance to make of their lives what they will." Finally, given this proclamation, an excessively long history of reports, and recent follow-up, we as editors of this volume seek to ask new questions based on recent research and policy in order to provide better answers.

Exactly why the goal of closing the achievement gap has been unfulfilled in the United States has remained unclear. There is without doubt a lack of clarity in the best approaches to be used and outcomes to be expected (see Foorman, Kalinowski, & Sexton, 2007; Gamoran, 2007; Howard, 2010; Noguera & Wing, 2006; Sadovnik et al., 2008). Many have argued that the methods used to enforce standards and to repeatedly test and classify readers in order to close the gap have been counterproductive.

First, our concern in this volume is that there has not been a close examination of the achievement gap—in reading—in one volume—one that would allow for close analysis of the most fundamental activity underpinning all learning and reasoning and that would benefit schooling in the 21st century. This is also the practice which sets the foundation and processes for higher order thinking that gives students the tools to advance confidently in their education. As there have been efforts to bring *equality* of opportunity for reading development, there also have been, concurrently, efforts to establish *excellence* to school reading, with these sometimes operating at cross-purposes in elementary, secondary schools, and also, of late, institutions of higher education.

Second, when we refer to "closing the achievement gap in reading," the goal that we are addressing is for *all* children, adolescents and youth, regardless of race, parental income level, ethnicity, or gender, to become competent and proficient in reading. Of course, mastery of reading is part of the larger goal of closing an achievement gap. Further, the goal is for all groups to compete economically in our society and have the literacy tools and related intellectual skills, motivations, and habits needed for advancing in content fields and work opportunities.

Even if the education system improves dramatically, we will not be able to educate in such a way that everyone will desire or be suitable for the most advanced programs of study in some fields. However, we believe that there is no reason why we cannot educate everyone so that all of our groups that previously have been left behind will be able to participate successfully in our society. In this way, the gap is redefined as a level at which all groups can compete economically in our society and have the literacy tools needed for building a good and thoughtful life in the 21st century.

The fact that the gap has not closed does not mean that there has been a complete failure in progress of any kind. Some groups have been successful in increasing the number of students who graduate high school and attend college. But despite these gains, and there have been gains, the stark differences in reading achievement among particular groups remain visible—on national testing, class-room test scores, courses assigned and selected, teacher-based evaluations, and in beginning and later developing reading processes and competencies.

The Solutions are Identifiable but Complex

The questions that we are asking about a national literacy in the United States have not been resolved. The answers provided in this volume, we believe, are identifiable and practical. The chapters in this volume offer policy makers and researchers avenues for clear reasoning and the possibility of new practices. The issues we address are important for teachers on the front lines.

In 1965, Lyndon B. Johnson signed the *Elementary and Secondary Education Act* to ensure success and graduation of all students. At this time, the *Head Start Program* was initiated. Its goal was to assist children who came from backgrounds where funds, parenting, and health care were lacking. Head Start was invented to help children who were born into poverty become familiar with the ideas and routines of school at a young age. However, being born into an impoverished society, as was the case of children who attended Head Start, meant that they were born at a disadvantage in relation to their peers from more affluent homes in resources and school-related knowledge. At the same time, *The Coleman Report* (Coleman et al., 1966), one of the largest studies ever undertaken in American history, argued that (a) the quality of the student body of a school and (b) teacher expectations were the significant factors in influencing achievement for non-dominant students. But the busing of students that followed did not reduce the achievement gap. Subsequently, Borman and Dowling (2010) conducted a partial re-analysis of reading achievement data originally collected by Coleman. Borman and Dolman showed a substantial difference in how well schools meet the needs of different populations, consistent with Coleman's work, but also argued for social context as a predictor in achievement. Critical comments of Borman and Dolman's work by Dominigue et al. (2011) proposed that the effects of schools on reading and their ability to overcome reading achievement gaps may be more bound by the social contexts and the cultures of the neighborhoods in which these schools exist and students live. These social factors must be addressed and are beginning to receive attention in the new century in conjunction with the structure of schools and the teaching community.

Some have taken the unpopular position that the gap has not closed because our society has not really wanted to close the gap. The argument given is that by not closing the gap, we have a population that we can justify paying less money for the work they do. A counter-position that represents what most educators believe is that given the ideals of a democratic society in which the rewards of that society are based on what one can contribute to society, all groups deserve the opportunity to have an excellent education. Education is viewed as a key factor in determining what a person can do to contribute to American society. Education is also the means for a stable and physically active life.

Educators today are trying to help *all* children in the United States become proficient in reading in order to close academic achievement gaps, but at the present time we do not have one single book that focuses on this problem and the problem of achieving not only beginning reading but advancing to the higher level of literacy needed for today's rapidly changing, technologically driven, complex society.

In order to help educators close the gap in reading, we have brought together a group of prominent scholars, experts in their respective fields and highly skilled in the research they conduct. These include senior scholars, some who have worked throughout their lifetime, for over 50 years, in educational research, half a century, to address the problems we describe, and, thereby, who bring years of writing, speaking, and wisdom to their thinking to solve the problem at hand. They work in very diverse settings and address educational and reading research with exceptional talent from varied perspectives. They share with us, in this volume, what in their learned opinion, based on research, it will take to close the achievement gap—with attention to reading. One concluding chapter will address a history of federal efforts to close achievement gaps by experts who have regularly communicated with federal leaders determining school policy. The editors provide a last chapter in the present book that will synthesize these recommendations to demonstrate common threads or consistent arguments that run through these scholarly reports of past and recent research.

As we view the achievement gap by grade level, there is agreement, from scientific data, but also historical, ethnographic, or personal accounts, that demonstrate that gaps, and reading gaps in particular, widen with time. However, there have been few *longitudinal* studies that follow the same students over several years to determine what influences the gap in reading per se as students move across grades and school reading assignments nationally or even in international locations (see recent longitudinal work by Kieffer, 2011, and Horowitz's discussion of international PISA data, and limits of longitudinal data, 2017, in this volume). Further, as conveyed by some National Academy of Education member reflections, research produced over the past 50 years may not have used the most telling designs and measures or may not be ready for implementing changes inside or outside of schooling (Feuer, Berman, & Atkinson, 2015).

Overview

Part I. Cases of Specific Demographics and Economics

Chapter 2, Poverty's Powerful Effects on Reading Achievement and Achievement Gap by David Berliner, begins this volume. He addresses head-on factors associated with poverty, often overlooked by researchers and policy makers, yet primary in limiting student achievement. Berliner presents two issues. First, he focuses on the distinction between reading performance test scores at an individual level and mean scores for whole classrooms and aggregated data. Secondly, he notes poverty is only "modestly related" to achievement scores, through other factors. Research argues "for early reading skill development as the most important ... of the entering characteristics a student brings to school" (Berliner, 2017, in this volume).

He argues that while an outstanding teacher may have tremendous influence on individual student accomplishments inside school and life outside of school, there is more to be considered beyond teachers in ameliorating or at least reducing group achievement gaps! For one, he reviews international research that suggests that reading, math, and science scores can be elevated when poor children do *not* attend classes with large numbers of other poor children. Rather, their experiences in classrooms with successful, high performing learners, likely to serve as positive learning models, will elevate the economically poor child's school performance and oftentimes their life opportunities (see Berliner, 2017, this volume; 2012). Berliner contends that our poorest children go to school with other poor children, due to increasing segregation in American schools. San Antonio, Texas schools are a confirmation of this proposition—as there are examples of poverty schools throughout the 17 school districts where 99 percent of the students are Hispanic. In these schools, there are buildings that only recently have installed air-conditioning units, lunches have not been nutritiously balanced, and space/resources for student outdoor or indoor social activities are limited. As we read Berliner's chapter, we are confronted with how poverty is related to other life quality out-of-school problems that inhibit or obstruct school learning. Demographics do matter. Berliner alerts us that when living in poor neighborhoods, children are subject to poor housing, greater rates of illness, high crime, mental health issues, and physical health issues such as premature births, low birth weights, unclean facilities, and incapacitating illnesses. Relatedly, there is less food and less sleep. Considering the lives of those in such poor neighborhoods presents a heart-wrenching, painstaking picture of impediments faced by poor children in America, and in other nations throughout the world as well, which block education and possible opportunities in life on a daily basis.

Data from the Program for International Student Assessments (PISA), Trends in International Mathematics and Science Study (TIMSS), and the National Assessment for Educational Progress (NAEP) make the case that the poverty/achievement relationship is present in all countries but is greater in its effects when income inequality is worst, as it is in the United States compared with other wealthy nations. In fact, Berliner emphasizes that the highest level of childhood poverty among the wealthy nations of the world is found here in our United States. Furthermore, Berliner contends that the policies that it has adopted for reducing the achievement gap are exactly those *not* recommended by the Organization for Economic Cooperation and Development (OECD) for improving national educational systems.

In sum, Berliner argues that the policy environment has done little to reduce the large achievement gaps in the United States. He argues the growth in data collection demonstrates how our nation switched its educational policies from caring about equal educational opportunity, a concern about the inputs to the schools and the lives of the children outside of school, to focus instead on the achievement gap, with attention to output such as standardized testing, an approach to education of its poor and its wealthiest students that is counterproductive to the American dream of equality and equity.

In Chapter 3, Creating Responsive Teachers of Hispanic and Bilingual Students Learning English, Robert Jiménez and coauthors Sam David, Mark Pacheco, Victoria Risko, Lisa Pray, Keenan Fagan, and Mark Gonzales are convinced that a more radical approach than traditionally has been applied is necessary to close the achievement gap and that the new approach must build on the cultural and linguistic strengths of the students learning English. Their chapter addresses teacher education practices with Hispanic students. Sociocultural theorists contend, as do applied linguists, developmental psychologists, and other disciplines, that language is a key tool for mediating and accelerating learning. They agree. Just as certain linguistic tools make it possible for mono-lingual learners to extend their conceptual reach, so too can bilingualism offer strengths that provide a variety of hitherto unrecognized cognitive resources. In this chapter, the authors develop the notion that bilingualism can, under the right conditions, facilitate comprehension and reduce the achievement gap. Research has shown that bilinguals, for example, activate both of their languages as they take in linguistic input. The activation of two languages during reading, especially if meta-linguistic and metacognitive prompting are involved, may stimulate more effective access to prior knowledge of the sort needed for comprehension, learning, and achievement. It can be, in other words, enriching. Chapter 3 concentrates specifically on students in the intermediate (4, 5, 6) to middle-school grades (5, 6, 7), namely pre-adolescents who are able to converse fluently in a language other than English and use this language with family and friends. The chapter considers those students who are growing in English skill, but not yet achieving in English reading comprehension. What is important is these students are capable of high achievement—which they have not yet attained in English reading due to immigration, prior schooling, or lack of quality instruction.

Jiménez and colleagues consider teacher education and the need for teacher expertise with cultural and linguistic knowledge of the populations that they teach. Further, today's teachers must teach English *and* content at the same time, an arduous task and one for which most teachers are not professionally prepared. Particularly important are dispositions of teachers, the beliefs, attitudes, and expectations that teachers hold for students from culturally different backgrounds. Validation of student's language, culture, and potential for learning is described by way of a translation method for guiding vocabulary knowledge. Jiménez suggests English language learners can learn to use their first language for academic purposes, for accessing prior knowledge and learning new words and concepts. Recommendations posed for teacher training include experiences with learning a new language, travel abroad, and interacting with others using the acquired language in ways that will benefit classroom instruction.

Chapter 4, Motivating and Instructing African American Students in Classrooms, by John Guthrie and Angela McRae, examines African American student motivations for reading and effective classroom supports for reading engagement. They argue that reading is *the* determining factor in academic achievement.

They report on the motivation qualities of high achieving African Americans who obtain standardized test scores at the same level as high achieving European Americans. An abundance of empirical studies from grades 3 to 12 show that highly achieving African American students are *behaviorally engaged* in school and reading. These students express dedication through good work habits of *effort, time, and persistence* in school reading, which generates high achievement. Guthrie and McRae argue for homework completion, class attendance, and participation. These habits will be best sustained when students possess clear goals and aspirations, e.g., for higher education. Lower achieving African American students are less dedicated. They find this factor is more significant for African American than European American students.

Guthrie and McRae argue that African American student dedication to reading depends on placing a high value on reading which in turn fosters engagement in reading. Namely, they must believe that reading is important and value it not only for now but their lives in the future. Guthrie and McRae point to research that shows low achieving African American adolescent students devalue reading and education *more* than low achieving European American students. Guthrie and McRae's five-year research program with 1,200 seventh grade students showed two instructional practices, whereby the teacher assures relevance of reading and emphasizes the importance of reading, can increase student behavioral engagement and the dedication of African American students.

Guthrie and McRae report examples of classroom practices that emphasize cultural relevance. They propose *Concept-Oriented Reading Instruction* (CORI) for teaching low-achieving African American students to attain the reading motivation, engagement, and expertise of their higher achieving peers. This is accomplished through building relevance into activities, choice, success in matching student to text, collaboration, and big idea thematic units. Finally, they advocate for a "culturally receptive educational science," that is, incorporating culturally relevant content and social interaction.

In Chapter 5, Closing the Reading Achievement Gaps for Indigenous Children, Jay S. Blanchard and Kim Atwill present a much-needed chapter on Native American children's achievements in reading. Clearly, families, schools, teachers, and child friendships all are influential, in different ways, in shaping reading. Understanding how each of these contributes to reading achievement and the achievement gap has been the subject of study for quite some time—and much is known. *Unfortunately, this is not true for Native Americans.*

Until the end of the last century, there was little empirical research about how families, schools, teachers, and children contribute to reading achievement and the achievement gap for Native American children. However, that situation has slowly begun to change. The seminal 2005 study *Status and Trends in the Education of American Indians and Alaska Natives* from the IES, NCES, and US Department of Education brought important data to the foreground. Since that time, interest about the achievement gap has increased as noted in the 2007 and the 2009 *National Indian Education Study.* Yet, despite this interest, empirical research has only slowly begun to appear. *The National Literacy Panel on Language Minority Children and Youth* (2006) shows scant attention is paid to Native American children.

The Blanchard and Atwill chapter examines, first, the relationship between school readiness and reading achievement. Second, they discuss how the school readiness relationship to Indigenous children and their families should be carefully developed to incorporate scientifically based programs that include the language and cultural practices, beliefs and values. Third, the high-quality Indigenous education programs examined include Native American Indian teachers and coaches, native language speakers, continuous monitoring, and engagement with families. This chapter reviews the extant empirically based literature through 2010 and discusses trends and issues in that literature. In addition, the chapter offers suggestions about improving the reading achievement of Native American children and closing achievement gaps of this population. Blanchard and Atwill call for culturally responsive intervention that incorporates the language, song, dance, arts, and activities of the Native American Indian children within the formal curriculum of schooling.

Part II. Conceptualizing and Measuring the Achievement Gaps in Reading

In Chapter 6, Why the Achievement Gap?, Edmund Gordon and Paola Heincke, present a different approach to the achievement gaps: Quality of life and access to education in communities and families, which are social divides, are foregrounded.

They emerge out of Gordon's 65-year life-long dedication to equity with his astute historical perspective. The consideration of these out-of-school factors, must be addressed in educational planning. Gordon pinpoints sources of error in educational policy and practice that he argues account for the modest progress made in closing the achievement gap:

> *A Focus on Race, Racism, and Possible Genetic Deficiencies,*
> *An Exclusive Focus on the Quality of Teachers and Schools,*
> *A Neglect of Relationship between Quality of Life and Access to Several Education Relevant Forms of Capital,*
> *A Service and Remedial Treatment Approach to Education such as in Physical Health Maintenance,*
> *A Belief that Public Health Supportive Context and Personal Attitudes and Behaviors may be the Intervention of a Personal Choice.*

After discussing the history and current status of these possible explanatory errors, Gordon calls for a reconsideration of a wide array of influences, opportunities, and resources that are *not under the control of teachers and schools.* He advances the argument that the availability and use of public health resources function as an approach to the problems of equalizing educational achievement. In this strategy, Gordon places considerable emphasis on strengthening the capacities of communities and families to support the academic and personal development of children for a comprehensive concept of gaps. It is proposed that we must go beyond our notions of school reform. While parents may have high aspirations for their children, Gordon argues that they often do not know how to navigate the educational system as a source of opportunity nor of the available resources for their children. Gordon and Heincke, suggest shaping the conversations parents have with children and monitoring the individuals to whom their children are exposed. Access to education in communities and families have not been addressed in a unified manner by educational researchers today. The approach that Gordon and Heincke take is broad in scope, interdisciplinary in approach, and requires a new conceptual, theoretical model.

Chapter 7, Including Differences in Variability in Assessing the Achievement Gap in Reading, by Michael Harwell looks at measures of achievement critical to this volume. Harwell argues there is compelling evidence of differences in reading achievement involving students from economically disadvantaged families, major ethnic groups, and students with disabilities and limited English proficiency. Harwell provides concise definitions of terms used in addressing the achievement gap. He argues that is important to state outright that there is *not a single achievement gap in reading* that is applicable to all students; *rather, there are different gaps of varying magnitude with different antecedents for different groups of students.*

This chapter summarizes quantitative results characterizing the nature, direction, and magnitude of differences in reading achievement for different student groups using nationally representative datasets (e.g., *Early Childhood Longitudinal Study, National Assessment of Educational Progress, Progress in International Reading Literacy Study*). Harwell focuses his chapter on the Black-White differences in achievement. A central tenet of the chapter is that **equal** attention must be paid to characterizing differences in achievement *using averages (means)* as well as differences in *variability* in Black-White reading performance. Understanding the implications of, and possible responses to, White students performing on average one-third of a standard deviation higher than a comparable group of African American students is enhanced by also knowing that, for example, the *variability of reading outcomes* for African American students is much less (or more) than that of White students. Harwell presents different methods of assessing differences in variability within Black-White comparisons. He concludes that "If the variation of reading scores of Black and White students is equal then inferences about an average difference in reading achievement are not likely to be distorted; if the variation differs then such inferences can be seriously distorted." In sum, the chapter provides a comprehensive characterization of historical and current differences in reading achievement for various student groups. It calls for a more careful and in depth understanding of reading achievement gaps based on standardized testing and variability in group scores. Harwell departs from traditional approaches by adopting the Hedges and Nowell (1999) definition of the achievement gap as "a difference in score distributions for Black and White students." The important point is that not only are means considered in comparisons of performance but variances are also addressed. Another consideration of importance is that much of the comparative data is from the National Assessment of Educational Progress (NAEP) studies, which are cross-sectional data and not longitudinal. This prevents us from seeing how Black and White students grow or reverse in reading performance over time inside or outside of schools.

Interestingly, the reading achievement gap narrowed in the 1970s through the mid-1980s, when there was little change among White students but those of Blacks increased. Thereafter, the gap began to increase, once again. Harwell notes that the gap in reading "is smaller than that observed 40–50 years ago," given Reardon et al. (2013), but "it is still three-quarters of a standard deviation or the equivalent of four years of learning in middle or high school."

Chapter 8, International Brain Wars: Adolescent Reading Proficiency, Performance, and Achievement from a Competitive Global Perspective, by Rosalind Horowitz (2017, this volume) focuses on adolescent reading proficiency, specific performance, and achievement. Attention is given to the comparisons and contrasts identified in international large-scale assessments. These are typically driven by short-term end goals of economic productivity. Horowitz notes that throughout the world adolescents have become the subject of research, after numerous years of neglect in the research literature. However, it is noted that adolescent weaknesses are accentuated with little attention to achievements in the sciences and arts by adolescents who show high reading ability and academic success.

This chapter addresses PISA data of 15-year-olds, a neglected population in reading and psychological research until of late. Rank-ordering of different levels of reading performance, from literal reading to application type reading, places nations in a competition with one another, although the culturally based beliefs about reading and goals may vary. Those countries who have excelled in reading have tended to be Asian nations, and Finland, for many years. Those countries that have not performed well on standardized measures of reading have been Latin American countries. The chapter concludes with highlights of the ways in which the PISA data may have been detrimental and short-changed our thinking about achievement worldwide. It calls for a cautionary approach to large-scale international assessments and a reconsideration of the competitive model for advancing quality of life and reading, and offers a cooperative model that will showcase the strengths and accomplishments of various nations, cultures, and societies that have potential for international collaboration for the good of the whole. This calls for a new vision of uses of international data, a shift in the purposes of international assessments by recognizing oral-based versus literate-based cultures and practices, a linguistic contrast that has implications for ways of thinking and has been of importance in Horowitz' research for decades (see Horowitz, 2007, 2015, an account of the role of oral language in meeting the Common Core Standards in the United States).

Part III. Explaining and Reducing the Achievement Gaps in Reading

In Chapter 9, The Talk Gap, Terrance Paul and Jill Gilkerson address the important role of talk in the family in advancing language development, reading, and reading achievement in schools. The Betty Hart and Todd Risley research reported in *Meaningful Differences in the Everyday Life of Young American Children* (1995) argued, based on scientific research, that the language and cognitive divide between the haves and have-nots is explained not by race, socioeconomic status, or parent education, but rather by the quality of a child's early home oral language environment and, concomitantly, the quantity of parent–child talk.

It is noted that Hart and Risley led the most comprehensive research project ever conducted on the home language learning experiences of young children. In this study of 42 families, Hart and Risley showed that children, 7 months to 3 years, from professional homes, with language ability heard 32 million more words and engaged in hundreds of thousands more conversations with their parents from birth to age 3 than children with poor language abilities and from welfare homes. The research described in this chapter presents the importance of parent–child interaction, not only number of words used by mothers but the quantity of turn taking in interactions. It shows ways of accelerating language and cognitive development, for academic success. The chapter (a) calls for education and training of parents that is designed to increase parent talk and parent–child interactions together with dialogic book reading, (b) promotes the value of providing books to parents who possess limited resources, and (c) emphasizes the importance of direct measurement of the early language environment and feedback so parents and clinicians can track progress in home language. This chapter provides evidence to support the claim that early dialogic book reading coupled with direct measurement and parent feedback are the missing links necessary for reducing and perhaps removing the achievement gap in reading among poverty children.

In Chapter 10, Summer Reading Loss Is the Basis of Almost All the Rich/Poor Reading Gap, Richard Allington and Anne McGill-Franzen argue that the achievement gaps we face in reading are due to poverty, with specifically a disparity in summer reading among the economically poor and the more financially secure in the United States. Allington and McGill-Franzen argue that we have good research evidence that a primary source of the current reading achievement gaps that exists between children from more and less economically advantaged homes is created by the summer vacations that the children experience, termed *Summer Reading Achievement Loss*. By the twelfth grade there is a four-year gap between the more and less affluent students. That primary source is termed *Summer Reading Setback*. That is, upper income students actually participate in summer enrichment programs and, thus, experience gains in reading across the summer. On the other hand, the lower socioeconomic status children who do not participate in these enrichment programs actually experience *achievement loss* by the end of the summer. The evidence available indicates that 80 percent of the achievement gap can be attributed to a summer setback. In general, children from economically advantaged families add a month's reading achievement during the summer. Children from economically disadvantaged families lose two months, thus creating a three-month gap every summer with this gap increasing as the students advance to the higher grades. This gap persists even when the school's high and low socioeconomic status children attend schools of roughly comparable effectiveness.

In fact, Allington and McGill-Franzen argue that children from low-income families gain as much reading growth as children from middle- and higher-income families during the school year. Numerous studies support this. These studies also provide evidence that it is in the summer when poor children do not attend school and do not have access to books that the rich/poor gap emerges and grows year after year.

If we want children to read during the summer they must have easy access to books and encouragement to read. In a series of recent studies whereby simply providing poor children with appropriately difficult books to read during the summer months, such an effort halted summer reading loss. This low-cost book distribution strategy has proven as effective as summer school attendance and Allington and McGill-Franzen argue this should be more widely adopted by school districts and individual schools across the nation.

Allington and McGill-Franzen report that "schools today are less successful in educating poor students than schools were in the 1980s when a *Nation at Risk* was produced, when the rich/poor reading achievement gap was widening." They find reading choice, self-selection, and allowing children to keep books rather than lend them to the children increased reading engagement of low-income children and summer reading.

Part IV. Contradictory Efforts and Commonalities in Attempts to Close the Gaps in Reading Achievement

In Chapter 11, The Federal Effort: How Five Different and Sometimes Contradictory Efforts Have Been Made to Close the Achievement Gap, Richard Long and Alan Farstrup have collaborated on this closing chapter to our volume. They convey how the power of the federal government to influence educational goals and patterns of instruction has been expanding ever since President Johnson signed the *Elementary and Secondary Education Act* into law in 1965. Central to that involvement has been the idea that reading is both the key element of success in school and the symbol of federal program effectiveness.

In order to help children living in areas of high poverty and who suffer from low achievement, the federal government added two additional categories of need: The first was to help children whose home language was not English. The second was the creation of a Federal definition of learning disabilities as part of the Education for the Handicapped Act. Each of these categories generated its own set of advocates and professional development programs.

In the 1980s federal policy in reading began to branch out to include non-academic issues as critical to making a measurable impact on the problem, yet in the 1990s this policy was amended by adding a set of five elements of reading—phonemic awareness, phonetics, vocabulary, fluency, and comprehension—that for all practical purposes became an emphasis on phonemic awareness, phonics, and fluency. This emphasis created no greater effect on closing the achievement gap.

As the first decade of the new millennium came to a close, the nation's reading policy was again shifting—this time to formally link reading and writing, and to link reading to academic course work. Long and Farstrup remind us that no longer will children in the fifth grade be drilled in vocabulary and spelling tests, but rather they will be measured by how well they perform in reading tasks in their academic courses. This is evident in the formation of the *Common Core Standards* and the *Every Student Succeeds Act* (ESSA, 2015) initiatives (Berman, 2015).

The Long and Farstrup chapter provides a historical review of federal efforts to close the achievement gap. It identifies five major trends of the federal government, over time. Long and Farstrup's historical review of federal efforts indicate shifts of attention centered on the school, the teacher, and the child, and a movement from federal to state flexibility in school improvements, but lack of a cohesive, comprehensive effort.

In Chapter 12, Synthesis, Discussion, and Recommendations: What We Can Do to Advance Reading Achievement, the editors, Rosalind Horowitz and S. Jay Samuels, synthesize and discuss each of the authors' key ideas and *Spotlight Recommendations*. We identify common threads, where there is agreement, among many of the proposals for addressing achievement gaps in reading, and also identify differences in emphases and contradictions in efforts.

We have found some unique and powerful suggestions within this volume depending upon the author's perspective on advancing reading achievement. The chapters have policy implications for school districts, state and federal levels, and parents and neighborhoods that are discussed. This synthesis offers perspective and suggestions that also may be useful to researchers and for Colleges of Education and teacher training—particularly as faculty design new courses to address the beginning and high levels of reading achievement needed in today's schools and for schools of the future.

References

Balfanz, R., Herzog, L., & MacIver, D. (2007). Preventing student disengagement and keeping students on the graduation track in high-poverty middle-grade schools: Early identification and effective interventions. *Educational Psychologist*, 42(4), 223–235.

Berliner, D. C., (2012). Effects of inequality and poverty vs. teachers and schooling on America's youth. Teachers College Record, 116(1). Retrieved March 1, 2013 from www.tcrecord.org/content.asp?contentid=16889.

Berliner, D. C. (2017). Poverty's powerful effects on reading achievement and the achievement gap. In R. Horowitz & S. J. Samuels (Eds.), *The achievement gap in reading: Complex causes, persistent issues, possible solutions* (pp. 23–37). New York and London: Routledge/ Taylor & Francis.

Berman, R. (2015, November 25). Congress prepares to launch a new era in education policy. A bipartisan agreement to replace George W. Bush's signature *No Child Left Behind Law* could pass next month. *The Atlantic*.

Borman, G. & Dowling, M. (2010). Schools and inequality: A multilevel analysis of Coleman's Equality of Educational Opportunity Data. *Teachers College Record,* 112(5), 1201–1246.

Coleman, J. S., Campbell, E.Q., Hobson, C. J., McPartland, J., Mood, A. M., Weinfield, F. D., & York, R. L. (1966). *Equality of educational opportunity*. Washington, DC: U. S. Department of Health, Education, & Welfare, Office of Education.

Common Core State Standards for English Language Arts & Literacy in History/Social Studies, Science, and Technical Subjects (2010). Common Core State Standards Initiative. Preparing America's Students for College & Career. National Governor's Association Center for Best Practices. Council of Chief State Officers.

Daly, A. J. & Finnigan, K. S. (Eds.). (2016). *Thinking and acting systematically. Improving school districts under pressure*. Washington, DC: American Educational Research Association.

Dominigue, B., Thomas, S., Ruhan, C. K., & Camilli, G. (2011, September). Schools and inequality: A multilevel analysis of Coleman's Equality of Educational Opportunity Data. Commentary on Borman & Dowling (2010). www.tcrecord.org/Content.asp?ContentId=16544.

Every Student Succeeds Act (ESSA) (2015, December 10). Washington, DC.

Feuer, M. J., Berman, A. I., & Atkinson, R. C. (Eds.). (2015). *Past as prologue: The National Academy of Education at 50. Members reflect.* Washington, D.C.: The National Academy of Education.

Foorman, B., Kalinowski, S. J., & Sexton, W. L. (2007). Standards-based educational reform is one important step towards reducing the educational achievement gap. In A. Gamoran (2007). *Standards-based reform and the poverty gap. Lessons from No Child Left Behind.* (pp. 17–42). Washington, DC: Brookings Institute Press.

Gamoran, A. (2007). *Standards-based reform and the poverty gap. Lessons from No Child Left Behind.* Washington, DC: Brookings Institute Press.

Hart, B. & Risley, T. (1995). *Meaningful differences in the everyday life of young American children.* Baltimore, MD: Paul H. Brooks Publishing Company.

Hedges, L.V. & Nowell, A. (1999). Changes in the Black-White gap in achievement test scores. *Sociology of Education,* 72(2), 111–135.

Horowitz, R. (1995, November/December). A 75-year legacy on assessment. Reflections from an interview with Ralph W. Tyler. *Journal of Educational Research, Seventy-Fifth Anniversary Issue.* 89(2), 68–75.

Horowitz, R. (Ed.) (2007). *Talking texts: How speech and writing interact in school learning.* New York: Routledge/Taylor & Francis Group.

Horowitz, R. (2015). Oral language: The genesis and development of literacy for schooling and everyday life. In P. D. Pearson & E. H. Hiebert (Eds.), *Research-based practices for teaching Common Core Literacy* (pp. 57–75). New York & London: Teachers College, Columbia University & Newark, Delaware: International Literacy Association.

Horowitz, R. (2017). International brain wars: Adolescent reading proficiency, performance, and achievement from a competitive global perspective. In R. Horowitz & S. Jay Samuels (Eds.), *The achievement gap in reading: Complex causes, persistent issues, possible solutions* (pp. 123–147). New York & London: Routledge/Taylor & Francis.

Howard, T. C. (2010). *Why race and culture matter in schools. Closing the achievement gap in America's classrooms.* New York: Teachers College Press.

Hoynes, H.W., Page, M. E., & Stevens, A. H. (2006, Winter). Poverty in America: Trends and explanations. *Journal of Economic Perspectives,* 20(1), 47–68.

Kahneman, D. (2011). *Thinking, fast and slow.* New York: Farrar, Straus and Giroux.

Kieffer, M. J. (2011, October). Converging trajectories: Reading growth in language minority learners and their classmates, Kindergarten to grade 8. *American Educational Research Journal,* 48(5), 1187–1225.

Long, R. & Farstrup, A. (2017). The federal effort: How five different and sometimes contradictory efforts have been made to close the achievement gap. In R. Horowitz & S. Jay Samuels (Eds.), *The achievement gap in reading: Complex causes, persistent issues, possible solutions* (pp. 187–200). New York and London: Routledge/Taylor & Francis.

McDonnell, L. M. & Weatherford, M. S. (2016, May). Recognizing the political in implementation research. *Educational Researcher,* 45(4), 233–242.

National Commission on Excellence in Education (1983). *A nation at risk: The imperative for educational reform.* Washington, DC: United States Department of Education.

National Indian Education Study Part II. (2007). The Educational Experiences of American Indian and Alaska Native Students in Grades 4–8. Statistical Analysis Report. National Center for Education State Institute of Education Sciences. Washington, D.C.: United States Department of Education.

National Reading Panel (2000). *Teaching children to read: An evidence-based assessment of the scientific research literature on reading and its implications for reading instruction.* Washington, DC: United States Department of Education.

Newkirk, T. (2012). *The art of slow reading: Six time-honored practices for engagement.* Portsmouth, New Hampshire: Heinemann.

Noguera, P. & Wing, J. Y. (Eds.). (2006). *Unfinished business: Closing the racial achievement gap in our schools.* San Francisco, CA: Jossey-Bass.

Reardon, S. F., Valentino, R. A., Kalogrides, D., Shores, K.A., & Greenberg, E. H. (2013). Patterns and trends in racial academic achievement gaps among states, 1999–2011. Retrieved from http://cepa.stanford.edu/sites/default/files/reardon%20et%20al %20state%20achievement.

Sadovnik, A. R., O'Day, J. A., Bohrnstedt, G. W., & Borman, K. M. (Eds.) (2008). *No Child Left Behind and the reduction of the achievement gap. Sociological perspectives on federal educational policy.* New York: Routledge/ Taylor & Francis.

US Department of Education (2008). *A nation accountable: Twenty-five years after A Nation at Risk.* Washington, DC: US Department of Education. www2.ed.gov/rschstat/research/pubs/accountable/accountable.pdf.

Vinovskis, M. A. (2009). *From A Nation at Risk to No Child Left Behind: National education goals and the creation of federal education policy.* New York: Teachers College Press.

PART I

Cases of Specific Demographics and Economics

2

POVERTY'S POWERFUL EFFECTS ON READING ACHIEVEMENT AND THE ACHIEVEMENT GAP

David C. Berliner

There are two issues that are often overlooked when discussing the role that poverty plays in the achievement scores obtained on various reading tests taken by US students. First is the distinction between reading performance at the individual level, and that of the mean scores for classrooms and other aggregated data, such as the mean scores obtained by schools, districts, and nations. Second is the fact that poverty is only modestly related to reading achievement directly: Poverty more frequently and quite powerfully produces its effects on a broad set of student achievements, including reading test scores, through its interactions with other factors—its correlates and its sequelae. Understanding the implications of these two issues is important.

Poverty's Effects on Aggregate Measures of School Achievement

At the individual level teachers exert great influence on our children and youth, particularly during the elementary grades. Teachers can affect an individual child's life, mostly in positive ways, but occasionally in negative ways. While they may not "touch" every student they encounter, they affect the lives of many, and in that way they do "touch eternity." No better example of this can be found than the remarkable story of Ms. A (Pedersen, Faucher, & Eaton, 1978). Every child who left her first grade class not only could read but held advantages over other children in the grades that followed and into adulthood. Ms. A's effects on her students, unlike so many teacher and school effects on students, did not fade after a few years. Her students attained higher social status than did similar students who were assigned other first grade teachers at the same school. Ms. A worked magic at the individual and at the classroom level. Her skills as a reading teacher, diagnostician, and motivator of children and youth made her an exemplary elementary classroom teacher for the lower social class children with whom she worked. The effects associated with this one teacher are found also in large scale data sets: A good start to reading has carryover effects to other curriculum areas, and to life outside of school, in ways that other school subjects do not (Master, Loeb, & Wyckoff, 2014; Konstantopoulos, 2011). This argues for early reading skill development as the most important of the primary school subjects to teach, or as the most important of the entering characteristics a student brings to school.

We have known for years that those possessing appropriate reading skills on entry to school are often the children of professionals, not of lower social class families (Hart & Risley, 2004). Thus, economically and socially better off children more often present the reading skills that help them in all their subjects, while lower class and racial minority children without the desired reading skill set on entry fall behind in all their subjects. Worse, lower class and racial minority children are frequently tracked. It is not uncommon for the weakest students in academic subjects to be assigned teachers that are lower in quality. There are no Ms. A's for them, thus making it even harder to compete with the children of families that are better off (Desimone & Long, 2010). Nevertheless, teachers of poor children may still touch and affect the lives of the individuals in their charge, but it is the rare teacher of poor children who affects the life chances of whole classrooms, as did Ms. A. This is because the mean scores of classrooms are primarily determined by the composition of the classrooms. This is also referred to as the peer or cohort effect.

The Ms. A's of the world, those wonderful super teachers who affect the test scores of a whole class are, in fact, rare. Their numbers are far less than is commonly believed. Many politicians and the nation's opinion makers keep searching for supermen (and women) to fix our classrooms and schools, apparently forgetting that those superheroes are fictitious characters! Persuasive evidence, not comic book fantasies, supports the idea that classroom mean performance, along with school, district, state, and national aggregate reading test scores, are greatly influenced by demographics. Peer or cohort or composition effects are more powerful than teacher effects on aggregate measures of reading, science and mathematics. The belief that the effects of poverty on school achievement can be overcome for whole classes or entire schools by great teachers must be revealed for what it really is—a rather low probability event, closer to fantasy than to reality, though it occasionally happens. But exceptions should not be the basis of policy. Some heavy smokers live well into their 80s without lung cancer or other illnesses. Such exceptions do not change the fact that cigarette smoking is causally related to many illnesses, among which is lung cancer.

Cohort characteristics are powerful conditioners of school achievement. For example, McEwan (2003), in Chile, found that mothers' education is the most important peer determinant of achievement in a classroom. His data suggest that a one standard deviation increase in mothers' mean educational level leads to over a one-quarter standard deviation rise in student performance in Spanish Language Arts.

In addition, there were effects on aggregate scores in Spanish Language Arts for fathers' education, but the effect was smaller. McEwan found that even small changes in the number of Indigenous students in the class changed the mean score of the class considerably. These are cohort or peer or compositional effects on reading achievement, independent of the teachers' effects. In the US, Fantuzzo, LeBoeuf, and Rouse (2014) found a similar effect when studying Philadelphia schools. In their study, the most important determinant of student and school achievement was the educational level of the mother.

Looking at school effects in England, Lavy, Silva, and Weinhardt (2009) showed that a large fraction of low achieving peers at school, as identified by students in the bottom 5 percent of the national ability distribution, negatively and significantly affect the cognitive performance of *all* the other students in the school. Because the students of impoverished families are more frequently the students with the lowest test scores, poverty, through its correlation with test scores, affects every child's reading score in the school, *independent of the teacher*. As is true of other researchers, these scholars found that the percent of boys or girls in a class affects classroom aggregate test scores. More girls in elementary classrooms make some teachers look like they are better at teaching reading than others, but it is quite likely that the ratio of girls to boys, a composition factor, not the teachers' skill, is affecting the reading scores in each classroom.

In Denmark, Schneeweiss and Winter-Ebmr (2005) used PISA data (the Program for International Student Assessment) for estimating student social class and achievement. They made use of a composite of home talk about political or social issues; discussions of books, films, or TV programs; and listening to classical music at home. This is not a poverty/wealth scale, but it is a measure that is highly correlated with family income, data the PISA researchers could not get directly. Their results suggest that if you moved the *average* student to a new peer group one standard deviation higher on this social class index, you can expect the student's reading achievement to rise by about 5 points on the PISA scale. And, if you are low in the index of cultural and social variables, and somehow find yourself in a class where there is an increase of a standard deviation in the quality of the peers you go to school with, then you will show an increase of about 10 PISA reading points. That is, the scores on reading, mathematics, and science tests for poor children rise considerably when they do *not* take their classes with large concentrations of other poor children.

Schindler-Rangvid (2003) in Denmark, and Levin (2001) in the Netherlands, found that low ability students substantially benefit from a high quality peer group. On the other hand, high-ability students are not influenced much when being mixed with low-ability students. Oakes (2005) reported similar findings when she studied detracking in the US. In general, compositional effects of classrooms and schools are more powerful in the lives of the least academically talented, our lowest social class students, and the ones we worry most about. It is their plight that launched the American (and now worldwide) obsession with describing effective teachers. But as I am pointing out, such efforts may be in vain. Aggregate scores in reading and other tested domains are less likely the result of a student's teachers and more likely the result of scholastically and socially effective or ineffective classmates. The reason I chose examples from around the world is to illustrate the pervasive nature of this phenomena.

It is precisely this underlying confusion about causality in determining school achievement that motivates assertive parents to pursue districts, schools, and classrooms that they believe have higher mean test scores. They know, without research informing them, that their own child's scores will go up because of compositional effects, which they typically confuse with teacher effects. They are in search of better teachers for their children, as any parent might, but they think those teachers are in better schools and neighborhoods with social and cultural indices that are higher than where they presently live or where they school their children now. These upwardly mobile parents, the tiger moms out there (Chua, 2011), have a correct understanding of the *effects* of their moves to "better neighborhoods." But their understanding of the *cause* of those effects may not be accurate. Increased student achievement in their new neighborhood may not be as much a function of better teachers as much as it is caused by the composition of the classrooms and schools in which their children find themselves. Parents, like almost everyone else in the US, may be overestimating the teacher effects and underestimating the compositional or peer effects in the search for effective classrooms and schools to teach literacy, numeracy, and other school subjects.

Because housing patterns determine schooling experiences for so many people we find that wealthy children and poor children go to school primarily with other wealthy and poor children. This helps the wealthy child achieve at higher levels than might otherwise be the case, and this depresses the scores for the poorer child than might otherwise be the case, *independent of the quality of the teachers to which they are assigned*. In the US we engage in what Jonathan Kozol calls "apartheid-lite," segregation by housing, not by law. For example, a little known fact about the US, a nation that prides itself on democratic traditions and its "melting pot" cultural heritage, is this: 40 percent of Hispanic children, almost 40 percent of Black children and 20 percent of American Indian children attend schools that are 90–100 percent minority (Orfield & Lee, 2005). Our poorest minorities go to school with other poor minorities, assuring through housing policies that the peer culture in most of these schools is likely not to be as supportive of high levels of literacy and numeracy as we educators would like. In contrast, under 1 percent of white children attend schools that are 90–100 percent minority. Although many of the schools that poor white children attend are low achieving, again because of housing patterns related to income, they are not so patently racially segregated. It is not illogical to argue that the greatest increase in reading scores for America's poorest children can be obtained through social policies that integrate housing by social class. But that will never happen in the US and that makes teaching in schools that primarily serve the poor all the more difficult.

Further examples of this cohort effect independent of the teacher effects on school achievements of all kinds are found in four studies using PISA data. The first of these contrasts the US with Finland, one of the consistently high achieving countries on PISA tests of reading, mathematics, and science. But the US, compared to Finland, has a very high GINI coefficient, the measure of the degree of inequality in income in a nation. In fact, among the developed nations, the US has the highest level of income inequality. This results in a startling rate of childhood poverty in the US, a rate approaching 25 percent. Finland, on the other hand, has a childhood poverty rate of under 5 percent. These data, not surprisingly, lead to differences in PISA scores. On one of the tests Finland scored 546, well above the average for PISA nations. On that same test the US scored 474, well below the international average. The newspapers and politicians, of course, blamed America's teachers and administrators. But Condron (2011) used regression models to ask what would happen if the degree of inequality in the US and Finland were switched? In this way childhood poverty rates would be quite different, and we could examine the predicted effects on PISA scores were our social policies designed to do that. If we switched the poverty rates then the US would have a predicted score on the PISA test of 509, above the international average, and Finland would have a score of 487, considerably below the international average. It is likely that we would get those higher scores in reading, science, and mathematics without firing a lot of our teachers, or putting in a common core, or buying iPads, or increasing the length of the school day, or busting the teacher unions. Inequality and it sequelae—high rates of poverty—has a big effect on school achievements of all kinds (see Wilkinson & Pickett, 2010).

So besides changing housing patterns as a way of improving reading in the US we can add another factor that seems supported by the data: reduce inequality in our society. Obviously this will be as hard to do as it would be to change housing patterns, but both these policies have strong data to support their likely positive effects on the school achievement of America's students.

Another contrast between Finland and the US was provided in the 2012 PISA results (OECD, 2013). In that study the variation in PISA scores attributable to between school variation was looked at. If schools vary a lot in their student composition because of rigid housing policies associated with family income and the quality of their buildings, staff, and curriculum, then a lot of the variance in students' achievement scores will be due to this between school variation. On the other hand, if the composition of the schools in a nation are similar, with less children segregated in housing patterns by family wealth, and school quality relatively constant across a nation's communities, than the percent of variance in scores attributable to differences in a nation's schools will be smaller. The results? Fifty-eight percent of the variation in student scores on one of the PISA tests was accounted for by school composition and school quality in the USA. In Finland the variance accounted for was 38 percent, a reduction in the effects of school cohort and school quality on achievement of 65 percent.

In the US your fate as a school achiever is tied to your neighborhood and neighborhood school, but that is much less true of Finland. Demography is much more likely to be destiny in the US than in Finland or any of the Northern European countries: nations that achieve more meritocratic outcomes in schooling and lifetime wealth than we do here in the US. As a side issue, to be addressed again later in this chapter, note that if about 60 percent of the variance between schools is primarily accounted for by cohort effects, only 40 percent of the variance is left unaccounted for. The usual estimates (Haertle, 2013) of the source of that variance are that 20 percent of the variance in students' scores on tests is accounted for by what happens in schools. And that is probably evenly split between teachers and school-level variables affecting instruction. Twenty percent of the variance in these aggregate scores is commonly error or unexplained variance. So teachers, who currently get so much blame for the outcomes of our schools, are probably accounting for only about 10 percent of the variance in those outcomes. In general, outside-the-school factors are three times more powerful in affecting aggregate achievement test scores than are inside-the-school factors; and outside-of-school factors are six times more powerful than are teachers when aggregated test scores are analyzed. We will return to this issue in the next section of this chapter.

A third PISA study also shows how the effects of poverty and housing work jointly to produce reading achievement scores that are either quite high or quite low independent of the quality of the teacher. Table 2.1 presents these data from Australia (Perry & McConney, 2013), but their results seem quite generalizable.

This table displays a number of important aspects associated with the relationship between a child's family income and reading achievement. First, looking at *all* the columns, we see that as family income goes up, student scores also

TABLE 2.1 PISA reading scores by income level of the student's family and income level of the families that the school serves (Perry & McConney, 2013).

Income Level of Child's Family	Income Level of the Families that the School Serves				
	Lowest	Low middle	Middle	High middle	Highest
Lowest Income	**458**	464	472	494	**535**
Low Middle	482	489	497	512	524
Middle Income	492	500	**510**	527	546
High Middle	499	503	526	537	561
Highest Income	**513**	529	527	549	**584**

go up. Family income predicts children's score on this PISA reading test (and almost all other tests) quite well. Second, if you read across all rows you find that as schools serve more and more advantaged families, PISA reading scores go up. The income of the families that are served by the school is a strong predictor of PISA reading test scores (and scores on most other tests). Third, we see in this table that a child who is poor and goes to school with other poor children receives a PISA score of 458 (cell 1, 1). But the same child in a school that serves the wealthy scores 535 (cell 1, 5), about three-fourths of a standard deviation higher. The tiger moms are right (Chua, 2011). Teacher effects of this magnitude rarely occur, but cohort effects of this size commonly do occur. Who you go to school with is a powerful influence on achievement in reading and in other school subjects. The opposite effect is seen, as well. Children of the wealthy, attending a school with lots of poor children (cell 5, 1) score about three-fourths of a standard deviation lower than they do in schools that primarily serve their social class (cell, 5, 5). But the fourth issue revealed in this table is perhaps the most startling. If you look at cell 1,1 and cell 5, 5 you see that poor children that attend schools serving poor children and wealthy children attending schools that serve the wealthy are a standard deviation and a half apart on this reading test. This is a huge difference. It is likely that most of the opportunities for social and economic success in our knowledge economy will flow to one of these subgroups and not the other. The chances of going to a good college, or any college, and finding good employment, or steady employment, are vastly different in the two populations. Although most Americans do not like to hear it, these data confirm quite convincingly that, indeed, demography really is destiny.

PISA provides still more international evidence that poverty is a strong factor in determining test scores in reading and other school subjects by looking at "resilient students." These are students in the *bottom* quartile of the social class distribution, but in the *top* quartile in the achievement test distribution. These are 15-year-olds who seem to break the shackles imposed by family and neighborhood poverty. In the US, about 6 percent of the children do that. So 94 percent of youth born into or raised in that lower quartile of family culture and resources do *not* make it into the top quartile of school achievers. Other countries—Belgium, Canada, Finland, Turkey, Portugal, among many others—produce at least 40 percent more "resilient kids" than we do. Could it be because the class lines are more hardened here in the US? Whatever the cause, family poverty along with its correlates and sequelae severely limit the life chances of most children in the lower quartiles, quintiles, and deciles on measures of social standing and family income.

The final PISA study I want to cite also dramatically documents these context effects on achievement around the world. Willms (2006) found that on average, across nations, if a child of *average* SES, in whatever nation, attended one of their own nation's high performing schools, or instead attended one of their own nation's low performing schools, the difference at age 15, the age of PISA testing, would be equivalent to about four grade levels! Thus a tenth grader of average SES who can attend a high performing school is likely to score at about the twelfth grade level (a grade level approximation from PISA data). And if that same child were to attend a low performing school, he or she would score at about the eighth grade level.

In sum, in this section of the chapter I have argued that there is no escaping the powerful context, cohort, peer, or compositional effects on aggregate assessment scores when we measure reading, science, and mathematics. In our society teacher effects on aggregate scores are overimagined, and cohort effects are underemphasized: The problem of not recognizing these facts is to make policy that is wrongheaded, at best, and harmful at worst. An example of this is the spread of Value-Added Models—VAMs—in which teachers are held responsible for student test score growth. Without taking into account a myriad of variables related to a child's social life, the equations used to determine value-added scores will be unreliable, and therefor invalid (Berliner, 2014).

Given a view of the world that stresses these compositional effects, it may well be that the search for effective reading programs is less likely to change aggregate school achievement than is a rise in the minimum wage. The Common Core State Standards are likely to have less effect on the performance of poor children than an increase in the local rate of employment. Professional fighting over the role of phonics and/or the power of extensive oracy in family life on later reading comprehension may be less important in influencing a child's reading scores than is the quality of the neighborhood in which that child lives.

Poverty's Correlates and Sequelae

The second point I want to make is to expand our quite common understanding that family income is related to a wide variety of achievement test scores. But family income may work its beneficial and pernicious effects through numerous other factors that have substantial effects on achievement. Thus it is not merely poverty (or wealth) that affects measured school achievement, but the correlates and sequelae of poverty (and wealth) that we need to explore. This is important for policy work.

Whether we see these other variables as correlates or sequelae is less important than recognizing their presence in the life of the impoverished at much higher rates than in the lives of the wealthy. In medicine, sequelae are what follow from a disease or condition. Thus, paralysis is one of the sequelae of poliomyelitis. In social science we see that post-traumatic stress disorder may be sequelae after rape or war. Sequelae, of course, are correlates of a disease or an event, but implicit in the term sequelae are both causality and lag. The state or condition of poliomyelitis, or of trauma, is causally linked to effects we see afterwards. But it is not uncommon for a time lag to occur: Sequelae may not follow immediately. For example, a correlate of wealth and poverty almost everywhere in the Western world is housing value. The associated neighborhood norms that develop as a neighborhood becomes poorer are sequelae of increasing poverty. Another characteristic associated with wealth and poverty is access to medical care. Vastly different life expectancies for the wealthy and the poor are sequelae associated with that differential access. As a person enters into poverty, say through job loss or divorce, physical and mental illness may exhibit themselves more frequently. Entering into poverty often leads to family violence, divorce, child absenteeism from school, food insecurity, and the like (Berliner, 2012). Sequelae in medicine are the secondary effects from a disease. Sequelae associated with poverty are similar; they follow and are causally related. Policy may not be able to eliminate poverty, but if the mechanisms through which poverty works its pernicious effects on achievement are known, perhaps the effects of poverty can be mitigated through policies addressing these associated effects.

For example, while SAT scores increase monotonically as family income increases, a trend that has long been known, the effects of family income on SAT scores is considerably magnified for Black students (Dixon-Román, Everson, & McArkdale, 2013). In general, compared to white middle class children, poor white children show a deficit on the SAT of 44 points. But poor Black children show a deficit of 77 points. Poverty's negative effects on Black Americans are more powerful than its effects on white Americans. Thus, policy for increasing SAT reading scores (and almost any other test scores) for poor Black children might focus on their ghettoization in contemporary America, while policy to increase the reading scores for poor white children might focus on something else, perhaps parent education or design of tutoring programs. Because poverty's effects differ, the methods of combatting poverty's pernicious effects must also differ: One size remedies do not fit all.

Poverty often exhibits its pernicious effects through its sequelae. That is, poverty increases the odds of other factors occurring that more directly impair school achievement. The simplest example of this is the rush by over a dozen states to retain in grade children who are not reading well by third grade. In Arizona this legislation is called "Move on When Reading"; in Florida it's called "Just Read, Florida." But the evidence from research in this area is quite one-sided, finding that retention in grade policies, that is, flunking children, is ineffectual, if not actually mean spirited. In fact, if you had identical twins who were equally deficient in reading, and you left one behind but passed the other one on, the latter child is much more likely to be ahead in school achievement and enjoy school more. Leaving children back harms parent–child relationships, results in more negativism toward school by the retained student, produces greater absenteeism, and produces greater dropout rates for those left back (Berliner, Glass, & Associates, 2014). The consequences of dropping out due to being left back also increases the chances that the dropout will be a burden on the community because that child will likely not be a big taxpayer and may, in fact, need fiscal support during periods of unemployment, and is far more likely to be incarcerated later in life. On top of all these negative effects, retention policies in the US are discriminatory. Poor Hispanic and poor African Americans suffer the most from this wrongheaded policy, but poor whites are affected in large numbers as well.

On the other hand, middle and upper social class families who have children identified as slow to read get them tutors. Middle class families have the resources for that kind of help. Tutoring is a powerful treatment. Thus middle class children are rarely the ones that are left back. In that way, poverty works its pernicious effects on the achievement of poor children. It's not poverty per se that hurts them, it's a lack of provision for tutoring if they are behind in reading that hurts them. Tutoring is also part of the reason that upper class children do better on the SAT than do lower-class children. It's not the poverty per se that dooms the lower class student to scores that may be 50 points or so lower than their middle class peers who received tutoring for the SAT. It's the lack of tutoring for these children that hurts them, pushing them to lower quality colleges, if they go to college at all. Note that in a more just society tutoring could be offered for modest costs. Instead, poverty affects achievement though our failure to provide this kind of support for poor children. In so doing we keep the poor, poor.

As noted previously, income is a powerful determinant of where you live. In that way, housing doesn't just determine the school one attends, it also affects rates of illness, rates of crime in the neighborhood, rates of mental health in the community, and so forth. Again, income per se is not the issue. Poverty works some of its pernicious effects on school achievement through American housing policies, or perhaps, better said, a lack of such policies. The result of so little concern for housing policy locally or nationally is stratification of housing by income throughout the US. That creates illness problems that affect the poor much more than the wealthy. Asthma, for example, affects huge numbers of children, but among those afflicted, poor children are overrepresented. For example, Berliner (2005) reports on a survey in the impoverished South Bronx. A fourth grade classroom was found where 12 of 30 students have asthma, and 8 of those have to bring their breathing pumps to school every day. The estimates of school days missed per year because of asthma is 10.5 million, with many children missing 20 to 40 school days a year because of their asthma, and many others having severe problems sleeping, making school learning even harder than it usually is for urban poor and minority children, a large proportion of the population affected. While children of all social classes get asthma, it is much more prevalent among the poor, who until our nations' recent provision of health insurance had little access to medical help for alleviation of their symptoms.

Asthma's effects on children from middle-income families are not nearly as severe as they are on the children of low-income families. Time-on-task, as we all know, is one of the strongest predictors of learning in schools. So it is no great leap of logic to point out that poor children, compared to their middle class counterparts, miss a lot more school because of asthma, and thus will be learning a lot less. Again, it is not poverty per se that hurts the achievement of low-income children, it's poverty's relation to housing that is substandard (mice, rat, and cockroach droppings, indoor air pollutants, fumes from urban trucks and busses) and the limitations imposed by poverty on visits to allergists and obtaining their prescriptions.

There is another medical problem that is directly related to poverty. Much more common among the poor are premature births and low birth weight children. Neural imaging studies show that premature and low birth weight children are several times more likely to have anatomic brain abnormalities than do full-term, full birth weight controls (see Berliner, 2005). Quantitative comparisons of brain volumes in 8-year-old children born prematurely, and age matched full-term control children also found that brain volume was less in the prematurely born. The degree of these morphologic abnormalities was strongly and inversely associated with measures of intelligence. Unfortunately, in hundreds of studies, birth defects have been found to be significantly correlated with social class. Some of the relationships seem associated with lifestyle problems (drug and alcohol use, vitamin deficiencies), while some seem neighborhood related (waste sites, lead, pesticides). But in either case, poverty is associated with mothers and their children frequently being in dysfunctional families or neighborhoods. That may be a causal factor in those women having a higher incidence of low birth weight children who display cognitive and social problems on their entrance to public schools five years later. And it is not just the child of low birth weight who suffers; that child affects the scores of every one of the other students at their school.

Again, it's not poverty per se that is the problem; rather it's poverty's correlates and sequelae that hurt our students and our schools. Capitalizing on a unique data set, Fantuzzo, LeBoeuf, and Rouse (2014) recently estimated that for over 10,000 third grade children in Philadelphia, 77 percent of the variance in the reading test scores was accounted for by poverty's correlates and sequelae. The predictors were two sets of variables. The first set were school-level demographic variables such as, race, gender, and degree of economic disadvantage. These variables predicted 63 percent of the between school variance, quite close to the usual estimate of 60 percent of variance in student achievement scores accounted for by such demographic variables. These data, then, are similar to what Haertle (2013) and other researchers find when demographic variables are put into regression equations like these, bolstering the validity of this study.

But here is what is unique about this study. Fattuzo et al. (2014) also were able to put into their equations student-level variables, as well as the usual group demographic variables. At the level of the student they knew whether the child was pre-term or low birth weight, had inadequate prenatal care, had a mother who was a teen, had high lead exposure, had ever been reported as being maltreated, had ever been homeless, and had a mother with less than a high school degree. Each and every one of these student-level variables was a negative predictor of test scores, and all but one was statistically significant. But two things stood out after they put in these student-level variables.

First, the between school variance in reading test scores increased to 77 percent when the group demographics and student-level variables were in the equation together, raising the question of what percent of the variance in student test scores are affected by teachers. Instructional variables related to teachers and schools have a maximum of 23 percent of the variance left to show their effects. But equations have error too, the unaccounted for variance. So it is more likely that the variance that can be attributed to the children's teachers and schools is in the neighborhood of 10–15 percent, and if teachers are thought of as responsible for half that, they would be accounting for 5–7.5 percent of the variance we see in the aggregate scores of these Philadelphia schools. Demography trumps instructional competence!

Teachers almost always move children and class scores up. School children do grow in competence over the school year. But other variables associated with poverty and wealth may well limit or expand a teacher's influence on the aggregate score a class or a school attains. In a district such as Philadelphia, where so many of the public school students are poor, there is not much variance unaccounted for, suggesting that teachers are not nearly as powerful an influence on aggregate scores as politicians and business people demand they be.

The second thing that stands out in this study is that two variables had very strong relationships with reading achievement—mother's education and child maltreatment. For policy work, this suggests that a lot more effort on these two characteristics associated with poor mothers would have greater payoff than leaving back children not reading well at third grade, or adding hours to the school day, or imposing the Common Core State Standards with its purportedly more rigorous curriculum and more difficult tests. Those approaches will be weak in their effects because the sources of reading problems exhibited by many poor children are in their homes, not in their schools, suggesting that social programs not educational programs might help more in improving reading achievement. Arizona, for instance, was found recently to never have investigated 6,000 phone calls reporting child abuse made to the state agency in charge of child safety. Yet against all research evidence, Arizona leaves back children who are not reading well. Clearly the state thinks the problems of reading achievement are mostly inside their schools, and not outside of them, and they are wrong.

Policy alternatives for helping poor children to read better exist, and might even be more helpful than many of today's programs. A leading scholar of literacy for decades, Tom Stitcht (2011), notes that the education of poor mothers in literacy building techniques and child care has already shown powerful effects. He quite rightly notes that if we were really serious about attaining long-lasting increases in student achievement, we have to look beyond the school, to the home. While the nation is finally coming around to understanding the importance of early childhood education, especially for the poor, it ignores early parenthood education for mothers at risk of hurting their children through ignorance or circumstances (covariates or sequelae of poverty). Early parenthood education should take its place alongside early childhood education as a primary means of getting education right from the start.

American public schools now have 15 million or so children performing about as well as do the students in any other country, and much better than most. These are children in schools serving families where under 25 percent of the children are in poverty. In reading, especially, on the PIRLS tests (Progress in International Reading Literacy Study), our children in schools that serve the middle and upper classes beat every other nation in the world. But in schools where poor children and racial minorities are attending school with those like themselves, where 50–74 percent of the children live in poverty, or over 75 percent of the children live in poverty, our students are failing. Early parenthood education for these mothers, if melded with high quality early childhood education, might well yield better results than will leaving back third graders slow to pick up reading skills.

Spotlight Recommendation

Two important aspects of poverty and its relationships to reading and other subject matters have been discussed. The first was poverty's powerful effect on a broad range of a child's achievements when melded with that of other children in poverty. The peer or compositional effects in classrooms, schools, districts, and nations are strong determinants of the aggregate scores obtained from a plethora of national and international tests. The conclusion from this analysis is that teachers have little power to make big differences in aggregate scores, though occasionally they do just that. But exceptions should not be used to make policy. In general, teachers affect the test scores obtained by individual students more than they do the reading test scores of classes, and they have even smaller effects on the test scores obtained by schools and other larger aggregations of students.

The second point made was that poverty (and wealth) has correlates and sequelae that are the real culprits or promoters of achievement. For example wealth can purchase tutoring, saving a child from being left back or helping that child add 50 extra points on his or her SAT. Poverty can bring absenteeism from school, a high crime rate in a neighborhood that traumatizes children and their families, illnesses that are debilitating, and so forth. And these factors, more than the poverty itself, is what negatively affects students' achievements in school.

The upshot of points one and two is that policies to raise literacy by concentrating on the schools, or that blame the teacher, are likely to have little effect on raising achievement in literacy or other school subjects. In fact, most current federal, state, and local policies that concentrate on raising test scores, such as the huge investment in the Common Core State Standards and their associated tests, will likely not be successful in changing the distribution of scores on aggregate measures of achievement. The solutions to America's unhappiness with the achievements of many of its poor citizens are to be found primarily in social policies not educational policies. Is there any backing for this thesis—you bet there is! One example can make this point concrete. When the families of poor Cherokee children in North Carolina were given a new source of income, the lives of their children, who had terrible school results and awful social lives, improved dramatically. In addition, minor crimes committed by Cherokee youth declined while on-time high school graduation rates improved. Psychiatric services were also markedly reduced in this community, solving an old argument about whether mental illness causes poverty, or whether poverty causes mental illness. While the former is likely to be true, we now know that the latter is equally true, and thus mental illness can be counted among poverty's sequelae (Costello, Erkanli, Copeland, & Arnold, 2010). The teachers of these poor children did not change all that much, but the changed social policies made a big difference in the effects of schooling on these poor children. This one study makes the point of this chapter: We too often expect schools to change the achievements of poor children without trying to fix the lives they and their families live. It's time for broader visions of what might help all of America's children to succeed in school.

References

Berliner, D. C. (2005). Our impoverished view of educational reform. *Teachers College Record*, 108(6), 949–995. Retrieved March 7, 2014 from www.tcrecord.org/content.asp?contentid=12106.

Berliner, D. C. (2012). Effects of inequality and poverty vs. teachers and schooling on America's youth. *Teachers College Record*, 116(1). Retrieved March 1, 2013 from www.tcrecord.org/content.asp?contentid=16889.

Berliner, D. C. (2014). Exogenous variables and value-added assessments: A fatal flaw. *Teachers College Record*, 116(1). Retrieved March 7, 2014 from www.tcrecord.org/content.asp?contentid=17293.

Berliner, D. C., Glass, G. V & Associates (2014). *50 myths and lies that threaten America's public schools*. New York: Teachers College Press.

Chua, A. (2011). *Battle hymn of the tiger mother*. New York: Penguin Books.

Condron, D. J. (2011). Egalitarianism and educational excellence: Compatible goals for affluent societies? *Educational Researcher*, 40(2), 47–55

Costello, E. J., Erlanli, A., Copeland, W., & Angold, A. (2010). Association of family income supplements in adolescence with development of psychiatric and substance use disorders in adulthood among an American Indian population. *Journal of the American Medical Association*, 303(19), 1954–1960.

Desimone, L. & Long, D. A. (2010). Teacher effects and the achievement gap: Do teacher and teaching quality influence the achievement gap between black and white and high- and low-SES students in the early grades? *Teachers College Record*, 112(12), 3024–3073. Retrieved March 3, 2014 from www.tcrecord.org/library/abstract.asp?contentid=16047.

Dixon-Román, E. J., Everson, H. T., & McArdle, J. J (2013). Race, poverty and SAT scores: Modeling the influences of family income on black and white high school students' SAT performance. *Teachers College Record*, 115(4), 1–33. Retrieved March 3, 2014 from www.tcrecord.org/content.asp?contentid=16925.

Fantuzzo, J. W., LeBoeuf, W. A. & Rouse, H. L. (2014). An investigation of the relations between school concentrations of student risk factors and student educational well-being. *Educational Researcher*, 43(1), 25–36.

Haertle, E. H. (2013). *Reliability and validity of inferences about teachers based on student test scores*. 14th annual William Angoff lecture. Princeton, NJ: Educational Testing Service.

Hart, B. & Risley, T. R. (2004). The early catastrophe. *Education Review*, 77(1), 100–118.

Konstantopoulos, S. (2011). Teacher effects in early grades: Evidence from a randomized study. *Teachers College Record*, 113(7), 1541–1565.

Lavy, V., Silva, O., & Weinhardt, F. (2009, December). The good, the bad and the average: Evidence on the scale and nature of ability peer effects in schools. NBER Working Paper 15600. Cambridge, MA: National Bureau Of Economic Research. Retrieved March 29, 2012 from www.nber.org/papers/w15600.

Levin, J. (2001) For whom the reductions count? A quantile regression analysis of class size and peer effects on scholastic achievement. *Empirical Economics*, 26, 221–246.

Master, B., Loeb, S., & Wyckoff, J. (2014, January). Learning that lasts: Unpacking variation in teachers' effects on students' long-term knowledge. Washington, DC: National Center for Analysis of Longitudinal Data in Education Research. CALDER Working Paper No. 104.

McEwan, P. (2003). Peer effects on student achievement: Evidence from Chile. *Economics of Education Review*, 22, 131–141.

Oakes, J. (2005). *Keeping track: How schools structure inequality* (2nd ed.). New Haven, CT: Yale University Press.

OECD (2013). *PISA 2012 results: Excellence through equity: Giving every student the chance to succeed* (Volume II). PISA, OECD Publishing. http://dx.doi. org/10.1787/9789264201132-en

Orfield, G. & Lee, C. (2005). *Why segregation matters: Poverty and educational inequality*. Los Angeles, CA: University of California at Los Angeles, The Civil Rights Project. Retrieved July 21, 2007 from http://escholarship.org/uc/item/4xr8z4wb.

Pedersen, E., Faucher, T. A., & Eaton, W. W. (1978). A new perspective on the effects of first–grade teachers on children's subsequent adult status. *Harvard Educational Review*, 48(1), 1–31.

Perry, L. B. & McConney, A. M. (2013). School socioeconomic status and student outcomes in reading and mathematics: A comparison of Australia and Canada. *Australian Journal of Education*, 57(2), 124–140.

Schindler-Rangvid, B. (2003). *Educational peer effects. Quantile regression evidence from Denmark with PISA 2000 data*. Aarhus, Denmark: Ph.D. thesis, Aarhus School of Business, Denmark.

Schneeweis, N. & Winter-Ebmer (2005, April). Peer effects in Austrian schools. Vienna, Austria: Department of Economics and Finance. Instutut für Höhere Studien.

Stitcht, T. G. (2011, Fall). Getting it right form the start. The case for early parenthood education. *American Educator*, 35(3), 35–39.

Wilkinson, R. & Pickett, K. (2010). *The spirit level: Why more equal societies almost always do better: Why equality is better for everyone*. London: Penguin.

Willms, J. D. (2006). *Learning divides: Ten policy questions about the performance and equity of schools and schooling systems*. Montreal, Canada: UNESCO Institute for Statistics.

3

CREATING RESPONSIVE TEACHERS OF HISPANIC AND BILINGUAL STUDENTS LEARNING ENGLISH

Robert Jiménez, Sam David, Mark Pacheco, Victoria J. Risko, Lisa Pray, Keenan Fagan, and Mark Gonzales

In this chapter, we examine the linguistic, literate, and cultural resources brought to the activity of reading comprehension by students who we describe as linguistically diverse. These students are alternatively referred to as limited English proficient, English language learners (ELLs), culturally and linguistically diverse (CLD) students, or emergent bilinguals. All of these categories have the effect of focusing one's attention on what these students can do with language(s). Although language is only one piece of a person's life, we see potential in highlighting this aspect of students' identity because language is "the tool of tools" (Dewey, 1958, p. 168) with respect to thought and all human activity. As a result, we see great value in helping students learning English to think about and use it in ways that help them develop deeper insights into its nature. We also believe that better understandings of students in terms of their linguistic abilities and potential holds the key to developing more effective instructional methods and programs for this population of young people.

For our purposes, we focus on students in the intermediate grades (4, 5, 6) and middle school (5, 6, 7, 8) who are conversationally fluent in a language other than English and who use that language regularly with family members, friends, or others in their respective communities. We are also interested in these same students who are gaining increasing command of English but who, for one reason or another, are not achieving at their expected grade level in terms of English reading comprehension. We see these students as fully capable of high levels of achievement but who, because of their histories of immigration, prior schooling, or lack of access to high quality instruction, have not yet attained full command of literacy in English.

Highly Skilled Instruction in Which the Teacher and the Students Share Two Languages

In the following example, four such middle school students (Carla, Ronnie, Joyce, and Celina) read a young adult book titled, *Brothers in Arms* (Langan & Alirez, 2004). These students were identified as reading two years below grade level by their teachers and here they are engaged in an activity that we call TRANSLATE (Teaching Reading and New Strategic Language Approaches to English learners) (Jiménez et al., 2015). In this activity, students are asked to read literature that has been assigned to them in their English language arts classes (usually 2 or 3 pages), identify a sentence or two that represent what is most important within that segment, and then with their peers, translate this text into their first language. It is clear from looking at the following transcript that Carla, and probably the other students as well, do not understand the sentence they are reading, most specifically the word *league*. The reference to Little League has them stumped for both decoding and cultural/historical reasons. These students do not seem to understand what the term Little League refers to and they pronounce the word as *ledge*.

> TEXT: One of them was a tiny photo of Huero in his Little League uniform. I loved that kid.
> Carla: What is league (she pronounces this word as if it is "ledge") uniform?
> Instructor 1: I think that's league.
> Carla: League.
> Instructor 1: Little League. You know what Little League is? That's, does anybody know what Little League is? It's kids' baseball teams.
> Carla: Baseball teams?
> Joyce: So how do you say league?
> Ronnie: That's hard.
> Instructor 1: One thing, do you ever watch soccer?
> <All students say Yes.> We play soccer.
> Instructor 1: And when you have a bunch of soccer teams, it's called in Spanish, *La Liga*, right?
> Carla: Like a football league.
> Ronnie: Oh! *Como la liga mexicana* (like the Mexican league)
> Instructor 1: Little League, league is Spanish, *Liga*.
> Carla: Oh, you should have told me, cause I was thinking about *una liga, yo tambien* (a league, me too).

In this situation, the instructor speaks and understands Spanish and can use this information to support the students as he skillfully scaffolds their interaction with the text. It is important to recognize that the students are motivated to comprehend the text, but they mispronounce a key word and this mispronunciation indicates an obstacle to comprehension. Any teacher working with these students would need to make some quick decisions concerning what to do next. Should students, for example, be corrected on their pronunciation? Should they be told to practice pronouncing the word? Such a decision could have negative consequences since students might interpret such a move as humiliating, especially if native-English speaking students were present. How then, should teachers respond to students who clearly do not understand grade-level appropriate text but who are doing their best to understand it? How can teachers most effectively recruit students who are learning English into the world of literate English speakers? Alternatively, how can teachers of students learning English avoid alienating these young people with respect to school literacy activities and at the same time provide them with the instruction they need to better comprehend the kinds of materials they will increasingly face as they move into high school?

In this situation, our instructor first vocalized the word in question, modeling correct pronunciation. He did not, however, belabor this point but rather immediately moved to checking whether the students understood the meaning of the word *league*. In other words, his emphasis was on how best to move students toward comprehending the text. He also explicitly told the students that the term Little League refers to kids' baseball teams; however, the students did not seem to pick up on this information. Because he knew something about the students' cultural backgrounds and because he knew Spanish, he was able to use both for this purpose. He linked the unknown word to something he knew they understood (soccer) and then he provided the students with the Spanish language cognate of the word in question, *liga*.

This instructor was able to combine his knowledge of the students and their communities with highly responsive instruction to their reading of the text. Of even more interest, after the instructor got the students to consider the cognate word, *liga*, Carla immediately made a connection to football leagues, something with which she is familiar. Ronnie, building on these comments, then translated what had been said back into Spanish, connecting it to her own background knowledge about the Mexican soccer [or fútbol] league. Carla responded by informing the group that she had intuitively made the appropriate cross-linguistic connection as she attempted to decode the word, but either she hadn't trusted this intuitive leap, or she didn't have a strategy for using her knowledge of Spanish to work through English text. Her admonishment ("You should have told me!") implies that she thinks these kinds of cognate relationships ought to be part of her literacy instruction.

We are aware that few teachers in US classrooms know the languages of their students. We are also aware that US classrooms contain students who speak dozens of languages. Even so, we wanted to start with this example because it shows how a knowledgeable teacher who is also well-informed concerning literacy instruction can guide students toward better comprehension of English-language text. In addition, notice how the instructor does not monopolize the floor and encourages student talk. Also, he does not assume that these young people are incapable of comprehending the text. He believes in them and finds ways to support their learning. This combination of beliefs and attitudes, informed understanding of literacy instruction, and the ability to enact necessary teaching is recommended by experts in the field of literacy (Risko & Walker-Dalhouse, 2012).

In many other classrooms, students might have spent all of their time focused on learning to pronounce the word *league*. In this situation, students not only ended up comprehending the text, they also began to develop tools to help them comprehend many other texts. These tools include a conceptual framework that Spanish and English share many words that mean essentially the same thing, an understanding that knowledge of Spanish is useful for comprehending English-language text, and the idea that bilingualism is a healthy and desirable achievement. These are all potential outcomes from skilled and informed teaching, especially if they are sustained over time by a teacher with high expectations for his or her students, with a high degree of knowledge of good teaching, and who knows how to put that knowledge into practice.

While it would be highly desirable if all teachers knew the languages spoken by their students, this is not always possible and so the question arises, how can we help those teachers who do not speak the languages of their students to be as responsive to their cultural and linguistic backgrounds as well as to their specific needs so that they become high-performing readers of English text? In the following example, another instructor works with students who are speakers of the Somali language, Mushunguli. In this example, the instructor is clearly unable to do the same kinds of things that occurred in the Little League example, yet he does end up guiding the students to better understanding of the text they are reading.

Highly Skilled Instruction in Which the Teacher and the Students Share Only One Language

Here, the instructor was working with Zed and Moheen, two Somali students who were unsure of how to translate the phrase *western guests* from *The All American Slurp* (Namioka, 1987) into Mushunguli, a Somali dialect. The instructor used two important teaching strategies. These included drawing students' attention back to the text and asking specific questions to help students understand what the word *western* meant in the story's context:

> TEXT: Since we had western guests, she set the table with large dinner plates, which we never used in Chinese meals (Namioka, 1987, p. 9).
> Instructor 2: What do we know about the characters in our story?
> Moheen: They are from two different places.

Instructor 2: Okay. Where are they from?
Moheen: China.
Instructor 2: Who is from China?
Zed: The family.
Instructor 2: Okay. What about the Gleasons? Where are they from?
Zed: The west.

Our instructor helped students infer the meaning of *western* by drawing on their understandings of where the characters were from in the story. Using the text to support translation mirrors what good readers often do when they summarize or clarify what they have read in order to identify possible meanings of new vocabulary words or predict outcomes in a story.

While this strategy helped Moheen and Zed understand the meaning of *western* in English (the source language), they were unsure how to say this word in Mushunguli (the target language). Clearly, the instructor could not tell them how to translate the word, but he was able to help them identify possible synonyms in English:

Instructor 2: Okay, right here. So, what does that tell us? What could *western* mean?
Moheen: America.
Instructor 2: Why do you say that?
Moheen: Because people in China, they say, like, to the other side of the map, it's the west side.
Instructor 2: And who's on that side?
Zed: USA.
Instructor 2: So what can we put for *western*?
Moheen: Um, USA, or American. American guests. That makes more sense now.

When students learning another language wish to express a concept for which they do not have a vocabulary word, they might use a paraphrasing strategy to "talk around" the word. This paraphrasing strategy is also useful when there might not be a word in the students' heritage language that directly corresponds with the English word. For example, if a translator does not know how to say the word *octopus* in the target language, they might say, "it's the animal that has eight legs" (Atkinson, 1987). The instructor prompted Moheen and Zed to try this strategy, and they decided that *American* worked as a translation given the context of the story.

In this example, the instructor encouraged students to use the text and to use a paraphrasing strategy to assist with translation. In doing so, Moheen and Zed not only honed their understandings of the text, but also developed important reading comprehension strategies. When they struggled to understand what western meant in English, they used context clues within the story. When they then needed to consider what western meant in their heritage language, they used a paraphrasing strategy that can support ELLs to express difficult concepts orally and in writing. Having students implement these strategies facilitates their reading comprehension. Taking things a step further by naming the strategies and reflecting on why they promote reading comprehension could help students acquire comprehension tools that they could use over and over again.

While we consider this to be an example of successful instruction, the instructor was unable to use understanding of the Somali culture or information derived from the students' first language to help them comprehend the English language text. It is very possible, for example, that the discourse concerning what is considered western and what is considered eastern does not resonate within Somali culture. Only someone with knowledge of this group could mesh a Somali perspective with skillful instruction for the purpose of promoting these students' reading comprehension. We include these two examples to recognize both the importance of methodologically informed teachers as well as those who combine teaching expertise with cultural and linguistic knowledge. We argue that all teachers, both monolingual and bilingual, can grow in all three areas: attitudes and beliefs about students, knowledge of teaching, and the ability to implement that knowledge with particular attention to the teaching and learning of culturally and linguistically diverse students.

Review of Research on Professional Development for Teachers of English Learners

So, the question arises, how do teachers—like our two instructors above—learn how to successfully teach students learning English? This question is important since there are growing numbers of students from linguistically diverse backgrounds. While the numbers of ELLs have increased between 80 and 90 percent over the last ten years, overall student populations have increased at a more modest pace—around 11 percent—and even declined in some states (OELA, 2004). This growth has highlighted the need for well-prepared teachers to meet these students' needs.

The current US student population is the most ethnically, racially, and linguistically diverse ever seen (NCES, 2005; Tienda & Mitchell, 2006). Unfortunately, these changes have not influenced parallel changes in teacher education programs. Perhaps as a result, 71 percent of ELLs from 2004–2007 were performing below grade level and are among the nation's lowest-performing students (NAEP, 2007; Lee, Grigg, & Donahue, 2007; Short & Fitzsimmons, 2007). Many teachers who work with ELLs are ill prepared to instruct them (NCES, 2002; Zimpher & Ashburn, 1992). Additionally, current teacher education research has not established how best to prepare future teachers to work with these students (Clark & Medina, 2000; Sleeter, 2008), nor do we know how best to support practicing teachers who wish to more effectively teach students learning English.

Noting an increase of research on multicultural teacher education during the last two decades, reviewers of this work (e.g., Hollins & Guzman, 2005; Risko, Roller, Cummins, Bean, Block, Anders, & Flood, 2008) concluded that it is narrow in scope and consequently has had little impact on teacher education reform. On the whole, findings are inconclusive, interventions are short-term (occurring in one semester or less), positive outcomes are generally reported on single measures (that are typically results of self-reporting), and assessment tools are inadequate. Lucas and Grinberg (2008) point out that the most obvious challenge facing teachers of English learners is that they must learn how to teach English and content (English language arts, math, science, social studies) at the same time. These authors add that few programs of teacher education prepare future teachers for this task.

To be fair, teaching English and content at the same time requires high levels of professional knowledge and a good deal of teaching skill. Valdés (2001) describes teachers who with the best of intentions struggled with this task:

> The task of actually teaching subject matter to students who did not understand any English at all, however, was challenging indeed. Interviews with teachers revealed that they spent hours preparing presentations with accompanying visuals in order to get across only one or two main concepts. (p. 70)

Sadly, few practicing teachers have completed any sort of coursework designed to prepare them to teach English language learners. Lucas and Grinberg (2008) report that a great majority of US teachers (74 percent) have no recent professional development for working with ELL students.

Despite limitations of current research, it is useful as a stepping-off point for thinking about how to provide high quality literacy instruction to students like Ronnie, Carla, Joyce, and Celina and Moheen and Zed. Our links to this body of literature provide a much-needed historical continuity that too often is overlooked by researchers (Risko et al., 2008; Wideen, Mayer-Smith, & Moon, 1998).

In the following, we present our understanding of the research on the professional development of teachers of ELLs. This work draws on the research of Darling-Hammond and Bransford (2005), as well as ELL teacher educators (de Jong & Harper, 2005; Wong-Fillmore & Snow, 2000), and other teacher educators, such as Shulman (1998), who proposed six commonplaces of professional development (e.g., service to society, body of scholarly knowledge, engagement in practical action). Taken together, there is considerable support for conceptualizing teacher education as a process that addresses simultaneously the development of teachers' dispositions, pedagogical knowledge, and practical teaching skills.

Dispositions

Studies have shown that teachers, especially those who are White, often have lower expectations for English language learners and other minority students (Garas-York, 2010; Marx, 2000; Terrill & Mark, 2000). Marx (2000), for example, compared the beliefs, attitudes, and perceptions of groups of White pre-service teachers (PSTs) and Hispanic PSTs, showing that Hispanics believed their Mexican-origin students were capable and could succeed academically, while their White peers indicated relatively low expectations and predicted school failure. Although research has shown that preservice teachers' beliefs and belief systems are difficult to change (Hollins & Torres-Guzmán, 2005; Wideen et al., 1998), especially over the course of a single semester, there is some evidence that PSTs can benefit from highly focused instruction designed to reduce prejudices (Obidah, 2000) and increase awareness of the benefits of culturally responsive teaching (e.g., Ball, 2000; Tadesse, Hoot, & Watson-Thompson, 2009). Worthy and Patterson's (2001) provision of carefully supervised tutoring experiences influenced noticeable shifts of PSTs dispositions, from deficit thinking to positive expectations for students and confidence for teaching culturally diverse students. In other studies, direct involvement with children (reading to students in community centers, writing family stories, tutoring) has been shown to have positive mediating effects on negative dispositions and expectations (Kidd, Sanchez, & Thorp, 2002; Wolf, Ballentine, & Hill, 2000; Xu, 2000).

Pedagogical Knowledge

Our conception of pedagogical knowledge for teaching ELLs draws in part on Shulman's (1998) idea of pedagogical *content* knowledge, which he describes as "the ways of representing and formulating the subject that make it comprehensible to others," as well as "an understanding of what makes the learning of specific topics easy or difficult: the conceptions and preconceptions that students of different ages and backgrounds bring with them to the learning of those most frequently taught topics and lessons" (p. 9). In other words, what do teachers need to know about their subjects and their students to be able to represent subject matter in a way that will be understood?

Many researchers in the field of culturally responsive pedagogy (CRP) have identified what they consider to be effective instructional practices for ELLs (Banks et al., 2005; González, Moll, & Amanti, 2005; Katz, 2000; Ladson-Billings, 1995; Nathenson-Mejía & Escamilla, 2003; Torok & Aguilar, 2000). A fundamental tenet of this approach is that teachers recognize and draw on students' linguistic knowledge and cultural backgrounds. However, few empirical studies focus on how teachers, either pre-service or in-service, learn to apply this knowledge (for a rare example, see Rymes, 2002).

We include learning a second language within the category of culturally responsive teaching because doing so provides teachers with insight and information useful for working with ELL students. Pray (2013), for example, illustrated how PSTs came to understand the demands and challenges of learning a new language while simultaneously struggling to acquire grade-level appropriate content. She took a group of PSTs to Mexico for an extended immersion experience where students studied Spanish, completed coursework to prepare them to teach English learners in the US, and taught English to local Mexican children. As second language learners of Spanish, they often had to struggle to be understood because of their incomplete understanding of the language. As a result, they began to understand how important one's first language is to learning a second language. Early on, many of them voiced firm and settled beliefs that immigrant students must learn English, they must learn it quickly, and they must use it at all times. As they went through the process of learning some Spanish, they began to change their views and voiced comments such as the following:

> I now understand how my students sometimes feel in my math class. I know how frustrating it is for my English language learners to not fully understand what is being asked of them. (p. 15)
>
> Yesterday I about started crying in my Spanish class. The frustration of trying to learn a new language is immense. I cannot express [enough] my desire to flush Spanish down the toilet. (p. 14)

These PSTs recognized that they needed the occasional comfort of another English speaker to ease their anxiety. They became quite vocal about their right to use English when they so desired and they clung to friends with whom they could share familiar cultural experiences. Findings such as these compel us to recommend that all teachers working with English learners complete at least two years of foreign language study. Alternatively, at least a semester spent living abroad learning another language also provides teachers with the experiences necessary to understand and empathize with persons learning a new language.

Lucas and Grinberg (2008) also build a compelling case that successful teachers of English learners need to have specific understandings and experiences with language to be successful with ELL students. These researchers have synthesized the research and concluded the following: Teachers of ELL students need to engage in formal study of language and possess knowledge of how it operates, they need proficiency in a second language, and they need to have engaged in extended contact with persons who speak languages other than English. They add that teachers need to have a good working knowledge of their students' linguistic backgrounds, experiences and proficiencies.

An Instructional Approach that Supports Positive Dispositions, Knowledge of Literacy Instruction, and Pedagogical Applications

We conclude our chapter by presenting one approach to instruction that fosters positive teacher dispositions, requires and leverages knowledge of literacy instruction, and provides ongoing opportunities to implement that knowledge. TRANSLATE, as an instructional approach, embodies culturally responsive pedagogy in that it "privilege[s] language resources that students bring from their everyday linguistic practices and repertoires outside school" (Lee, 2008, p. 275), and sets high expectations by working with grade-level texts. Fillmore and Fillmore (2012) point out that English learners seldom have access to complex texts in English and that such access is essential to discover how academic language works.

Of course, there are many other ways that teachers can learn about and make use of their students' language resources, but TRANSLATE provides a relatively straightforward means for accomplishing this goal. Students have multiple opportunities while engaging in TRANSLATE to inform the instructor concerning their perceived language proficiencies, their prior schooling abroad, and their levels of literacy in their first language. Although perhaps surprising, teachers from mainstream backgrounds do not typically inquire about these matters, perhaps because they hold to frameworks that position students' first languages as impediments to learning English.

While CRP is an exciting innovation in the field of education research, to date there is a paucity of unequivocal demonstrations of its effectiveness. Sleeter (2012), a noted authority in multicultural education, for example, argues that more and better research on CRP is necessary. She states:

> First, there is a clear need for evidence-based research that documents connections between culturally responsive pedagogy and student outcomes that include, but are not necessarily limited to, academic achievement. Politically, it is difficult to build a case to change approaches to teaching without strong evidence. Small-scale case studies illustrate what is possible, but we also need research on the impact of scaled-up work in culturally responsive pedagogy, *including research showing how teachers can learn to use it in their classrooms.* (p. 578)

Engagement: Choosing Academic Excellence

Excerpt 1: "Que es un elf?"
Carla: Look at her.
Ronnie: xx. Es un duende
Carla: No, really. xx Aquí no! Mira (Not here! look.)

Ronnie: xxx ¿Qué dijiste? That's xxx..Ahí es un duende ... las orejas (What did you say? That is an elf [dwarf, goblin] ... the ears).
Carla: xxxte Dije que ya no. (I said no, not any more.)
....
Instructor: What'd you think about this?
Carla: It's a girl. She's a girl, <and then she>
Ronnie: <They're> best friends.
Instructor: They're best friends.
Carla: And she turns into a ... un duende (an elf).
Instructor: Una? (A?)
Carla: An elf.
Instructor: An elf? OK.
Ronnie: That's not an elf.
Carla: ¿Qué es un elf? (What is an elf?)
Ronnie: Es una de esas cositas verdes. ¿Cómo se llaman esas cositas? (It's one of those little green things. What do they call those little things?)
Carla: Un duende. (An elf.)
Ronnie: No.
Instructor: Like a leprechaun?
Ronnie: Yes. Una leprechaun.
Carla: No.
Ronnie: Es una leprechaun. (It's a leprechaun.).
Carla: It isn't a leprechaun. [Laughing.]

Clearly, there is a need for more and better research on CRP. Using a design research approach, my colleagues and I have begun the work of determining how TRANSLATE makes possible the instructional conditions that support students' participation and learning. We did this to answer the question: What pedagogical moves lead to increased student strategy use, comprehension, and engagement with curricular texts? We also wanted to know whether our instructional approach leads students learning English to enhance their use of reading comprehension strategies, improve their reading comprehension, and increase their engagement with curricular texts. If so, how and in what ways?

The findings from our project focused on three specific goals of CRP: increasing engagement, teaching disciplinary modes of reasoning, and empowering students to think about their cultural practices as resources for learning. These goals deal primarily with pedagogical applications but they also touch on teacher knowledge and their dispositions toward students learning English.

We posited that by using translation, students became more engaged during reading because they appreciated schoolteacher recognition of their first language. Translation provided opportunities for peer interaction about dual language processing, which validated students' bilingualism while promoting deeper understanding of both English and native languages.

In the preceding example, Ronnie and Carla interact with each other and the instructor a total of 18 times. For ten of those interactions, the girls switch into Spanish or speak entirely in Spanish and eight are entirely in English. While this instructor spoke Spanish, he was much more fluent in English and only occasionally addressed students in Spanish. Notice too that the instructor took only four turns in this segment. Students were looking at several books and trying to decide which they would like to read. They did not translate text, only the words for elf, leprechaun, and *duende*. What is interesting here is that Ronnie and Carla move back and forth across their two languages searching for information on little green magical creatures. They note that the book they are interested in is about a girl who transforms into a *duende*, which they translate as elf. Ronnie argues that the girl does not turn into an elf but rather something else and she accepts the instructor's suggestion of a leprechaun. Translation triggered translanguaging and this resulted in significant student participation.

Disciplinary Modes of Reasoning: Reading Like a Scholar

Excerpt 2: "His heart had turned grey"
Celina: Dentro de mi si yo estuviera … (Inside of me, as if I were …)
Carla and Celina: Corno si mi corzón se hubiera puesto … (As if my heart had become …)
Celina: Cambiado, Carla (Changed, Carla)
Carla: Como si mi corazón estuviera cambiandose en gris, gris (As if my heart had changed to gray, gray)
Ronnie: I think that's how you spell it.
Carla: How do you say turn in Spanish?
Ronnie: Me voltié? (I turned [around]) Turned, like turned
Carla: Turned, like my heart had turned gray.
Ronnie: Oh! y mi corazón se volteó (Oh, and my heart turned around).
Carla: No, that doesn't make sense.
Ronnie: That doesn't make sense. Xxx. Cambió
Carla: Volvió a gris (Turned to gray).
Instructor: ¿Cambió (Changed?).
Ronnie: Y se volvió. (And it changed.)
Instructor: ¿Se volvió? (It changed?).
Carla: Como si estuviera cambiado (As if it had changed.)
Instructor: So what are these two translations telling us about the story and telling us about what's going on with Marty?
Ronnie: He was cold. He didn't care about anybody. He just wanted to kill the person that killed his brother. He wanted to feel the pain. <He wanted>, the person who killed his brother, the pain's he's going through cause he killed him.

Instructor: OK.

Ronnie: That didn't make sense.

Instructor: No, it did make sense. You said he's turning cold. I thought that was an interesting way to put it. He just wants to kill, and make the person feel the sadness.

Carla: <He's just sad.> Estoy apagada. (I'm turned off.)

Ronnie: <[the person feels]>

Joyce: Deprimido. (Depressed.)

In terms of disciplinary modes of reasoning, translation required our participants to engage in the kind of close reading employed by experts in many fields, particularly authors who consider the needs of their audience. Close reading encouraged students to engage in a back and forth movement between the original text and their developing translation. Students talked explicitly about vocabulary and the range of meanings of words—or the microstructure of text (Kintsch & Rawson, 2005)—and they discussed central concepts, phrases, metaphors and idioms. This talk was optimal for discussing theme, plot, or character development within narratives, and relationships among details and central concepts in informational texts. One effect of translation included its ability to prompt students to make more connections to their prior knowledge.

Here the students move back and forth across the two languages and they try out a translation. *Voltearse* means to turn but more like turn around, physically as in, "I turned to see what was happening in the street." Ronnie provides *voltearse* when asked how to translate the verb *turn*. She then clarifies by saying in English, *turned*, in the past tense. Carla adds more context and it is clear that the range of meaning for the word *turned* in English overlaps but is not entirely continuous with that of the verb *voltearse*, which leads to Ronnie saying that the translation does not make sense. Here we can see that the translation, *mi corazón se volteó*, or *my heart (physically) turned*, leaves Ronnie with an incomprehensible statement. Her recognition that one's heart cannot turn by itself leads to the production of two alternatives, *volverse* and *cambiar*. Either one is suitable for this purpose but the students settle on *cambiar* in its participle form. The question here would be whether the students, because of the translation, came away with a deeper, more fully developed understanding of the original English text. Does their understanding remain at the sentence level? Are they able to use this understanding in terms of building a larger envisionment of the text? Later statements on the part of the students, particularly Ronnie, indicate that the translation work seemed to move them towards better comprehension.

Ronnie's reasoning is very deeply embedded in and indebted to her knowledge of Spanish and her knowledge of English. In other words, translation triggered something cognitive. The understanding depends on the fact that the Spanish words *voltearse* and *cambiar*, and the English word *turn*, have overlapping but distinct ranges of meaning. This kind of thinking is evidence that students were beginning to employ their full range of linguistic competence to engage in disciplinary modes of reasoning. In other words, the students were engaged in careful word selection, just as an author does when thinking about a particular audience. Without a very conscious effort involving both languages, and without an opportunity to compare and contrast these lexical items, Ronnie probably would not have arrived at the understanding she did.

Empowerment: Transforming Student Attitudes

While collaborative translation activities helped students understand more of the reading required by school, our underlying goal was for students to leverage their full linguistic resources for a variety of reading tasks in and out of school. This entailed a transformation in the way they thought about the practice of translation. As our student participants mastered the TRANSLATE approach they begin to think of translation not just as a way to render words in another language, but as a way to control their own learning. Lee (2008) argued that CRP can give students the tools to overcome obstacles created by hegemonic school practices. Our position is that, for linguistically diverse students, this can happen when students feel empowered to use their first language resources.

In some of the groups we worked with, students appeared to make a fundamental shift in the way they thought about the affordances of using their first language for academic purposes. When Zed was asked at the beginning of the intervention what piece of text is a "good" line to translate, he responded that it would have no difficult words in Somali or in English. A good line of text, in essence, was an easy line of text. After participating in the TRANSLATE intervention for two weeks, these students began to understand the activity's payoff for deepening their understanding of Somali, English, and the text they were working with. At this point, the students' definitions of a good sentence to translate shifted dramatically. Towards the end of the intervention we asked them again what might be a good line to translate. Zed wrote that the sentence would "describe words that you don't understand" and Moheen wrote that it would be "a sentence that makes you think" and one that affords the opportunity to "learn new Somali and English words." The goal for students, as they appropriate the tools and become aware of their potential, changes from simply converting meaning from one language to another, to leveraging their native language and cultural backgrounds for new kinds of learning.

Conclusion

There is growing awareness of the importance of language for the academic achievement of ELL students. This importance extends to teacher knowledge of language, primarily for the purpose of helping ELL students learn about language and then use these understandings to drive their academic learning. We conclude, on the basis of our own research and our review of available literature, that students learning English need instruction that leads them to be aware of all their linguistic resources. Teachers that know the most about language, particularly bilingualism and the language learning process, are best positioned to help students become aware of these resources.

Students can develop what are called meta-level understandings of language as they engage in the activity of translation. Their translating, however, requires instruction and activities designed to help them move back and forth across their two languages for the purpose of comprehension. The more students engage in these activities, the more likely they are to reflect on their actions and develop tools that facilitate comprehension. Carla asserted that knowing the cognate vocabulary tied to the term *Little League* would have helped her to make sense of the book she was reading. Zed and Moheen came to the realization that the activity of translating led them to think more about their reading, and also that their first language was useful to their thinking.

The students' insights about language were the result of teaching grounded in positive dispositions about these students. In other words, their teachers assumed they could be successful readers and then supported their learning with the necessary teaching. Their teachers also knew that these young people needed to be shown what to focus on in a text, as well as how to make use of their first language to process that information. Finally, as teachers led their students to think bilingually about reading comprehension, they as teachers learned more about how to enact effective literacy instruction with their bilingual students.

We conclude by noting that students learning English can develop their reading comprehension abilities. They need and deserve, however, teachers who believe in them and know about their unique needs and abilities, and who can implement effective literacy instruction.

Spotlight Recommendation

The two examples that we used to begin this chapter show that students who are learning English can analyze language. Specifically, students develop meta-linguistic awareness as they compare and contrast differences across their two languages, reason about text, and draw conclusions based on familiar information. All of these activities are higher-level thinking and students learning English receive very few opportunities to think in these ways in school during typical instruction. While students learning English often engage in higher level thinking outside of school, we encourage teachers to find ways to more frequently tap into their thinking abilities. We also recommend that teachers and students take these efforts further and develop their own personal strategies grounded in their own experiences.

1. In our first example, the teacher pronounced the word *league* after students mispronounced it. Then, the student, with prompting from the teacher, produced the Spanish equivalent and cognate of the word *league*, *liga*. The teacher connected the words *league* and *liga*. We recommend that, to the extent possible, teachers work with students and guide them to explain the general principal that cognate relationships exist across their two languages and also how they might use that knowledge strategically. Across the examples, teachers promoted comprehension (beyond word knowledge only) explicitly with strategies of connecting words/text ideas to students' prior knowledge, "talking around words" to help students access the context, paraphrasing ideas in their own words, and focusing on key concepts that connect to details. Teachers encouraged students to move back and forth across their two languages to generate meanings and confirm understandings.

    Similarly, the Somali students benefited from a teacher who held high expectations for her students and who assumed that they were capable of reasoning about texts and that their language and cultural backgrounds were an important source of information.

2. The work of Pray (2013) and that of Lucas and Grinberg (2008) point out the importance of teachers' personal language learning efforts. We recommend that teachers reflect on these efforts to learn a second language. Why did the pre-service teachers in Pray's research get so upset about learning Spanish? What factors were most influential in determining their attitudes? How do people in your school and district respond to students and parents with less than native-like proficiency in English? How can these experiences and reactions be shaped for more positive outcomes?

3. An important research finding concerning English learners is that they don't have many opportunities to practice using English in US schools. Consider your own instruction and compare the amount of talk that you produce as a teacher vs. the amount of talk your students produce. TRANSLATE is grounded in the idea that students bring valuable language resources to the task of learning. This approach creates opportunities for students to share what they know about their first language with other students and the teacher, thus providing them with opportunities to talk. We recommend that teachers and other educators identify the benefits that accrue when students talk more and have opportunities to learn from their peers, realizing the power of collaborative learning.

4. Teachers should listen carefully to what students say as they work through a translation. While engaged in a discussion of how Spanish marks nouns as either feminine or masculine, one of our student participants noted how a fellow student's language was marked by regional differences. She asked where she and her family lived in their country of origin. We inferred that this student had an inherent understanding that region of origin influences

one's language use. Her insight had to be inferred, of course, but an astute teacher could help students recognize what Carol Lee calls tacit knowledge and help students convert this into explicit knowledge or academic language.

References

Atkinson, D. (1987). The mother tongue in the classroom: A neglected resource? *English Language Teaching Journal*, 41(4), 241–247.

Ball, A. F. (2000). Teachers' developing philosophies on literacy and their use in urban schools: A Vygotskian perspective on internal activity and teacher change. In C. D. Lee & P. Smagorinsky (Eds.), *Vygotskian perspectives on literacy research: Constructing meaning through collaborative inquiry* (pp. 226–255). New York: Cambridge University Press.

Banks, J., Cochran-Smith, M., Moll, L., Richert, A., Zeichner, K., LePage, P., Darling-Hammond, L., & Duffy, H. (2005). Teaching diverse learners. In L. Darling-Hammond & J. Bransford (Eds.), *Preparing teachers for a changing world: What teachers should learn and be able to do* (pp. 232–274). San Francisco: Jossey-Bass.

Clark, C., & Medina, C. (2000). How reading and writing literacy narratives affect preservice teachers' understandings of literacy, pedagogy, and multiculturalism. *Journal of Teacher Education*, 51(1), 63–76.

Darling-Hammond, L. & Bransford, J. (2005). *Preparing teachers for a changing world: What teachers should learn and be able to do.* San Francisco, CA: Jossey-Bass.

de Jong, E. & Harper, C. (2005). Preparing mainstream teachers for English language learners: Is being a good teacher good enough? *Teacher Education Quarterly*, 32(2), 101–124.

Dewey, J. (1958). *Experience and nature* (Vol. 1). New York: Dover.

Fillmore, L. W. & Fillmore, C. J. (2012). What does text complexity mean for English learners and language minority students? In K. Hakuta & M. Santos (Eds.), *Understanding language: Language, literacy and learning in the content areas* (pp. 64–74). Palo Alto, CA: Stanford University.

Garas-York, K. (2010). Overlapping student environments: An examination of the home-school connection and its impact on achievement. *Education and Urban Society*, 42(4), 430–449.

González, N., Moll, L. C., & Amanti, C. (Eds.). (2005). *Funds of knowledge: Theorizing practices in households, communities, and classrooms.* Mahwah, NJ: Lawrence Erlbaum Associates.

Hollins, E. & Guzmán, M. T. (2005). Research on preparing teachers for diverse populations. In M. Cochran-Smith & K. Zeichner (Eds.), *Studying teacher education: The report of the AERA Panel on research and teacher education* (pp. 477–548). Mahwah, NJ: Lawrence Erlbaum Associates.

Jiménez, R. T., David, S., Fagan, K., Risko, V. Pacheco, M., Pray, L., & Gonzales, M. (2015). Using translation to drive conceptual development for students becoming literate in English as an additional language. *Research in the Teaching of English*, 49(3), 248–271.

Katz, S. R. (2000). Promoting bilingualism in the era of Unz: Making sense of the gap between research, policy, and practice in teacher education. *Multicultural Education*, 8(1), 2–7.

Kidd, J. K., Sanchez, S. Y., & Thorp, E. K. (2002). A focus on family stories: Enhancing pre-service teachers' cultural awareness. *National Reading Conference Yearbook*, 51, 242–252.

Kintsch, W. & Rawson, K. (2005). Comprehension. In M. J. Snowling & C. Hulme (Eds.), *The science of reading: A handbook* (pp. 209–226). Malden, MA: Blackwell.

Ladson-Billings, G. (1995). Toward a theory of culturally relevant pedagogy. *American Educational Research Journal*, 32(3), 465–491.

Langan, P. & Alirez, B. (2004). *Brothers in Arms*. West Berlin, NJ: Townsend Press.

Lee, C. (2008). The centrality of culture to the scientific study of learning and development: How an ecological framework in education research facilitates civic responsibility. *Educational Researcher*, 37(5), 267–279.

Lee, J., Grigg, W., & Donahue, P. (2007). *The nation's report card: Reading 2007*. Washington, DC: National Center for Education Statistics, Institute of Education Sciences, US Department of Education.

Lucas, T. & Grinberg, J. (2008). Responding to the linguistic reality of mainstream classrooms: Preparing all teachers to teach English language learners. In M. Cochran-Smith, S. Feiman-Nemser, D. J. McIntyre, & K. E. Demers (Eds.), *Handbook of research on teacher education* (3rd ed.) (pp. 606–636). New York: Routledge.

Marx, S. (2000). An exploration of preservice teacher perceptions of second language learners in the mainstream classroom. *Texas Papers in Foreign Language Education*, 5(1), 207–221.

Namioka, L. (1987). The all-American slurp. In D. Gallo (Ed.), *Visions* (pp. 32–42). New York: Bantam Doubleday.

Nathenson-Mejía, S. & Escamilla, K. (2003). Connecting with Latino children: Bridging cultural gaps with children's literature. *Bilingual Research Journal*, 27(1), 101–116.

National Assessment of Educational Progress (2007). *The nation's report card: 2007*. Washington, DC: Institute for Education Sciences, US.Department of Education.

National Center for Education Statistics. (2002). Schools and staffing survey, 1999–2000. Overview of the data for public, private, public charter, and Bureau of Indian Affairs elementary and secondary schools. Washington, DC: US Department of Education, Office of Educational Research and Improvement.

National Center for Education Statistics (2005). *The condition of education 2005: Indicator 5 Language minority school-age children*. Washington, DC: US Department of Education/ Institute of Education Sciences.

Obidah, J. (2000). Mediating boundaries of race, class, and professional authority as a critical multiculturalist. *Teachers College Record*, 102(5), 1035–1060.

OELA (2004). *The biennial report to Congress on the implementation of the Title III State Formula Grant Program school years 2004–06*. Washington, DC: US Department of Education.

Pray, L. (2013). Developing an intercultural orientation in an ESL endorsement program: A journey from resistance to affirmation. In C. T. Cowart & G. Anderson (Eds.), *Teaching and leading in diverse schools, 8th monograph edition*. Arlington, VA: Canh Nam Publishers.

Risko, V. J., Roller, C. M., Cummins, C., Bean, R. M., Block, C. C., Anders, P. L., & Flood, J. (2008). A critical analysis of research on reading teacher education. *Reading Research Quarterly*, 43(3), 252–288.

Risko, V. J., & Walker-Dalhouse, D. (2012). *Be that teacher!* New York: Teachers College Press.

Rymes, B. (2002). Language in development in the United States: Supervising adult ESOL preservice teachers in an immigrant community. *TESOL Quarterly*, 36(3), 431–452.

Short, D. & Fitzsimmons, S. (2007). *Urgent but overlooked: The literacy crisis among adolescent English language learners*. Washington, DC: Alliance for Excellent Education.

Shulman, L. S. (1998). Theory, practice and the education of professionals. *The Elementary School Journal*, 98(5), 511–526.

Sleeter, C. E. (2008). Preparing white teachers for diverse students. In M. Cochran-Smith, S. Feiman-Nemser, & J. McIntyre C.E. (Eds.) *Preparing White teachers for diverse students. Handbook of research on teacher education* (3rd ed.) (pp. 559–582). New York: Routledge.

Sleeter, C. (2012). Confronting the marginalization of culturally responsive pedagogy. *Urban Education*, 47(3), 562–584.

Tadesse, S., Hoot, J., & Watson-Thompson, O. (2009). Exploring the special needs of African refugee children in U.S. schools. *Childhood Education*, 85, 352–356.

Terrill, M. & Mark, D. L. H. (2000). Preservice teachers' expectations for schools with children of color and second-language learners. *Journal of Teacher Education*, 51(2), 149–155.

Tienda, M. & Mitchell, F. (2006). *Multiple origins, uncertain destinies.* Washington, DC: National Academies Press.

Torok, C. E. & Aguilar, T. E. (2000). Changes in preservice teachers' knowledge and beliefs about language issues. *Equity & Excellence in Education*, 33(2), 24–31.

Valdés, G. (2001). *Learning and not learning English.* New York: Teachers College Press.

Wolf, S. A., Ballentine, D., & Hill, L. A. (2000). "Only connect!": Cross-cultural connections in the reading lives of preservice teachers and children. *Journal of Literacy Research*, 32(4), 533–569.

Worthy, J., & Patterson, E. (2001). "I can't wait to see Carlos!": Preservice teachers, situated learning, and personal relationships with students. *Journal of Literacy Research*, 33(2), 303–344.

Wideen, M. F., Mayer-Smith, J., & Moon B. (1998). A critical analysis of the research on learning-to-teach. *Review of Education Research*, 68(2), 130–178.

Wong-Fillmore, L. & Snow, C. E. (2000). *What teachers need to know about language.* Washington, DC: US Department of Education.

Xu, H. (2000). Preservice teachers in a literacy methods course consider issues of diversity. *Journal of Literacy Research*, 32(4), 505–531.

Zimpher, N. & Ashburn, E. (1992). Countering parochialism in teacher candidates. In M. Dilworth (Ed.), *Diversity in teacher education* (pp. 40–62). San Francisco, CA: Jossey-Bass.

4

MOTIVATING AND INSTRUCTING AFRICAN AMERICAN STUDENTS IN CLASSROOMS

John T. Guthrie and Angela McRae

An Educational Perspective on Reading Engagement

Many scholars who study achievement in underrepresented populations, such as African Americans, emphasize structural and cultural forces in society. For example, William Julius Wilson in *More Than Just Race: Being Black and Poor in the Inner City* (2009) referred to two traditional forces in sociology. One force is the social act, such as discrimination in hiring, admission to educational institutions, or job promotion. Aligned with social acts are social processes, which refer to joblessness, declining wages, and technological changes in the workplace that challenge those with lower educational opportunities. For example, African Americans are overrepresented in low skilled jobs, such as in the food service industry. Sociological variables of poverty, joblessness, and inadequate educational opportunities resulting in low skills that characterize a large proportion of African American families are associated with low educational attainment, and specifically with low reading achievement. Sociologists have often attributed low achievement of students to these structural barriers faced by low-income families. However, it is equally possible that low reading achievement produces barriers to jobs and higher education. We suggest that the variables of achievement and economic forces are reciprocal. Because of this reciprocity, and because it is not within the power of teachers or school administrators to increase jobs or decrease poverty, educators must look beyond sociological variables for solutions to the achievement gap.

The cultural perspective on achievement has been explored by Cynthia Hudley and others in a 36-chapter volume entitled *Handbook of African American Psychology* (2009). Joined by others, Hudley (2009) emphasized that the motivations of students are essential to their cultural identities. These motivations include goals, dispositions, and behaviors that direct students' lives. Hudley stated, "I explore the extent to which motivationally relevant variables including self-beliefs and perception of barriers to success account for individual differences in African American student achievement" (p. 188). Regrettably, attempts to explain achievement by comparing levels of African American and European American motivations have been frustrating for these cultural analysts. For example, the level of reading self-efficacy of African American students is equal to the level of self-efficacy of European American students. This contradicts the expectation of psychologists who expected that African American students' self-efficacy would be lower than that of European American students. A majority of the comparisons of motivations and beliefs of African American and European American students have not led to cogent explanations of low achievement for African American students (Hudley, 2009). The exception to this pattern is the valuing of education, which is lower for adolescent African American students than European American students (Graham & Hudley, 2005).

Among educational researchers, a popular perspective on African American students' learning in schools is the cultural historical framework. Kris Gutiérrez featured this perspective in her 2011 AERA Presidential Address in New Orleans. In this framework, effective teachers empower students to appropriate practices of literacy that are widely used by members of their communities. Students learn social practices such as reading complex text for authentic purposes, including building models, creating posters of their knowledge in a domain, or participating in a debate. As Gutiérrez and Vossoughi (2010) said, "We argue that social design experiments organized around expansive forms of learning, powerful literacies, dialogic exchange, situated practice, and evidence-based observations of children's learning can help promote instrumental uses of theory, through which novice teachers can develop and sustain thoughtful, robust, and informed understandings of learning, and come to value learning over teaching and joint activity over individual learning arrangements" (pp. 111–112).

A limitation of this cultural historical perspective on collaborative action in teaching is that investigators have not taken the step of examining whether these particular forms of education enable students to gain expertise in reading or in a knowledge domain, in comparison to other approaches. To determine whether the proposals drawn from the cultural historical perspective are valuable in education, simple comparisons are needed between conventional education and these innovative approaches. Yet the scientific step of making quantitative comparisons between the proposed innovations and other comparable forms of teaching has not been forwarded. Although this perspective is powerful, the next stage of this line of inquiry will be to identify specific teaching arrangements and document their comparative utility in fostering expertise for African American students.

To understand the optimal educational contexts for increasing reading achievement of African American students, it is imperative to focus on empirically established pathways of learning for these students. Instead of attending to the differences between African American and European American students, it is fruitful to identify the ways in which high-achieving African American students can be contrasted with their lower-achieving African American peers. To the extent that motivations within the African American student population impact achievement, the argument that achievement is attributable to structural or cultural forces is weakened, and the emphasis on individual resilience is strengthened. This leads us to look for the qualities of African American students that correlate to their achievement.

As contended by sociologists such as Wilson (2009) and Eugene Robinson, a Pulitzer Prize winning journalist, there are four groups of African Americans rather than one "Black America" in the United States. According to Robinson (2010), African Americans form four groups consisting of (a) a transcendent group, which has enormous wealth, power, and influence; (b) a mainstream group, which is a middle class majority with full ownership stake in American society; (c) emerging groups consisting of individuals with mixed race and heritage and communities of Black immigrants; and (d) an abandoned minority with less hope of escaping poverty and dysfunction than at any time since the end of Reconstruction.

One prominent transcendent African American is former President Barack Obama, but he is joined by such luminaries as Oprah Winfrey, Earvin "Magic" Johnson Jr., who has become a media mogul, Robert Johnson, founder of Black Entertainment Television, John Johnson, a grandson of slaves who created *Ebony* and *Jet* magazines, Franklin Raines, who served as the CEO of Fannie Mae, and accomplished surgeon Dr. Ben Carson. These individuals transcended poverty, prejudice, and educational barriers. All of these individuals attained their transcendence through exceptional expertise in their lines of specialty, which relies on long-term devotion. As recounted in the *Road to Excellence* by Ericsson (1996), the acquisition of expertise in business, the arts, or sciences usually requires 10 years or 10,000 hours of disciplined participation.

Many transcendent African Americans distinguished themselves in reading and literacy. In a remarkable recounting of the books read by noted African American writers, Holloway (2006) concluded to her surprise that many African Americans read broadly as well as deeply. Holloway identified the books in the libraries and favorite reading lists of noteworthy luminaries such as W. E. B. Dubois, Ralph Ellison, Richard Wright, John Hope Franklin, Angela Davis, Malcolm X, Eldridge Cleaver, Maya Angelou, James Baldwin, Nikki Govanni, Langston Hughes, Leon Forrest, and Oprah Winfrey. Although she anticipated that these transcendents would focus on the factor of race in their professional or scholarly lives, she concluded that "the way to mark their uniqueness, education, and competence seemed to be to call attention to their immersion in a literature that is best identified as classic within the English and European American language traditions" (p. 181). Holloway says that "Malcolm X establishes his 'nearness' and his intimacy with books, the library, and the college-level quality of its presence as a way of indicating that he might share their credibility or at least that it might be passed on to him" (p. 83). In brief, transcendent African Americans have displayed rare expertise in reading and in the acquisition of universal perspectives through books.

A majority of transcendent African Americans point proudly not only to their expertise in literacy, but to their devotion to schooling. The world class African American surgeon, Ben Carson, was born in poverty-stricken urban Baltimore. He reported that he had no competition for being the bottom of the class in early elementary school. In Grade 5, his mother told him in no uncertain terms to turn off the television and read one book a week. After reading about geology he discovered he had more knowledge of rocks than anyone in the class and his teacher was paying attention to him with pride. From that moment, Ben Carson (1992) aimed to be more knowledgeable than anyone in his classes. He ultimately graduated with an M.D. from Johns Hopkins University and became a noted surgeon and writer. His pride in graduating from Harvard University and Johns Hopkins Medical School permeate his autobiography, *Think Big*. Likewise, in *Strength in What Remains*, an African adolescent named Deo recounted his escape from genocidal conflict in Burundi, landing in Harlem and making his way to medical school at Columbia University (Kidder, 2009). From war-torn Burundi he attained an M.D. at Columbia University and returned to build hospitals in Burundi. Both attributed their accomplishments to the power of literacy and schooling at all stages.

Transcendent African Americans have often followed a pattern charted by cultural anthropologists such as Scribner and Cole (1999) and Gutiérrez and Lee (2009). Individuals such as Ben Carson and Deo gain passionate affinities for learning through literacy. As partners with more experienced members of a community, they join in a common endeavor, share diverse forms of expertise, produce outcomes, and are proactive in their own learning. More broadly, these processes characterize the acquisition of language in all cultures, the learning of computers among young students, and the adoption of literacy in the transcendent achievers in the African American community.

This anthropological perspective suggests that when students or adults participate in a community of practice with diverse members, their learning will be more rapid and more permanent than the learning of individuals in other situations (Rueda, August, & Goldenberg, 2006). This hypothesis was tested and confirmed in a study of young adults, ages 21 to 25, representing a national sample in the United States which included substantial samples of African Americans, European Americans, and Hispanics. Individual interviews with all persons were undertaken to understand their diverse diet of reading and time spent with a wide range of topics and genre. Simultaneously, the reading level on a widely used measure by the National Assessment of Educational Progress (NAEP) was assessed for these young adults. One result of this national study was that the connection between the level of reading expertise, as shown in NAEP scores, and the breadth of reading activities was stronger for African American than European American students. African American students who were equal to European American students in their high volume of reading activity were equal in reading achievement. However, as the amount and variety of reading decreased among African Americans, their achievement declined more precipitously than it did for European Americans. Payoff for reading widely was higher for African American than European American students. Those who were most involved in culturally relevant practices of literacy showed the highest cognitive expertise in literacy. This relationship was stronger for African American than for European American students (Guthrie, Schafer, & Hutchinson, 1991).

A similar finding was observed in an international survey in 2009. Evidence from 70 countries confirmed that two broad factors enabled individuals to become experts in literacy across these cultural varieties. The two factors were (a) active literacy participation, which consisted of reading a variety of materials, enjoying reading, and professing to interact frequently around topics of reading; and (b) students' qualities of thinking about reading, which consisted of meta-cognitive strategies for reading comprehension. In other words, a common set of cultural literacy practices increased the cognitive literacy achievement of 15-year-old students worldwide (Brozo, Shiel, & Topping, 2007).

Culturally Receptive Educational Science

In the quest to understand how African American students can acquire literacies that will empower them in the 21st century, we believe it is advisable to sustain the social contract that educators have with society. All teachers are committed to helping their students. Educators do not merely attempt to take students in any direction that a current whim may suggest, but rather, aim toward educational targets that are valued by society. Parents, school boards, and professional groups generate ideas about desired reading competencies, which are written into standards. Teachers' social contract with their communities is to enable students to learn the literacies that are functional for health, safety, and economic welfare. These shared values lead to goals for literacy learning.

Part of the social contract is to design, intervene, and interact in classrooms in ways that foster progress toward success in mutually agreed-upon tasks. To document the social agreement, we need to display progress toward these goals. Thus, educators create assessments to examine whether students are gaining the expected expertise. Whether the assessments are optimally designed is beyond the scope of this book. Without assessments as benchmarks of success, educators cannot determine precisely whether the designed interventions are working. In a society with a social contract between educators and communities, there are two crucial elements to educational progress. The first element involves understanding which literacy practices are culturally relevant for a particular society and its students. Second is the agreed upon notion about educational contexts that effectively promote the students' attainment of these literacies. Therefore, we have adopted the approach of *culturally receptive educational science*. Literacy activities in schooling should be grounded in purposes that are authentic to the individuals and the communities in which they reside at present or may enter in the future. These contexts of schooling created to promote literacy are expected to be valuable and beneficial in predictable ways. Spending more time in the schooling context should enable learners to acquire broader, more proficient forms of literacy expertise. A scientific enterprise in education is not relevant unless it is culturally grounded. At the same time, the cultural perspective on literacy practices in education is not verified unless it is scientifically investigated. In this chapter on African American students' acquisition of literacy, we attempt to fuse these twin needs by pursuing the theme of culturally receptive educational science.

Engagement in Reading among African American Students

Three forms of engagement are interlocked. A highly engaged student is thinking deeply about her work and reflecting on how her learning connects with what she already knows. This is often termed cognitive engagement. Motivational engagement refers to students' interests, desires, or aversions to an academic activity like reading. Third in the mix of qualities is the learner's active behavior, which is putting forth effort, time, and persistence in learning. Essential engagement behaviors include concentration, focus, paying attention in class, attendance in school, and other characteristics that enable the person to sustain cognitive involvement with text (Fredricks, Blumenfeld, & Paris, 2004; Skinner, Furrer, Marchand, & Kindermann, 2008).

Behavioral engagement has been highlighted in recent studies of literacy and reading achievement. A host of investigations confirm that students who put forth effort, time, and persistence in reading activities are the highest achievers at all levels of schooling (Guthrie, Wigfield, & You, 2012). These enabling behaviors for literacy are seemingly obvious, but they are not trivial. Students who are behaviorally disengaged will inevitably be lower achievers and will not grow in other academic pursuits such as science or history (Greenleaf et al., 2011). The role of active participation in the development of expertise in reading has been confirmed with a range of correlational and experimental studies, as well as embraced by cultural perspectives on literacy that underscore the role of actively participating in culturally valued forms of social interaction. In our engagement model of reading development (Guthrie & Wigfield, 2000), behavioral engagement is intimately tied to the development of reading proficiency, and motivation is the primary energizer for these achievement-generating behaviors.

For African American students, investigations from a diverse array of journals point toward the power of behavioral engagement for achievement. Smalls, White, Chavous, and Sellers (2007) reported a study with 390 African American middle and high school students from the Midwest. Their indicator of engagement was students' attention, participation, effort, and persistence when presented with new reading material in the classroom. Students responded to questions with the following kinds of statements: "If I can't get a problem right the first time I just keep trying." "When I do badly on a test I work harder the next time."

Students who agreed with these statements were likely to have higher GPAs in English, Science, and Social Studies than students who were neutral or negative about these statements. At the same time, the investigators asked about forms of disengagement such as skipping a class without an excuse, being sent to the principal's office, or cheating on tests and exams. Students who reported these forms of disengagement from school reading were significantly more likely to have lower GPAs than other students. Positive engagements increased achievement and negative engagements decreased reading proficiency.

Classroom participation is a visible form of literacy engagement. Hall, Merkel, Howe, and Lederman (1986) reported classroom observations of students in five middle schools with European American and African American students. Observers recorded whether students were attending, on task, participating, and highly active in the academic activities of reading and writing in the classroom. Students who were actively observing, preparing, discussing, and reacting to text were regarded as engaged. These indicators of engagement correlated 0.72 with grades in school for African American males, 0.56 for European American males, 0.66 for African American females, and 0.81 for European American females. Engagement in the classroom interactions surrounding text was so strong that it predicted students' grades, even when the aspects of gender, race, and ability levels were accounted for statistically. It was the behavioral engagement, rather than demographic characteristics of learners, that most markedly impacted reading achievement.

Other studies have confirmed that behavioral engagement impacts achievement more strongly than demographic variables of gender and socioeconomic status. With an African American population of students from grades 7 to 12, Sirin and Rogers-Sirin (2005) reported that school grades in Language Arts and test scores of reading vocabulary were uniquely predicted by two qualities of behavioral engagement. The first quality was active participation in school, which consisted of paying attention in class and getting along well with teachers. The second quality was school expectations, which consisted of students' belief that they would continue their education beyond high school. African American students who were highly participatory and had solid expectations for future education were substantially higher achievers than students with less participation or lower expectations. Behavioral engagement was connected to achievement for both boys and girls at all six grade levels, irrespective of students' academic achievement in vocabulary or their background in the form of mothers' education. Behavioral engagement outdistanced all demographic variables, including gender, income, and academic aptitude in generating achievement for African American adolescents. Unquestionably, behavioral engagement is a pathway to attainment within the African American population in secondary schooling.

One form of behavioral engagement that is widely investigated is completion of homework and time spent daily on academic work assigned by the teacher. Amount of time spent daily on homework correlated significantly with reading achievement for African American students in 10th and 12th grades, as well as for European American and Hispanic students (Mau & Lynn, 1999). In a study of middle school students, Ferguson (2008) found that the behavioral engagements of completing homework and spending time on homework were two of the most powerful factors influencing GPA for African American males and females. High-achieving African American males and females were more likely to complete homework, spend sufficient amounts on time on homework, and make decisions to commit focused energy on homework more frequently than low-achieving African American males and females. Evidently, behavioral engagement is a pathway for excellence within the population of African American students of both genders. Even at the university level, African American students' GPA average is significantly impacted by the students' work ethic (Cokley, 2003).

Most poignant for our purposes is the observation that behavioral engagement eclipses demographic characteristics in its impact on achievement. In brief, behavioral engagement emerges as a prominent pathway for achievement among African American students. The key features of behavioral engagement are time, effort, and persistence in academic literacy. The structural variables emphasized by sociologists as obstacles to achievement can be surmounted through express behaviors that explicitly consist of active reading. For example, urban students from low income homes who are behaviorally engaged in reading are relatively high achievers. At the same time, sustaining these behaviors over time through consistent activities such as completing homework, attending class, and participating enthusiastically in classroom interactions are necessary to sustain reading growth. Behaviors of being a reader are fueled partly by proficiency in the skills of reading. High-proficiency students grow in engagement and highly engaged learners grow in proficiency. Synergy between engagement and achievement is noteworthy for primary age students (Morgan & Fuchs, 2007) and may also occur in middle and high school, although it has not been documented at those levels.

Motivation Effects on Achievement among African American Students

In contrast to the power of behavioral engagement as a pathway to achievement for African American students, there are several motivational characteristics of individuals that do not represent promising pathways. For example, Osborne (1997) proposed the concept of *disidentification* to describe adolescent African American students who remove themselves from emotional and psychological commitment to achievement in school. Empirical evidence offered by Osborne and others, such as Mickelson (1990), showed that for African American students, the quality of self-esteem (e.g., believing in one's self-worth) is disconnected from school achievement because it is not correlated with standard indicators of achievement such as grades or test scores. In other words, African American middle and high school students often believe they are worthy individuals without achieving highly in school. In comparison, European American students' self-esteem and school achievement correlate positively and significantly. The source of this disidentification, according to Osborne (1997), is African American students' need to protect themselves against the demeaning experiences associated with low reading achievement. By decoupling their self-esteem from achievement, they continue to believe in their self-worth. In terms of our quest for pathways, the role of self-esteem cannot be included as a source of academic growth for African American students. As we have argued elsewhere, African American students who are disengaged from school at an early age will likely be low achieving, and their disengagement in primary grades may be the actual starting point for a cycle of low achievement and ultimate disidentification from schooling in the adolescent years (Guthrie, Rueda, Gambrell, & Morrison, 2009).

Similar to self-esteem, the widely studied factor of intrinsic motivation does not appear to impact achievement for African American students in ways similar to its impact for European American students. According to at least two substantive investigations, the relationship of intrinsic motivation and achievement is much weaker for African American students than for European American students. Long, Monoi, Harper, Knoblauch, and Murphy (2007) and Guthrie and McRae (2011) found no significant association between intrinsic motivation (interest in reading) and achievement for African American students, despite a substantial correlation for European American students, which is confirmed by an extensive empirical literature (Gottfried, Fleming, & Gottfried, 2001). Although African American students clearly have interests in sports, clothing, and popularity similar to European American students (Ferguson, 2008), African American students as a group do not connect reading activities to their interests as tightly as do European American students.

A third motivational pathway is uncertain for African Americans. Several studies indicate that the correlation between self-efficacy and achievement is not as high for African American students as for European American students (Baker & Wigfield, 1999; Graham, 1994; Guthrie, Coddington & Wigfield, 2009; Stephenson, Chen, & Uttal, 1990). One possible explanation is similar to the explanation for disidentification. When African American students consistently encounter low evaluations of their performance in reading, they decide that their capacity for achievement in reading is not connected to their test scores or grades. Some students may believe they are adequate readers despite low evaluations of reading from teachers; other students may believe they are inadequate readers despite positive evaluations from teachers. Although some studies show a positive correlation of self-efficacy and achievement among African American students (Hudley & Gottfried, 2008), the evidence is mixed, and therefore, self-efficacy as a pathway to achievement is uncertain at best. The relative weakness of self-esteem, intrinsic motivation, and self-efficacy as correlates to achievement for African American students render them as less promising pathways than behavioral engagement for this ethnic group.

Another motivational pathway to achievement that appears to operate very differently for African American and European American students is value. In the motivational literature with European American students, valuing refers to believing that school is important, useful, and beneficial. Although valuing is positively correlated with achievement for secondary school students (Wigfield et al., 2008), the relationship appears to be reversed among African American students. Graham, Taylor, and Hudley (1998) examined the achievement values for African American males and females by asking students to nominate peers who they admired or wished to emulate. African American students most frequently nominated low achievers who wore "cool" clothing and participated in sports. High-achieving African American males were not recognized as individuals that other African American students wished to imitate. Taylor and Graham (2007) subsequently confirmed this result appeared for seventh graders but found it was not present for students in grades 2 and 4. In the elementary grades, African American students appear to value high achievement, whereas in the middle and high school grades, African American students appear to believe that achievement is neither valuable nor important for them. In an African American sample of urban students Long et al. (2007) found that valuing school correlated negatively with school achievement, even when other variables of gender, interest, and self-efficacy were statistically controlled. It is astonishing that these African American students (males and females) should view high achievement in school as an undesirable trait to be shunned. As we will report, our analyses corroborate this finding.

Impacts of Dedication on Achievement of African American and European American Students

We draw on several sections of our investigations into adolescent student literacy to investigate the connections of dedication and achievement empirically (see Guthrie, Wigfield, & Klauda, 2012). In a 5-year NICHD study of more than 4,000 students, we identified many aspects of African American students' reading through interviews with students, each of whom was interviewed on two occasions by an individual ethnically matched to the interviewee. In that work, we observed that the amount of reading reported by African American students both in school and out of school was substantially correlated with their level of reading achievement on the accountability test in the state. For school reading, this consisted of the amount of reading of textbooks, literature, classroom notes, overhead projections, and other forms of literacy artifacts within schools. For non-school reading, this included reading novels, the Internet, information books, newspapers, and magazines. The fact that both of these literacy domains were associated with achievement for African American students more highly than they were for European American students is intriguing. It suggests that the activity theory (Gutiérrez & Lee, 2009), which proposes that students gain cognitive skill in reading to the extent that they participate in practices shared by peers in their school and non-school communities, is confirmed by our statistical analyses. This relationship between the breadth of reading practice and achievement is consistent with expertise theory (Ericsson, 1996), which argues that extremely high amounts of disciplined practice in any pursuit are frequently associated with the highest levels of expertise. Just as violinists, basketball players, and chess masters who perform at the highest levels of proficiency spend the highest volumes of time in these activities, the most expert readers of school and non-school materials are the individuals who show the highest amounts of time and highest diversity of activities in reading and literacy.

Because behavioral engagement appears to be strongly related to achievement for African American students, we investigated whether it is sufficiently powerful to close the achievement gap between African American and European American students. To capture dedication we asked students about their willingness to work long and hard at reading and we connected that to the Gates-MacGinitie Reading Comprehension test. At the highest levels of dedication to reading, African American and European American students were equally high in standardized reading test performance. However, as dedication declined for both groups, achievement decreased more precipitously for African American than for European American students. At the lowest levels of dedication, there was a substantial gap in reading achievement.

To show that this finding was not peculiar to this sample or these particular measures, we compared it to an investigation of the reading dedication and achievement of young adults published in 1991, twenty years before this study. Effects of dedication on achievement were higher for African American young adults than for European American young adults. These data were drawn from a national sample of students with the achievement measure consisting of the National Assessment of Educational Progress (NAEP) and the indicator of dedication consisting of a measure of the self-reported breadth of reading taken during interviews with the sample of over 3,000 adults aged 21 to 25 years. For adolescents and adults alike, the most highly dedicated readers were equal in achievement across the two ethnic groups. However, when the ethnic groups were compared at the lowest level of dedication (or amount of reading variety), African Americans were significantly lower in achievement than European Americans. This may be interpreted as indicating that for African Americans, the neglect of reading has more deleterious consequences than for European American learners. The effect of dedication on information text comprehension is equally important to the effect of dedication on standardized test scores because adolescents are continually confronted with information text across their school curricula. We observed that the students' dedication, as shown in their questionnaires administered in 2009 and 2010, was highly associated with their literal comprehension of information text. This connection appeared irrespective of students' demographic characteristics of gender and family income and also irrespective of their motivations to reading, including eight different constructs. This shows that the behaviors of investing time, effort, and persistence in reading increased literal information text comprehension for African Americans, even when all other motivations were held constant. This is the characteristic that stands most prominently when a range of demographics and motivations are investigated. However, there was no statistically significant effect for dedication on literal information text comprehension for European Americans.

The benefits of dedication are extended to crucial cognitive components of reading expertise. For example, the positive effect of dedication on inferencing in information text comprehension tasks was similar to the effect of dedication on literal information text comprehension, discussed in the previous paragraph. That is, dedication increased inferencing for African Americans more than for European Americans, even when gender, income, and eight other motivational constructs were statistically controlled. We investigated the effect of reading dedication on fluency, which was measured according to the Woodcock Johnson Fluency indicator, and observed no influence of behavioral engagement on achievement for either ethnic group. In other words, behavioral engagement increased reading comprehension and inferencing in reading, which are higher order cognitive skills, but it did not influence the lower order process of fluency, which is typically acquired sufficiently in the elementary grades to assure grade level information text comprehension.

In our study, dedication in Reading/Language Arts strongly increased grades. Grades were impacted by dedication more highly than intrinsic motivation, self-efficacy, valuing, and pro-social interactions. This influence was equally apparent for African American and European American students. Teachers awarded higher grades for dedicated than for avoidant students. Because dedication increased standardized test scores and the state accountability test scores, it is possible that teachers' grades are reflecting this increase in students' expertise. However, statistical analysis controlling the effect of test scores showed that the impact of dedication on grades was undiminished. Dedication increased grades, regardless of its effect on actual reading proficiency. Teachers approve and reward dedicated behaviors of students in the classroom, apart from whether those students are highly achieving. Even among honors students, teachers rewarded the more dedicated individuals with higher grades than the less dedicated ones. Likewise, among struggling readers and Special Education students, teachers gave higher grades in Reading/Language Arts to students who showed more time, effort, and persistence in reading than students who were showing less dedication. Teachers attempted to encourage behavioral engagement in literacy tasks for both genders and at all levels of achievement across the diverse population.

Effects of Motivational Variables on Reading Dedication

In the previous section, we portrayed dedication as a cluster of behaviors consisting of putting effort into reading, spending time in reading, persisting in difficult tasks, and completing reading for schoolwork. In this regard, dedication is a set of observable behavioral interactions of the student with a text and other students or teachers. Students' reasons for performing this cluster of actions vary widely. Although it is evident that motivation increases effort (Wentzel, 1996), some students may read avidly because they are interested, whereas other students read avidly because they believe they must do it, irrespective of interest. The first group is intrinsically motivated, reading for its own sake. The second group is motivated by the value of reading apart from its connection to their interests. Students' reasons may impact persistence quite differently. A student who is reading primarily for interest is not likely to persist if the interest declines. A student who is reading primarily for value (believing in its importance for self) is likely to persist irrespective of interest. Persistence may be a consequence of valuing more than intrinsic motivation. In this regard, it is possible that African American and European American students commit to practices of reading for different reasons. Due to these relationships between dedication and various reading motivations, we distinguish between behavioral engagement (e.g., dedication) and motivation in this chapter.

As two sides of behavioral engagement, dedication and avoidance are complementary. Dedicated students invest high effort, time, and persistence into reading whereas the avoidant students retreat from effort, time, and persistence in reading. Although dedication reflects the extent to which students participate actively in text interaction, avoidance measures students' aversion to reading and to consciously performing non-reading activities. But these are not simple opposites. Some students express a middle ground in which they are not highly dedicated, but they are not remarkably avoidant either.

Avoidance is predicted most strongly by devaluing for both African American and European American students. When the motivations of devaluing, perceived difficulty, intrinsic motivation, and antisocial goals were used to predict levels of avoidance, devaluing emerged repeatedly as the strongest. Devaluing was more highly associated with avoidance for African American than European American students, although it was the strongest factor influencing avoidance for both groups.

The impact of devaluing on avoidance was extremely powerful. Students who devalued reading highly (who gave a score of 4 out of 4 to their level of devaluing) were the most avoidant (giving a score of 4 out of 4 to their level of avoidance). At the same time, students who reported the lowest level of avoidance (1) were also reporting the lowest level of devaluing (1). The extremes of being "totally avoidant" versus "not at all avoidant" were tightly tied to the full extremes of devaluing reading. In other words, high amounts of devaluing converted to total avoidance of reading information text by this adolescent population.

In middle school, the major reason students avoid reading is that they devalue it, believing that reading is not important to them. Devaluing equates to lack of usefulness. It is important to recognize that the students also avoid reading because they feel they cannot perform well. But the effects of devaluing on avoidance were free of the influence of perceived difficulty when they were both entered in the same statistical regression equation. Importantly, when students were equated statistically on antisocial motivation, devaluing continued to increase avoidance.

Connections among Dedication and Motivations Influencing Achievement

A network of connections among behavioral engagement and motivation impact information text comprehension (see Guthrie, Klauda, & Ho, 2013). In this framework, valuing increases reading comprehension through dedication. Students who valued reading most highly became highly dedicated to reading and this dedication increased their reading comprehension. At the same time, students who devalued reading were low in dedication and were relatively low achievers. Influences of self-efficacy on achievement were partly mediated by dedication. Some of the influence of self-efficacy on achievement operated through dedication and some of the influence was direct. When some students were more confident of themselves they became more dedicated, which increased their achievement. At the same time, some students scored higher on the information text comprehension tests due to their belief in their capacity to read well, even though their self-efficacy had not increased their dedication to reading. In sum, both valuing and self-efficacy impacted achievement at least partly through the influence on time, effort, and persistence to reading.

Educational Practices for Literacy Engagement

To formulate a set of classroom practices that may promote engagement, we constructed Concept-Oriented Reading Instruction (CORI). The practices were sufficiently specific that we could train teachers to implement them, fused with the teachers' personal preferences. Practices were limited in number to prevent overload on teachers or students, yet were abundant enough to increase cognitive reading skills and a range of motivational supports for engagement. As described further by Taboada, Guthrie, and McRae (2007), the engagement practices for elementary school consisted of the following:

- relevance (e.g., hands-on activities, text tied to hands-on activity, student questioning);
- choice (e.g., student selection of subtopics, text, partners, strategies for learning);
- success (e.g., text matched students' reading levels, feasible tasks, student goal setting);

- collaboration (partner read aloud, team projects, partner concept mapping); and
- thematic units (e.g., "big idea," question of the unit, daily questions, connected texts).

A meta-analysis of CORI's effects across 11 experiments with 75 effect sizes at the elementary school level (Guthrie et al., 2007) was revealing. CORI surpassed comparison treatments in increasing students' competence according to standardized tests of reading comprehension (ES = 0.90), two-day reading and writing tasks (ES = 0.93), passage comprehension (ES = 0.73), and reading fluency (ES = 0.59), as well as word recognition (ES = 0.75). CORI also fostered students' self-reported reading motivation (ES = 1.2) and teachers reported students' engagement in reading (ES = 1.0), as well as amount of reading (ES = 0.49). This confirms that an integrated cluster of motivational practices over extended time can increase students' performance on educationally significant measures of reading comprehension. Some of these instructional effects on achievement were mediated by behavioral engagement (Wigfield et al., 2008; see further discussion below). These effects were confirmed by investigators who showed that an intervention that added motivational supports to instruction in self-regulation increased students' self-regulated reading more effectively than instruction that did not include motivational practices (Souvignier & Mokhlesgerami, 2006). Investigators who have used some of these practices in instructional units on conceptual learning from text have reported them to be effective in comparison to other instructional practices (Block, Parris, Reed, Whiteley, & Cleveland, 2009).

To facilitate literacy engagement in middle school where valuing reading is crucial, we added one instructional practice to the set of instructional supports used in elementary school. We termed that practice "importance" to represent the teachers' emphasis on the importance of information book reading as a tool for students' school learning. To make the value of reading concrete during instruction, we emphasized how reading enabled students to explain a topic to a partner, successfully complete a concept map, and inform themselves to succeed in a debate about text-based topics (such as biodiversity or the Civil War). We believe that situated experiences will increase the value that students place on reading. We expect that the value will generalize to other texts and settings as a function of students' awareness and their direct experiences that reading benefits their interests, competencies, social interactions, and recognition for success in school. These projected benefits for middle school students are similar to the benefits of the *value rationale* that Jang (2008) provided to college students for reading texts.

Effects of CORI on Behavioral Engagement in Information Text Reading

As described previously, we conceive of behavioral engagement as students' time, effort, and persistence. Related to "grit" (Duckworth, Peterson, Matthews, & Kelly, 2007), behavioral engagement in reading refers to actions undertaken by the student that extend over time and reflect goal-directed commitments to literacy. There are two sides to this coin, one consisting of dedication, which refers to the positive attributes of high amounts of time, effort, and persistence. On the other side is avoidance, which refers to the students' attempt to minimize time, effort, and persistence in reading activities. But dedication and avoidance are not simple opposites. Statistically, they do not form two factors that are independent of each other. For example, a person may be dedicated to reading in general, but seek to avoid particular types of reading such as interacting with information text. An individual may be globally dedicated to literacy, but may have highly constrained periods of time in which she focuses energy on literacy activities. On the other hand, many individuals are dedicated and non-avoidant. Their time, effort, and persistence generalize across a wide range of texts and time periods. In middle school samples, achievement correlates more strongly with avoidance than dedication. Therefore, avoidance is the most prominent variable in our investigations of behavioral engagement.

In CORI classrooms, students who received a six-week unit on symbiosis and biodiversity decreased their avoidance of reading information books dramatically, in comparison to students in control classrooms who did not receive CORI. CORI was substantially effective in impacting behavioral engagement through decreasing avoidance. Consistent with the reports of Tatum (2005), this benefit occurred equally for both genders and for high, medium, and low levels of poverty.

Benefits of CORI for reducing avoidance were greater for African American than for European American students. The CORI framework enabled African American students to expand their commitment to literacy activities. African American students in the control group were more avoidant than European American students, whereas African American students in the CORI group were less avoidant than European American students.

In brief, if African American students' achievement is strongly influenced by avoidance, then a promising intervention for them would appear to be one that optimally reduces avoidance. Because CORI impacted avoidance more for African American than for European American students, and because avoidance influenced achievement in information book comprehension more for African American than for European American students, CORI emerges as a promising instructional design for African American students' information text comprehension.

Motivational Sources of CORI Effects on Behavioral Engagement

Why did CORI change students' behavioral engagement? The statistical analyses revealed that the effect of CORI on avoidance was not due solely to its effect on students' devaluing. Even when we held students' level of devaluing constant across ethnic groups, CORI still benefited all students. However, when we held devaluing constant, the interaction between ethnicity and CORI on behavioral engagement disappeared. This can be explained by the effect of CORI on devaluing. CORI decreased the devaluing of reading which increased the dedication of middle school African American students more strongly than it did for European American students.

An alternative explanation is that students become more behaviorally engaged when books are easily readable. However, the effect of CORI on avoidance was not dramatically reduced when we statistically controlled the students' perceived difficulty of reading. It is also possible that the CORI experience increased dedication by increasing students' social interaction, because collaboration was part of the CORI framework. However, the statistical analyses showed that CORI's effect on avoidance was not explained by its influence on students' social motivations. What influenced the effect of CORI on avoidance more for African American than for European American students was devaluing. In other words, the benefits of CORI on African American students' time, effort, and persistence were attributable to the fact that they decreased their devaluing of information books.

Effects of CORI on dedication were very similar to its impacts on avoidance. CORI increased dedication more markedly than a control group, which complements the finding that CORI decreased avoidance. However, there was no interaction between ethnicity and CORI in its effects on dedication. CORI's effects on dedication were similar for both ethnic groups. Benefits of CORI for dedication, furthermore, were not explained by any single motivation of perceived difficulty, intrinsic motivation, social motivation, or valuing. Rather, CORI impacted several motivations which increased dedication which, in turn, increased achievement in information text comprehension.

CORI might be most effective for students at certain levels of achievement. Dividing the middle school students into high, medium, and low groups, based on their scores on the state accountability test, formed three achievement groups. CORI significantly decreased the avoidance of all students, including high, medium, and low achievement groups. However, the CORI benefit for students was highest for the low-achieving group, second highest for the moderately achieving group, and lowest for the high-achieving group. CORI was more beneficial for low achievers than high achievers, although it improved behavioral engagement for all groups. Statistically speaking, there was an interaction between CORI and achievement group in their effects on information text comprehension. Effects of CORI on achievement in information text comprehension were similar for African American and European American students.

Designing Engaging Contexts for African American Students' Literacy Development

A prominent quality of the African American student population is the connection of achievement to their behavioral engagement in literacy. Referring to time, effort, and persistence in reading activities, behavioral engagement was highly associated with reading achievement for African American and European American learners, but the power of this characteristic was more prominent for African American students. When other motivational contributions to achievement were controlled, the behavioral engagement of African American students impacted their achievement more highly than it did for European American students. More specifically, time, effort, and persistence increased achievement for African Americans, whereas motivations such as self-efficacy were relatively stronger in influencing achievement for European American students.

Impacts of behavioral engagement on achievement for African American students were highly visible across the school year. Behavioral engagement was a strong forecaster of achievement growth across the academic year for African American students. The best forecast of African American students' end of year achievement was their level of behavioral engagement at the beginning of the academic year. For European American students, self-efficacy was a stronger predictor than this behavioral engagement.

This pattern may be attributable in part to the differences in income for the two ethnic groups, which can be estimated by whether or not students received free or reduced meals at school (FARMS). Impacts of behavioral engagement on achievement were substantial for both higher and lower income groups. For both African American and European American groups, low income students showed a stronger connection between behavioral engagement and achievement than higher income students. Income appeared to influence both ethnic groups similarly. Across the income groups for European American and African American students, the motivational variables predicted behavioral engagement in remarkably parallel forms. Income did not "explain away" the benefits of behavioral engagement. The grounding of behavioral engagement in valuing was also not "explained away" by income.

For the four groups consisting of low income African American, high income African American, low income European American, and high income European American, the most powerful predictor of behavioral engagement was valuing reading. Next strongest was intrinsic motivation, and third was self-efficacy as positive predictors of behavioral engagement for all four groups. The motivational contributors that are drivers of behavioral engagement were remarkably similar across ethnic and income groups.

What stands out is the contribution of behavioral engagement to reading comprehension and literacy achievement for African American students, when all other motivation variables are controlled. This prominence of behavioral engagement is not a one time finding. We have observed it across several cohorts of students in several different years in the investigation of grade 7 students.

Another way of describing African American and European American students is to say that African American students who achieve highly in reading devote effort and time, becoming behaviorally engaged in reading information text irrespective of their interest and confidence in reading. In contrast, European

American students who achieve highly are confident of their capacities for success and are more likely to enjoy the texts than lower achieving European American students.

Behavioral Profiles in Literacy Engagement

If African American students' achievement is influenced markedly by behavioral engagement, we should examine whether behavioral engagement is displayed in their home and community environments. What opportunities do African American students have for acquiring behavioral engagement through cultural appropriation? In 2004, the National Endowment for the Arts released a report on literary reading across a national sample of US adults. They included African Americans, Hispanic Americans, and European Americans at ages 18–75 in education levels from grade school through graduate school and family incomes ranging from $10,000 to $75,000 or more. The overall rate of reading literature with any reasonable frequency was 51 percent for European Americans, 37 percent for African Americans, and 26 percent for Hispanic Americans. For all ethnic groups, females were substantially more likely to read literature than males, which has been documented across many nations (PISA, 2010). Across the age span, the literary reading rates were consistently discrepant for European Americans and African Americans. In the 18 to 24 range, 49 percent of European Americans were reading literature, whereas only 35 percent of African Americans reported reading literature. This gap slowly widened to a 20 percent difference for 44- to 54-year-old adults and this difference was maintained for those 75 years or older. The difference of literary reading rates at a wide range of education levels favored European Americans by approximately 10 percentage points. For high school graduates, 40 percent of European Americans reported reading literature, whereas 30 percent of African Americans reported reading literature.

Income levels did not change the picture substantially. For those with incomes $30,000 to $40,000, approximately 49 percent of European Americans were literature readers, whereas 38 percent of African Americans were literature readers. This gap was sustained across the income span. This suggests that the opportunities for observational learning of the cultural practice of reading literature was lower for African American students than for European American students across all ages, all education levels, and all family income levels in contemporary America. A similar story emerged for literacy practices in the workplace. In 1985, a nationally representative sample of 3618 young adults ages 21 to 25 was studied. Data was collected through a 30-minute guided interview containing 123 questions, which were coded into 473 data points for each individual (Guthrie et al., 1991). The variety of different documents that appeared in the workplace was shown to be read more frequently by European American than African American young adults in this study. That is, European American young adults were more likely to read memos, letters, lists, messages, reports, diagrams, forms, charts, catalogues, and legal documents. In addition, documents such as reference books and manuals that tend to dominate workplace reading were more frequently read by European American than African American young adults. Although European American individuals reported reading more fiction than African Americans, an exception to the pattern was that African American young adults reported reading sports and recreation articles in newspapers and magazines more frequently than European American young adults. Across the socioeconomic spectrum, children of these adults would have less opportunity for observational learning and cultural modeling of literacy engagement if they were African American than if they were European American. If their behavioral engagement in reading is based on opportunity for observational learning, African American students would appear to be substantially challenged in acquisition of literacy engagement based on home and community experiences. Needless to say, this places a premium on effective school programs for literacy engagement for this ethnic group.

The bond between behavioral engagement and achievement was confirmed in a study of a national sample of young adults (Guthrie et al., 1991). For workplace literacy activities, which refer to the frequency of reading reference books, charts, diagrams, and business materials, there was a higher correlation between behavioral engagement and achievement for African Americans than for European Americans, even when controlling for parental education, parental occupation, and years of schooling for all individuals. Reading workplace documents widely and frequently increased reading achievement more strongly for African Americans than European Americans. The finding is consistent with the link of achievement and literacy engagement among adolescents. This nationally representative young adult literacy study confirmed the findings from this NICHD study of middle school students. In both studies, African American individuals show a tighter effect of behavioral engagement on achievement than European Americans.

Conclusion and Implications

The achievement gap between African American and European American students in literacy has been studied from historical, sociological, anthropological, and psychological perspectives. Using an educational lens, our purpose was to attempt to understand by attempting to improve the educational achievement of both groups with particular attention to African American students. For this, we adopted a two-stage approach of pathways and design. In the pathway stage we seek to identify student processes (variables) that are pathways to (correlates of) achievement for each group separately. For African Americans, it was evident that the pathway of dedication to information book reading was potentially powerful. Dedicated African Americans students showed information text reading comprehension that was equal to the most highly dedicated European American students. However, at lower levels of dedication, African Americans students revealed more rapid declines in achievement than European Americans.

Dedication is a pathway that is capable of closing the achievement gap between these ethnic groups in the United States. If schools were successful in empowering a high proportion of African Americans students to be highly dedicated to information text reading, it is conceivable that they would show parity with European American students in achievement. This is an astonishing possibility, but is promoted by data from a sizeable sample of African American and European American males and females from diverse income levels.

Assuming the link of dedication and achievement is confirmed by other researchers, educators should attempt to capitalize on this connection by creating adaptive designs for classroom instruction. Because devaluing was most highly correlated with dedication for both ethnic groups, we originally considered designing middle school CORI to emphasize the pathway of valuing. This would entail trying to increase students' sense of importance for reading. To follow this plan, the instructional goals would be focused on valuing. However, a pattern in the full set of motivation variables suggested a different design.

We observed a broader pattern of motivations that placed valuing as a centerpiece. The pattern (called the simplex) suggested that a developmental sequence for both ethnic groups consisted of self-efficacy, valuing, and peer valuing. In brief, a student initially needs to believe in himself (self-efficacy) as a reader; then, when he can succeed in reading, the student may be encouraged to develop positive values for reading (valuing); if he acquires some perceived benefits (values) for reading he may interact with peers regarding their reading opinions (peer values). Therefore we designed CORI for middle school to emphasize a sequence of the practices of success (for self-efficacy), importance (valuing), and collaboration (for peer valuing). Other engagement practices were included consisting of choice, collaboration, and thematic units to deepen the motivation support.

Not surprisingly, the fully implemented CORI increased dedication equally for both African American and European American students. CORI's impact on achievement in information text comprehension was also equal for both ethnic groups. However, CORI decreased the mirror construct of avoidance more for African American than for European American students. This is potentially beneficial because avoidance is an especially powerful pathway to achievement (or failure) for African American students. Due to the finding that devaluing is highly correlated with avoidance, we found that CORI decreased devaluing more for African American than for European American students. CORI influenced African American students to move from actively devaluing reading to positively valuing reading.

Students' dedication to achievement in academic literacy should be more profoundly endorsed and systematically nurtured for both African American and European American students. A solid database exists for this endeavor. The good news is that this pathway is especially powerful for African Americans, while fostering attainment for all. Our current challenge is to enable teachers to assure continual growth of literacy dedication for all students.

Spotlight Recommendation

Our chapter focused on literacy engagement as a driver of reading achievement for all students. Based on research showing that student motivations foster their engagement, we implemented Concept Oriented Reading Instruction (CORI) in grades 3 to 7. We concluded that elementary students' literacy achievement and engagement are supported by key instructional practices consisting of (a) relevance, (b) choice, (c) success, (d) collaboration, and (e) thematic units, accompanied by direct cognitive instruction. For middle school students, we observed it is particularly powerful to highlight instruction that emphasizes the importance of literacy to strengthen students' valuing of learning from text.

As effective classroom instruction is the proximal cause of improved reading achievement, the federal role in education should consist of funding states to implement evidence-based reading instruction. High quality teaching requires investment into teacher preparation and school resources. Yet, while US reading achievement trails Asia and Europe, US funding diminishes. The federal government should redouble its financial support for states and districts that embrace rigor in hiring, mentoring, evaluating, resourcing, encouraging, protecting and continually re-educating teachers.

International comparisons of reading for students at ages 9 (PIRLS) and 15 (PISA) show that socioeconomic status is more highly associated with reading achievement in the US than many other nations. Typically, top-performing countries have a low correlation of achievement and income. In these countries, emphasis is placed on early childhood education, teacher competency assessment, and professionalism such as planning time, academic commitment, and educational values. Sociological factors of income, housing, or health correlate with literacy in the US, but there is no strong evidence that social programs addressing them have merit for improving literacy. Our most promising leads are seen in the education sciences that reveal potent learning contexts for elevating literacy broadly.

References

Baker, L. & Wigfield, A. (1999). Dimensions of children's motivation for reading and their relations to reading activity and reading achievement. *Reading Research Quarterly*, 34, 452–477.

Block, C. C., Parris, S. R., Reed, K. L., Whiteley, C. S., & Cleveland, M. D. (2009) Instructional approaches that significantly increase reading comprehension. *Journal of Educational Psychology*, 101(2), 262–281.

Brozo, W. G., Shiel, G., & Topping, K. (2007). Engagement in reading: Lessons learned from Three PISA countries. *Journal of Adolescent & Adult Literacy*, 51, 304–315.

Carson, B. (1992). *Think big*. Grand Rapids, MI: Zondervan.

Cokley, K. O. (2003). What do we know about the motivation of African American students? Challenging the 'anti-intellectual' myth. *Harvard Educational Review*, 73, 524–558.

Duckworth, A. L., Peterson, C., Matthews, M., & Kelly, D. (2007). Grit: Perseverence and passion for long-term goals. *Journal of Personality and Social Psychology*, 92, 1087–1101.

Ericsson, K. A. (1996). *The road to excellence: The acquisition of expert performance in the arts and sciences, sports, and games*. Mahwah, NJ: Erlbaum.

Ferguson, R. F. (2008). *Toward excellence with equity: An emerging vision for closing the achievement gap*. Cambridge, MA: Harvard Education Press.

Fredricks, J. A., Blumenfeld, P. C., & Paris, A. H. (2004). School engagement: Potential of the concept, state of the evidence. *Review of Educational Research*, 74, 59–109.

Gottfried, A. E., Fleming, J. S., & Gottfried, A. W. (2001). Continuity of academic intrinsic motivation from childhood through late adolescence: A longitudinal study. *Journal of Educational Psychology*, 93, 3–13.

Graham, S. (1994). Motivations in African Americans. *Review of Educational Research*, 64, 55–117.

Graham, S., & Hudley, C. (2005). Race and ethnicity in the study of motivation and competence. In A. J. Elliot & C. S. Dweck (Eds.), *Handbook of competence and motivation* (pp. 392–413). New York: Guilford.

Graham, S., Taylor, A. Z., & Hudley, C. (1998). Exploring achievement values among ethnic minority early adolescents. *Journal of Educational Psychology*, 90, 606–620.

Greenleaf, C. L., Litman, C., Hanson, T. L., Rosen, R., Boscardin, C. K., Herman, J., Schneider, S. A., Madden, S., & Jones, B. (2011). Integrating literacy and science in biology: Teaching and learning impacts of reading apprenticeship professional development. *American Educational Research Journal*, 48(3), 647–717.

Guthrie, J. T., Coddington, C. S., & Wigfield, A. (2009). Profiles of reading motivation among African American and Caucasian students. *Journal of Literacy Research*, 41, 317–353.

Guthrie, J. T., Hoa, L. W., Wigfield, A., Tonks, S. M., Humenick, N. M., & Littles, E. (2007). Reading motivation and reading comprehension growth in the later elementary years. *Contemporary Educational Psychology*, 32, 282–313.

Guthrie, J. T., Klauda, S. L., & Ho, A. N. (2013). Modeling the relationships among reading instruction, motivation, engagement, and achievement for adolescents. *Reading Research Quarterly*, 48, 9–26.

Guthrie, J. T. & McRae, A. (2011). Reading engagement among African American and European American students. In S. J. Samuels, & A. E. Farstrup (Eds.), *What research has to say about reading instruction* (4th ed.) (pp. 115–142). Newark, DE: International Reading Association.

Guthrie, J. T., Rueda, R., Gambrell, L. B., & Morrison, D. A. (2009). Roles of engagement, valuing, and identification in reading development of students from diverse backgrounds. In L. M. Morrow, R. Rueda, & D. Lapp (Eds.), *Handbook of research on literacy and diversity* (pp. 195–215). New York: Guilford.

Guthrie, J. T., Schafer, W. D., & Hutchinson, S. R. (1991). Relations of document literacy and prose literacy to occupational and societal characteristics of young black and white adults. *Reading Research Quarterly*, 26, 30–48.

Guthrie, J., Wigfield, A. & Klauda, S. (2012). Adolescents' engagement in academic literacy. Retrieved March 20, 2012 from www.corilearning.com/research-publications/2012_adolescents_engagement_ebook.pdf.

Guthrie, J. T., Wigfield, A., & You, W. (2012). Instructional contexts for engagement and achievement in reading. In S. Christensen, A. Reschly, & C. Wylie (Eds.), *Handbook of research on student engagement* (pp. 601–635). New York: Springer Science.

Guthrie, J. T. & Wigfield, A. (2000). Engagement and motivation in reading. In M. L. Kamil, P. B. Mosenthal, P. D. Pearson, & R. Barr (Eds.), *Handbook of reading research, Vol. III*, (pp. 403–422). Mahwah, NJ: Erlbaum.

Gutiérrez, K. & Lee, C. D. (2009). Robust informal learning environments for youth from non-dominant groups: Implications for literacy learning in formal schooling. In L. M. Morrow, R. Rueda, & D. Lapp (Eds.), *Handbook of research on literacy and diversity* (pp. 216–232). New York: Guilford Press.

Gutiérrez, K., & Vossoughi, S. (2010). Lifting off the ground to return anew: Mediated praxis, transformative learning, and social design experiments. *Journal of Teacher Education*, 61, 100–117.

Hall, V. C., Merkel, S., Howe, A., & Lederman, N. (1986). Behavior, motivation, and achievement in desegregated junior high school science classes. *Journal of Educational Psychology*, 78, 108–115.

Holloway, K. F. C. (2006). *Bookmarks: Reading in black and white*. Brunswick, NJ: Rutgers University Press.

Hudley, C. & Gottfried, A. E. (2008). *Academic motivation and the culture of school in childhood and adolescence*. New York: Oxford University Press.

Hudley, C. (2009). Academic motivation and achievement of African American youth. In H. Neville, B. Tynes, S. Utsey (Eds.), *Handbook of African American psychology* (p. 187–199). Thousand Oaks, CA: Sage.

Jang, H. (2008). Supporting students' motivation, engagement, and learning during an uninteresting activity. *Journal of Educational Psychology*, 100, 798–811.

Kidder, T. (2009). *Strength in what remains*. New York: Random House.

Long, J. F., Monoi, S., Harper, B., Knoblauch, D., & Murphy, P. K. (2007). Academic motivation and achievement among urban adolescents. *Urban Education*, 42, 196–222.

Mau, W. C., & Lynn, R. (1999). Racial and ethnic differences in motivation for educational achievement in the United States. *Personality and Individual Differences*, 27, 1091–1096.

Mickelson, R. A. (1990). The attitude-achievement paradox among black adolescents. *Sociology of Education*, 63, 44–61.

Morgan, P. L. & Fuchs, D. (2007). Is there a bidirectional relationship between children's reading skills and reading motivation? *Exceptional Children*, 73, 165–183.

Osborne, J. W. (1997). Race and academic disidentification. *Journal of Educational Psychology*, 89, 728–735.

OECD (2010). PISA 2009 Results: What students know and can do – Student Performance in reading, mathematics and science, volume I. DOI: http://dx.doi.org/10.1787/9789264091450-en.

Robinson, E. (2010). *Disintegration: The splintering of black America*. New York: Doubleday.

Rueda, R. S., August, D., & Goldenberg, C. (2006). The sociocultural context in which children acquire literacy. In D. August & T. Shanahan (Eds.), *Developing literacy in second-language learners: Report of the National Literacy Panel on Language-Minority Children and Youth* (pp. 319–340). Mahwah, NJ: Erlbaum.

Scribner, S. & Cole. M. (1999). *The psychology of literacy*. Cambridge, MA: Harvard University Press.

Sirin, S. R. & Rogers-Sirin, L. (2005). Components of school engagement among African American adolescents. *Applied Developmental Science*, 9, 5–13.

Skinner, E. A., Furrer, C., Marchand, G., & Kindermann, T. A. (2008). Engagement and disaffection in the classroom: Part of a larger motivational dynamic? *Journal of Educational Psychology*, 100, 765–781.

Smalls, C., White, R., Chavous, T., & Sellers, R. (2007). Racial ideological beliefs and racial discrimination experiences as predictors of academic engagement among African American adolescents. *Journal of Black Psychology*, 33, 299–330.

Souvignier, E. & Mokhlesgerami, J. (2006). Using self regulation as a framework for implementing strategy instruction to foster reading comprehension. *Learning and Instruction*, 16, 57–71.

Stevenson, H. W., Chen, C., & Uttal, D. H. (1990). Beliefs and achievement: A study of black, white, and Hispanic children. *Child Development*, 61, 508–523.

Taboada, A., Guthrie, J. T., & McRae, A. (2007). Building engaging classrooms. In R. Fink and S. J. Samuels (Eds.), *Inspiring reading success: Interest and motivation in an age of high stakes testing* (pp. 141–166). Newark, DE: International Reading Association.

Tatum, A. W. (2005). *Teaching reading to black adolescent males*. Portland, ME: Stenhouse.

Taylor, A. Z., & Graham, S. (2007). An examination of the relationship between achievement values and perceptions of barriers among low-SES African American and Latino students. *Journal of Educational Psychology*, 99, 52–64.

Wentzel, K. R. (1996). Social and academic motivation in middle school: Concurrent and long term relations to academic effort. *Journal of Early Adolescence*, 16, 390–406.

Wigfield, A., Guthrie, J. T., Perencevich, K. C., Taboada, A., Klauda, S. L., McRae, A., & Barbosa, P. (2008). The role of reading engagement in mediating effects of reading comprehension instruction on reading outcomes. *Psychology in the Schools*, 45, 432–445.

Wilson, W. J. (2009). *More than just race: Being black and poor in the inner city*. New York: W. W. Norton & Co.

5

CLOSING THE READING ACHIEVEMENT GAP FOR INDIGENOUS CHILDREN

Jay S. Blanchard and Kim Atwill

Becoming a successful reader can be a challenge for Indigenous children (Atwill, 2014; Barnhill, 2013; Demmert, 2011; Demmert, Grissmer, & Towner, 2006; Dorer & Fetter, 2013; Faircloth & Tippeconnic, 2010; Faircloth & Tippeconnic, 2013; Huffman, 2010; Johnson, 2013; McCardle & Berninger, 2015; Obama, 2011, 2014; Reyhner & Hurtado, 2008).[1] Evidence of the challenge can be found in the reading achievement data of the National Assessment of Educational Progress (NAEP). In general, the NAEP 2013 reading scale score data for Grade 4 Indigenous children indicate the lowest performance across any race/ethnicity comparison (National Center on Education Statistics, 2013a). For example, using NAEP 2013 reading data, the Trial Urban District Report for Albuquerque, New Mexico indicated that for Grade 4 Indigenous children, 41 percent were at or above the *BASIC* level of performance (46 percent below BASIC), significantly fewer than both White and Hispanic children in Albuquerque, 77 and 46 percent respectively. In NAEP terms, BASIC means that children are able "…to locate relevant information, make simple inferences, and use understanding of the text to identify details that support a given interpretation or conclusion [as well as] interpret the meaning of a word as it is used in the text" (National Center on Education Statistics, 2013b, p. 6).

The reading achievement gap for Indigenous children is a complex issue with many historical, social, economic, and geographical variables at work that contribute to the gap (see Adams, 1995; McCardle & Berninger, 2015; Obama, 2014; Smith, 1999/2006, for discussion) including, for example, the fact that the gap is widest for children living in rural and remote areas (National Center for Educational Statistics, 2012; Williams, 2011). However, while the complexity of the issue can be daunting, educators must seek viable solutions that close the reading achievement gap. This chapter offers a solution: school readiness. This solution closes the achievement gap before it can open. Why is school readiness so important? Studies of early reading achievement across nations have consistently found that if children enter formal schooling lacking requisite school readiness skills, they frequently develop limited reading skills by the end of the early grades, and they are likely to have low reading achievement throughout elementary and secondary education (Annie E. Casey Foundation, 2014; Cunningham & Stanovich, 1997; Dockett, Perry, & Kearney, 2010; Duncan et al., 2007; Fiester, 2010; Gormley & Gayer, 2003; Halle, Forry, Hair, Perper, Wandner, Wessel, & Vick, 2009; Hanson & Farrell, 1995; Henry & Rickman, 2005; Juel, 1988; Klein & Knitzer, 2006; Lee & Burkam, 2002; National Early Literacy Panel, 2008; Schweinhart, 2004; Sparks, Patton, & Murdoch, 2014; United National Children's Fund, 2012; Venn & Frude, 2003; Venn & Jahn, 2004a; 2004b). The low achievement throughout formal schooling is mostly likely due to the "Matthew Effect" (Stanovich, 1986). In essence, children who get off to a bad start in reading avoid it and consequently do not develop the reading skills needed for elementary and secondary education. Thus, the achievement gap grows between them and children that get off to a good start (Neuman & Celano, 2006). An example of the Matthew Effect can be seen in the recent research of Dougherty and Fleming (2012). The researchers investigated the reading achievement gap among more than 300,000 4th to 12th graders in the United States and found that only six to seven percent of students were able to close the gap in reading achievement once it had arisen. As would be expected, the Matthew Effect and the resulting inability to the close the reading achievement gap have real consequences beyond elementary and secondary schooling and this extends into adulthood. For example, the results of the National Assessment of Adult Literacy (National Center for Education Statistics, 2006) found that adults with poor literacy skills are less likely to be employed. Thus to close the reading achievement gap before it can begin, Indigenous children must enter elementary school with the language and literacy needed to support elementary school, secondary school, and adult reading success.

The chapter is divided into three sections. The first section discusses the relationship between school readiness and the reading achievement gap. The second discusses the relationship in terms of Indigenous children and families. The third section examines two high-quality, comprehensive, evidence-based early childhood Indigenous education programs and their effects on school readiness. In the past, the research base of Indigenous studies has not included examinations of these types of programs because for the most part they did not exist. In fact, until 2003, the entire research base of investigations of Indigenous early childhood education in the United States was represented by only 36 studies and most of these were personal histories, interviews, and case studies (Department of Health and Human Services, 2004). Today the research base is slowly expanding amid heightened concern about school readiness and the reading achievement gap. Nevertheless, many more studies are needed and the entire area continues to be "woefully understudied" (Department of Health and Human Services, 2004,

p. 40; see also, McCardle & Berninger, 2015; National American Indian and Alaska Native Head Start Collaboration Office, 2013; National Indian Education Study, 2011; Regional Educational Laboratory for the Central Region, 2011; Spicer et al., 2012).

School Readiness and Reading Achievement

A high-quality school readiness program is needed to prevent the reading achievement gap before it can begin. Converging neurobiological, behavioral, and social science research support for this statement first appeared in the mid-1990s. Simply put, all early language experiences have powerful effects on school readiness including reading and overall literacy development and the effects are long lasting (National Early Literacy Panel, 2008; National Institute of Child Health and Human Development, 2000; Snow, Burns & Griffin, 1998; United National Children's Fund, 2012). Thus language skills gained early in life help children acquire later school readiness skills including reading and overall literacy (Carneiro & Heckman, 2003). As a corollary, school readiness skills missed early in life are difficult to rectify later, as shown in the studies of Hart and Risley (1995) and more recently in the Weisleder and Fernald study (2013; see also Schoon, Parsons, Rush, & Kaw, 2010). This fact supports the value of high-quality, comprehensive, evidence-based school readiness intervention programs, especially those that focus on emergent reading and literacy in the development of beginning reading skills (Barnett, 2011; Chrisler & Ling, 2011; Christie, Enz, & Vukelich, 2013; Dickinson, McCabe, Anastasopoulos, Peisner-Feinberg, & Poe, 2003; Justice, Kaderavek, Fan, Sofka, & Hunt, 2009; Lonigan, Farver, Phillips, & Clancy-Menchetti, 2011; National Early Literacy Panel, 2008; Vellutino & Zhang, 2008; Wilson, Dickinson, & Rowe, 2013; Zucker, Cabell, Justice, Pentimonti, & Kadervek, 2013). But the value of these school readiness interventions extends beyond beginning reading skills. There is now a general consensus among researchers, and many policy-makers, that the effects of high-quality school readiness programs "…can produce large effects on IQ during the early childhood years and sizable persistent effects on achievement, grade retention, special education, high school graduation … [T]hese effects are large enough and persistent enough to make a meaningful difference in the lives of children from low-income families: for many children, preschool programs can mean the difference between failing and passing, regular or special education, staying out of trouble or becoming involved in crime and delinquency, dropping out or graduating from high school" (Barnett, 1995, p. 43; see also Barnett, 2011; Ritchie, Bates, & Plomin, 2015; Waldfogel, 2014). The importance of high quality school readiness programs for children was echoed by President Obama in the 2014 State of the Union address: "…research shows that one of the best investments we can make in a child's life is high-quality early education" (The White House, Office of the Press Secretary, 2014).

What is a high-quality early childhood school readiness program? Today, examples of high-quality programs can be found in the US Department of Education's *Good Start, Grow Smart Initiative,* and *Early Reading First* grants. According to the Department of Education (and mirrored in *Public Law 110-134, Improving Head Start for School Readiness Act of 2007)* high-quality, comprehensive, evidence-based school readiness programs are those that generally feature (a) a scientifically based early literacy curriculum; (b) research-based activities that build language and literacy skills (speaking, listening, reading, writing); (c) extended school calendars; (d) response to intervention strategies for children struggling; (e) coaching by mentor teachers; (f) ongoing, targeted professional development; (g) continuous progress monitoring; and (h) engagement with families and communities. As a note, emphasis in the *Early Reading First* grants was placed on supporting emergent reading and literacy development (i.e., vocabulary, oral comprehension, phonological awareness, alphabet knowledge, print awareness, and writing).

School Readiness and Indigenous Children and Families

Any successful model of school readiness for Indigenous children and families must include a culturally responsive approach. While this may seem obvious to the reader, it has not been obvious in practice. In fact *The White House 2014 Native Youth Report* called for culturally responsive approaches across all grade levels as key "recommendations for change" (Obama, 2014, p. 27; for earlier discussions, see Barnhill, 2013; Bigfoot, 2011; Castagno & Brayboy, 2008; Demmert, 2011; Department of Health and Human Services, 2004; Dockett, Perry & Kearney, 2010; Dorer & Fetter, 2013; Gay, 2013; Gillard & Moore, 2007; Gutierrez-Gomez & Pauly, 2006; Marks, Moyer, Roche, & Graham, 2003; McCardle & Berninger, 2015; Niles, Byers, & Krueger, 2008; Nguyen, 2011; Paulson et al., 2003; Reyhner & Hurtado, 2008; Richards, Brown, & Forde, 2006; Spicer, Bigfoot, Funderburk, & Novins, 2012; Thompson, Hare, Sempier, & Grace, 2007). In terms of classroom instruction, a culturally responsive approach means that the traditional and contemporary cultural experiences of the children and their families, including their language, must be integrated and embedded into all materials and activities of the daily program including the curriculum, teaching strategies, assessment, professional development, and family engagement. It also means that teachers must know how to effectively teach using cultural experiences. As noted by the Regional Educational Laboratory for the Central Region (2011) "…educational interventions that incorporate American Indian cultures, values, and belief systems are not enough to produce positive educational outcomes if teachers don't know how to incorporate them into classroom instruction" (p. 1).

In most all cases a culturally responsive approach for classroom instruction means that "mainstream" school readiness materials and activities must be adapted to provide language, social, historical, geographical, and emotional links from the cultural experiences of the children and families to the materials and activities.

Another way of viewing the adaptation process is that it localizes the materials and activities so they can best support the needs and circumstances of the children, families and communities. This includes Indigenous ways of learning and knowing that are enabled by embedding traditional and contemporary crafts, songs, dances, ceremonies, legends, events, and oral stories into the daily materials and activities (Preston, Cottrell, Pelletier, & Pearce, 2011).

Successful Efforts

Pump Up the Volume in Preschool Program

One example of a successful school readiness program that served Indigenous children and their families was the *Pump up the Volume in Preschool* (PVIP) US Department of Education Early Reading First Grant in New Mexico (Blanchard & Burstein, 2015). The schools served by this program were composed entirely of Indigenous children living on rural and remote tribal lands (*remoteness* as defined by the Department of Health and Human Services, 2004).

As required for Early Reading First funding, the PVIP program implemented a comprehensive, evidence-based approach for three- to four-year-old preschoolers that included (a) a scientifically based early literacy curriculum; (b) a full-day, 42 week instructional year; (c) American Indian teachers and staff; (d) response to intervention strategies for children struggling; (e) coaching by American Indian mentor teachers; (f) ongoing, targeted professional development; (g) continuous progress monitoring; (h) engagement with family and community; and (i) ongoing fidelity of implementation assessment. Importantly and unique to PVIP, the program also featured much needed culturally responsive adaptations that were developed and implemented by the Indigenous teaching staff. These types of adaptations, that is, those that incorporate traditional and contemporary culture into daily materials and activities, are difficult and time-consuming, but they are critical for success.

Adapted Curriculum

As could be anticipated, much of the adaptation efforts focused on the materials and instructional activities. The PVIP program used a mainstream emergent literacy curriculum (i.e., *Where Bright Futures Begin,* Houghton-Mifflin Harcourt, 2005) that provided teachers with an ample amount of instructional materials, such as big books, regular sized children's books, vocabulary picture cards, and oral language discussion cards. These materials, however, were often distal to the daily experiences of the children in this rural area. For example, one of the big books focused on an underground subway in a large city; there are no subways in the children's community, just narrow highways and unpaved roads. An oral language card pictured a lush farm that had nothing in common with the high-altitude, arid lands where the children live. These and other materials were kept in the curriculum to widen the children's knowledge about the world, but adaptations were needed to enable the children to make connections to their own lives.

After experimenting with differing degrees of adaptation, the final program included developing and then embedding culturally responsive content into all aspects of the daily lesson plan materials and activities (i.e., morning message, large group, storybook time, small group, play). Indigenous, native-language speaking mentor coaches led the adaptation process. All classrooms had at least one staff member (teacher/instructional aide) that was native-language speaking and was a member of the same tribal nation as the children. The adaptations included adding vocabulary words from the children's native language that matched English words. For example, in the "Welcome to School" thematic unit, teachers introduced *shi k'is* (my friend) alongside the English word *friend*. The vocabulary picture discussion cards were expanded with images representative of experiences common to the children. For example, a yellow tribal fire truck was added to the discussion card picturing a red fire truck. Language, songs, and movement activities were also expanded through the use of the children's native language. During circle time, English rhymes such as "Mary Had a Little Lamb" were presented in English and the children's native language. This is an especially good example, because sheep and lambs are very common in the children's homes and communities.

Culturally responsive materials in the form of artifacts and props were also needed to adapt the learning centers that accompanied each thematic unit. Many of these came from the families and surrounding tribal communities. As just one example, to adapt the "My Community, My Family" thematic unit, the dramatic play center featured a rodeo theme and included a saddle, ropes, and all the trappings of an Indian rodeo. Since published books for young Indigenous children that have any relevance for the thematic units of the curriculum were almost non-existent, the staff and coaches created and printed their own books. For the "My Community, My Family" thematic unit, a book was created about a boy riding a sheep at a rodeo event, *Wooly Riders*, as well as a book about a visit to a livestock feed store. The books provided opportunities for shared storybook reading in content familiar to the children (for discussion, see Inglebret, Jones, & Pavel, 2008). It must be noted the thematic units changed monthly, requiring parallel changes in the content and activities of the adaptations, including the artifacts, materials, and props in the classroom environments including the various centers (i.e., writing, library, shared storybook, dramatic play, manipulative).

Adapted Professional Development

The PVIP model of incorporating culturally relevant adaptations into a high-quality, multi-component early literacy intervention required intensive and ongoing professional development. Mentor coaches worked in each classroom in order to monitor the implementation fidelity of program practices, such as daily instructional lessons, language modeling and shared book reading strategies, and the use of the culturally responsive adaptations (Fixsen, Naoom, Blase, Freidman, & Wallace, 2005). The mentor coaches were also able to identify specific strengths and weaknesses of the adaptations that could be immediately addressed. Monthly professional development meetings were designed to facilitate implementation and the interchange of ideas on the effectiveness of adaptations as well as the development of new adaptations for up-and-coming classroom materials and instructional activities.

Adapted Family Activities

Culturally responsive content was also developed and embedded into the activities for families. The activity adaptations were an especially important part of the PVIP model and designed to strengthen family interest and participation (Annie E. Casey Foundation, 2009). Families attended monthly in-school literacy nights, during which mentor coaches and staff modeled home-based embedded routines for learning that reinforced concepts recently presented at school. These nights also included shared book reading demonstrations in the tribal language and English. Families were also provided theme-related and culturally responsive books so that they could share literacy experiences with their children. As noted, many of the books were created and printed by the staff and mentor coaches.

Judging the Impact of PVIP

Sixty 4-year-old children enrolled in four PVIP preschool classrooms during the 2010–2011 school year were followed through the end of kindergarten (m = 30; f = 30). Preschool and kindergarten assessments were selected and administered by the school district pursuant to state directives. Results presented show preschool receptive vocabulary development and subsequent kindergarten emergent literacy skills.

Preschool Receptive Vocabulary

Children entered PVIP preschool with varying levels of receptive vocabulary skill as documented by the Peabody Picture Vocabulary Test (PPVT; Dunn & Dunn, 2007). The district admittance policy yielded a range of PPVT standard scores from 45 to 124, with only 11 of the 60 children scoring at or above age-appropriate performance (standard score of 100) and an overall mean of 86.02. By the end of the preschool year, the overall mean standard score increased to 98.15, marking a gain of almost one standard deviation. Most importantly, the 26 children who scored more than one standard deviation below age-appropriate at the beginning of the year showed a significant and robust gain of 18 standard score points, increasing from a mean of 72.50 to a mean of 90.04. Overall, children who experienced the PVIP program showed significant PPVT score gains across the preschool year.

Kindergarten Emergent Literacy

The children's emergent literacy skills, including initial sound recognition and phoneme segmentation, were assessed multiple times throughout the kindergarten year using the Dynamic Indicators of Basic Early Literacy Skills (DIBELS-Next; Good & Kaminski, 2011). The group means at first administration on the First Sound Fluency (FSF, fall) and Phoneme Segmentation Fluency (PSF, winter) subtests (12.58 and 34.59, respectively) revealed that the majority of the children entered kindergarten at or above the DIBELS Benchmark, suggesting that they had developed critical foundational skills needed to learn to read (DIBELS-Next; Good & Kaminski, 2011). Equally positive, the children's skills continued to grow across the kindergarten year, such that the group means continued to surpass each subtest's Benchmark. Of perhaps greater interest in terms of preventing a future reading achievement gap, more than half of the 26 children who began the PVIP preschool with receptive vocabulary scores more than one standard deviation below age-appropriate scored above "high-risk" on both administrations of FSF and above Benchmark on both administrations of PSF.

Rocky Boy Coalition Preschool Program

Like the PVIP program, an Early Reading First grant funded the Rocky Boy Coalition (RBC) program to improve the emergent literacy skills of Indigenous children living in rural Montana (Griffin Center for Inspired Instruction, 2015). The program was fortunate to have additional funds for professional development and on-site instructional coaching through a simultaneous Indian Education Demonstration grant. Across four years (2008–2012), the program served the instructional and support staff in two Head Start centers housing nine preschool classrooms. Each year, the RBC served approximately 150 three- and four-year-old children.

Adapted Curriculum

As an Early Reading First grantee, the RBC program also implemented a high-quality, comprehensive, evidence-based approach. As was the case with the PVIP program, RBC had to adapt a commercial curriculum to reflect the children's environment and culture. At the activity and material level, evidence-based instructional methods and materials were introduced to the staff and then the professional developers and staff worked together to adapt the materials and methods to better align with the tribal culture and language, yet preserve their instructional purpose. As just one example, color words for a math activity were printed in both English and the native language and staff were encouraged to alternate languages.

On a larger scale, entire classrooms were also adapted to reflect the tribal culture and language, as well as the children's environment. For example, for the "Welcome to School" unit the classroom theme was *school*, so the children went on a field trip within their school building, meeting people and touring areas outside of their classrooms that were important to the day-to-day functioning of the school. They met the cooks and toured the cafeteria. They went into the boiler room and listened as the janitors shared what they do. They visited with the office staff and watched as the receptionist typed on the computer and printed out a letter. They even went to the bus garage and watched the bus driver fill the bus with gas. After the "trip," the children and teachers worked together to transform each of their classroom's center areas into a part of their school. In one classroom, for example, the dramatic play area was transformed into the cafeteria, the manipulative area became the boiler room, the writing area became the front office, and so forth. Teachers and children added important vocabulary words and pictures of what they observed in each area so that they could enact the jobs and activities that they observed in these places that were integral to their school. Teachers and instructional coaches added an additional layer of print in both English and the local tribal language to expose the children to print and as a scaffold to remind the teachers to expose the children to higher-level vocabulary.

Similar to the PVIP program, the RBC struggled to find culturally responsive books to support their themes. The RBC Indigenous coaches had some success partnering with local libraries to support their searches. Once located, grant funds allowed for multiple copies of theme-based and culturally responsive books to be purchased and added to each classroom's monthly theme kits. Teachers and coaches also created their own books using pictures they took on their field trips and then adding text through a classroom language experience activity. When possible, text was presented in both English and the tribal language. These books were laminated and bound for use in the classroom or photocopied and sent home for children to share with their families.

Later in the year, the children took a field trip into "town" as a preview for the "My Community, My Family" unit. In this rural area, the town consisted of a gas station/general store on one corner, the elementary school on another, and the vacant tribal college building across the street. Between their school and town, they passed a horse ranch, a wheat farm, and the health clinic. As done during the school field trip, the children met and interacted with the people at each of these locations and learned about people's jobs (what the people said and did), and the teachers took pictures. The children and teachers then transformed their classroom to reflect their community and their family.

Adapted Professional Development

Throughout all four years of the program, instructional and support staff received professional development to support their adaptation and implementation of the curricular materials. Teachers and instructional aides were given opportunities to practice using the new materials and instructional methods with each other, allowing everyone an opportunity to experience the curricular activities in order to facilitate the adaptation process. Inherent to each professional development session was a circle dialogue for sharing perceptions regarding which elements of the project were and were not achieving the group's goals. The professional developer and classroom staff worked together to resolve the incongruence between some of the materials and the reality of the children's lives. For example, given that none of the children had been to a zoo or aquarium, and there were none within a day's drive of their school, the children had limited background knowledge to bring to the "Animals Everywhere" unit. As a result, the children took virtual field trips via YouTube. Using this information, the children and teachers transformed the areas of their classrooms into zoos and aquariums that highlighted the animals and fish common to their community in addition to those they viewed in the videos and could read about and see in books. Staff also consulted tribal elders for guidance about traditional animal myths that they could share during circle time. On the whole, classroom staff that remained in the program throughout its entirety showed marked improvement in their use and adaptation of curricular materials, quality of interaction, general knowledge of early childhood development, and enjoyment of the work in general.

Documenting the Impact of RBC

Data were available for two cohorts of four-year-old children, those completing preschool in summer 2011, and those completing preschool in summer 2012. All children enrolled in the RBC classrooms who matriculated into one of two local elementary schools were followed from the beginning of preschool through kindergarten entry. Preschool and kindergarten assessments were selected and administered by the school district pursuant to state directives. Results presented show preschool and kindergarten emergent literacy skills.

Preschool Skills

Children enrolled in the RBC four-year-old classrooms for two school years were administered a receptive vocabulary assessment at the beginning of the school year and the end. Standard scores across both cohorts revealed a diverse yet normally distributed range of receptive vocabulary skill as documented by the Peabody Picture Vocabulary Test-IV (PPVT; Dunn & Dunn, 2007). Across these two years, children entered preschool with an overall mean receptive vocabulary standard score of 91.6, with 36 of the 130 children (27.7 percent) scoring at or above age-appropriate performance (standard score of 100). After only seven months of preschool, children in both cohorts showed close to one year of growth in receptive vocabulary, allowing nearly half to achieve age-appropriate performance (64 children), and generating an overall mean standard score of 98.2. Most importantly, the 39 children who scored more than one standard deviation below age-appropriate at the beginning of preschool showed even greater PPVT score gains, increasing from a mean standard score of 76.0 to a mean of 85.2.

A similar pattern of growth is found for children's uppercase letter name knowledge. Children enrolled in the RBC four-year-old classrooms for the 2010–11 or the 2011–12 school year were also administered the Preschool Phonological Awareness Literacy Screening (PALS) in September and again in April. Results from the PALS show that children began the preschool year knowing an average of 6.7 uppercase letters, with 10.0 percent (13 children) knowing all 26. The goal for Head Start is that children "graduate" with the ability to correctly identify at least 19 letters. When reassessed in April, the results showed that children could identify an average of 18.9 uppercase letters, 69 children (53.0 percent) named all 26 letters correctly, and 83 children (63.8 percent) named 19 or more. Among the group of 39 children with lower receptive vocabulary skills upon preschool entry, the scores increased from 2.2 to 15.1 letters named correctly and 15 children (38.4 percent) correctly named all 26 uppercase letters at year's end. Overall, children who experienced the RBC program showed significant gains in PALS scores across the preschool year, especially those entering farther below their peers.

Kindergarten Emergent Literacy

The children's emergent literacy skills, including initial sound recognition and letter name knowledge, were assessed upon kindergarten entry using the Dynamic Indicators of Basic Early Literacy Skills (DIBELS-Next; Good & Kaminski, 2011). The group mean on the First Sound Fluency subtest revealed that more than half of the children entered kindergarten at or above the DIBELS Benchmark (mean = 13.2; 57.4 percent), suggesting that they had developed critical foundational skills needed to learn to read. Equally positive, the children's group mean on the Letter Name Fluency subtest showed that most children could identify letters quickly (mean = 19.3).

Conclusion

Becoming a successful reader can be a challenge for Indigenous children, but a high-quality, comprehensive, evidence-based school readiness intervention program like those implemented in both the Pump Up the Volume in Preschool and Rocky Boy Coalition can provide an effective means of ensuring that children develop the requisite school readiness skills needed to become successful beginning readers. Both projects ensured that children entered elementary school with the language and literacy skills needed for future reading success. To accomplish this, children and their families had access to preschool readiness programs that provided culturally responsive materials and activities that focused on the development of emergent reading and overall literacy (vocabulary, oral comprehension, phonological awareness, alphabet knowledge, print awareness, writing).

While the reading achievement gap is a complex issue with many variables at work, there is at least one viable way to close the reading achievement gap—school readiness. With school readiness intervention programs like of PVIP and RBC, the challenge of becoming a successful beginning reader can be overcome and the reading achievement gap can be closed before it begins. But a final word of caution! School readiness interventions like PVIP and RBS hold enormous promise for children, teachers, families, and communities at the beginning of formal schooling; however, overcoming the reading achievement gap for Indigenous children will be stillborn without "scaled up" changes beyond school readiness education. This means changes to elementary and secondary reading education that must include high-quality, comprehensive, evidence-based, culturally responsive approaches (National American Indian and Alaska Native Head Start Collaboration Office, 2013).

Spotlight Recommendation

To stop the reading achievement gap before it begins, Indigenous children and their families need access to high-quality, comprehensive, evidence-based, culturally responsive preschool programs beginning at age three. These preschool programs must be anchored by full-day, preferably year-round, classrooms staffed with highly qualified early childhood teachers (i.e., baccalaureate or higher) and aides (i.e., associate degree or higher). These programs must also feature culturally responsive curricula, materials, and practices that are either locally designed or locally adapted to meet these children's unique learning needs. These curricula must facilitate the development of fundamental language and literacy skills such as vocabulary, oral comprehension, phonological awareness, alphabet knowledge, print awareness, and emergent writing in English and, importantly, in the children's Indigenous language to the greatest degree possible. The programs must continuously monitor children's language and literacy skill progress, and include response to intervention strategies for children who are struggling. For teachers and aides, the programs must include coaching by mentor teachers and ongoing, targeted professional development. Finally, the programs must engage with families and the communities.

However, closing the reading achievement gap for Indigenous children will be stillborn without "scaled up" changes beyond school readiness education. This means changes to elementary and secondary reading education that must include high-quality, comprehensive, evidence-based, culturally responsive approaches; these approaches are recommendations for change in *The White House 2014 Native Youth Report*.

Note

1   The terms Indigenous, Aboriginal, Indian, American Indian, Alaska Native, First Nation Peoples, and Native American are often times grouped together or utilized interchangeably. The authors realize that an individual's identity may be honored when identified through Nation, Clan, or specific Tribe; however, the term Indigenous will be utilized in the chapter to identify communities who have sovereign status and treaty rights in North America.

References

Adams, D. (1995). *Education for extinction: American Indians and the boarding school experience 1875–1928*. Lawrence, KS: University Press of Kansas.

Annie E. Casey Foundation. (2009). *How families survive and thrive in the American Indian and Alaska native community*. Baltimore, MD: Author.

Annie E. Casey Foundation. (2014). *Early reading proficiency in the United States*. Baltimore, MD: Author.

Atwill, K. (2014). An analysis of kindergarten entry skills among American Indian children. Data from the Early Childhood Longitudinal Study-Kindergarten Cohort accessed via The Education Data Analysis Tool (EDAT). National Center for Education Statistics, Institute of Educational Sciences, US Department of Education: https://nces.ed.gov/edat/. Accessed January 12, 2014.

Barnhill, J. (2013). Literacy and illiteracy. In R. Lawson (Ed.), *Encyclopedia of American Indian issues today* (pp. 151–160). Santa Barbara, CA: Greenwood.

Barnett, W. (1995). Long terms effects of early childhood programs on cognitive and school outcomes. *The Future of Children*, 5(3), 25–50.

Barnett, W. (2011). Effectiveness of early educational interventions. *Science*, 333(6045), 975–978.

Bigfoot, D. (2011). The process and dissemination of cultural adaptations of evidenced-based practices for Indigenous children and their families. In M. Sarche, P. Spicer, P. Farrell, & H. Fitzgerald (Eds.), *Indigenous children and mental health* (pp. 285–307). Santa Barbara, CA: Praeger.

Blanchard, J. & Burstein, K. (2015). *A preliminary study of a cultural wrap around curriculum adaptation for the development of early literacy skills with Navajo children attending public preschools*. 20th Annual Navajo Studies Conference. May 28–30. Northern Arizona University Flagstaff, AZ (available from karen.burstein@louisiana.edu).

Carneiro, P. & Heckman, J., (2003). Human capital policy. IZA Discussion Paper No. 821. http://ssrn.com/abstract=434544. Accessed January 23, 2014.

Castagno, A. & Brayboy, B. (2008). Culturally responsive schooling for indigenous youth: A review of the literature. *Review of Educational Research*, 78, 941–993.

Chrisler A., & Ling, T. (2011). *What works for early language and literacy development: Lessons from experimental evaluations of programs and intervention strategies*. Child Trends (Fact Sheet 2011-18).

Christie, J., Enz, B., & Vukelich, C. (2013). *Teaching language and literacy: Preschool through the elementary grades (5th ed.)*. Boston: Pearson.

Cunningham, A. & Stanovich, K. (1997). Early reading acquisition and its relation to reading experience and ability 10 years later. *Developmental Psychology*, 33, 934–945.

Demmert, W. (2011). Culturally based education: Promoting academic success and the general well-being of Native American students. In M. Sarche, P. Spicer, P. Farrell, & H. Fitzgerald (Eds.), *Indigenous children and mental health* (pp. 255–268). Santa Barbara, CA: Praeger.

Demmert, W., Grissmer, D., & Towner, J. (2006). A review and analysis of the research on Native American students. *Journal of American Indian Education*, 45(3), 5–23.

Department of Health and Human Services. (2004). *Establishing a research agenda for Indigenous Head Start programs*. Washington DC: Department of Health and Human Services, Administration on Children and Families, Child Outcomes Research and Evaluation, Head Start Bureau.

Dickinson, D., McCabe, A., Anastasopoulos, L., Peisner-Feinberg, E., & Poe, M. (2003). The comprehensive language approach to early literacy: The interrelationships among, vocabulary, phonological sensitivity and print knowledge among preschool-aged children. *Journal of Educational Psychology*, 95(3), 465–481.

Dockett, S., Perry, B., & Kearney, E. (2010). *School readiness: What does it mean for Indigenous children, families, schools and communities.* Issues Paper No. 2. Canberra, Australia: Closing the gap clearinghouse, Australia Institute of Family Studies.

Dorer, B., & Fetter, A. (2013). *Cultivated ground: Effective teaching practices for Native students in a public school.* Cambridge, MA: Harvard University Native American Program.

Dougherty, C. & Fleming, S. (2012). *Getting students on track to college and career readiness: How many catch up from far behind?* ACT Research Report Series. Iowa City: ACT, Inc.

Duncan, G., Dowsett, C., Claessens, A., Magnuson, K., Huston, A., Klebanov, P., Pagani, L., Feinstein, L., Engel, M., Brooks-Gunn, J., Sexton, H., Duckworth, K., & Japel, C. (2007). School readiness and later achievement. *Developmental Psychology*, 43(6), 1428–1446.

Dunn, L. & Dunn, D. (2007). *Peabody Picture Vocabulary Test-Fourth Edition.* San Antonio, TX: Pearson.

Faircloth, S. & Tippeconnic, J. (2010). *The dropout/graduation rate crisis among American Indian children and Alaska Native students: Failure to respond places the future of Native peoples at risk.* Los Angeles, CA: The Civil Rights Project/Proyecto Derechos Civiles at UCLA.

Faircloth, S. & Tippeconnic, J. (2013). Leadership in indigenous education: Challenges and opportunities. *American Journal of Education*, 119(4), 481–486.

Fiester, L. (2010). *Early warning! Why reading by the end of third grade matters.* Baltimore, MD: The Annie E. Casey Foundation.

Fixsen, D., Naoom, S. Blase, K., Freidman, R., & Wallace, F. (2005). *Implementation research: A synthesis of the literature.* Tampa, FL: University of South Florida, Louis de la Parte Florida Mental Health Institute, The National Implementation Research Network.

Gay, G. (2013). Teaching to and through cultural diversity. *Curriculum Inquiry*, 43(1), 48–70.

Gillard, J. & Moore, R. (2007). An investigation of how culture shapes curriculum in early care and education programs on a Native American Indian reservation. *Early Childhood Education Journal*, 34(4), 251–259.

Good, R. & Kaminski, R. (2011). *DIBELS Next assessment manual.* Eugene, OR: Dynamic Measurement Group. https://dibels.org/. Accessed January 28, 2014.

Gormley, W. T. & Gayer, T. (2003). *Promoting school readiness in Oklahoma: An evaluation of Tulsa's pre-K program.* Washington, DC: Public Policy Institute, Georgetown University.

Griffin Center for Inspired Instruction. (2015). *Improving school readiness for American Indian children.* Snowmass, CO: Author.

Gutierrez-Gomez, C. & Pauly, N. (2006). Early childhood curriculum related to American Indians: Appropriate or not? *Childhood Education*, 82(4), 201–206.

Halle, T., Forry, N., Hair, E., Perper, K., Wandner, L., Wessel, J., & Vick, J. (2009). *Disparities in early learning and development: Lessons from the Early Childhood Longitudinal Study – Birth Cohort (ECLS-B).* Washington, DC: Child Trends.

Hanson, R. & Farrell, D. (1995). The long-term effects on high school seniors of learning to read in kindergarten. *Reading Research Quarterly*, 30, 908–933.

Hart, B. & Risley, T. (1995). *Meaningful differences in the everyday experience of young American children.* Baltimore, MD: Brookes.

Henry, G. & Rickman, D. (2005). *The Georgia Early Childhood Study 2001-2004.* Final report. Atlanta, GA: Georgia State University, Andrew Young School of Policy Studies.

Houghton-Mifflin Harcourt Publishers. (2005). *Where bright futures begin*. Orlando, FL: Author.

Huffman, T. (2010). *Theoretical perspective on American Indian education*. Lanham, MD: AltaMira Press.

Inglebret, E., Jones C., & Pavel, D. (2008). Integrating American Indian/Alaska Native culture into shared storybook time. *Language, Speech and Hearing Services in the Schools*, 39, 521–527.

Johnson, W. (2013). Public education: Current issues and legislation. In R. Lawson (Ed.), *Encyclopedia of American Indian issues today* (pp. 169–179). Santa Barbara, CA: Greenwood.

Juel, C. (1988). Learning to read and write: A longitudinal study of 54 children from first through fourth grades. *Journal of Educational Psychology*, 80, 437–447.

Justice, L., Kaderavek, J., Fan, X., Sofka, A., & Hunt, A. (2009). Accelerating preschoolers' early literacy development through classroom-based teacher-child storybook reading and explicit print referencing. *Language, Speech, and Hearing Services in Schools*, 40, 67–85. doi:10.1044/0161-1461(2008/07-0098)

Klein, L. & Knitzer, J. (2006). *Pathways to early school success: Effective preschool curricula and teaching strategies*. New York: National Center for Children in Poverty.

Lee, V.E. & Burkam, D.T. (2002) *Inequality at the starting gate; Social background differences in achievement as children begin school*. Executive Summary. Economic Policy Institute. Retrieved February 1, 2007 from www.epinet.org/content.cfm?id=6.

Lonigan, C., Farver, J., Phillips, B., & Clancy-Menchetti, J. (2011). Promoting the development of preschool children's emergent literacy skills: A randomized evaluation of a literacy-focused curriculum and two professional development models. *Reading and Writing*, 24, 305–337.

Marks, E., Moyer, M., Roche, M., & Graham, E. (2003). *A summary of research and publications on early childhood for American Indian and Alaska Native children*. Calverton, MD: ORC Macro. (Report for the Child Outcomes Research and Evaluation, Office of Planning, Research and Evaluation, Administration for Children and Families, US Department of Health and Human Services).

McCardle, P. & Berninger, V. (Eds.). (2015). *Narrowing the achievement gap for Native American students: Paying the educational debt*. New York: Routledge.

National American Indian and Alaska Native Head Start Collaboration Office. (2013). *Needs Assessment 2013 survey results*. Washington DC: Author.

National Center for Education Statistics. (2006). *The health literacy of American adults: Results from the 2003 National Assessment of Adult Literacy*. Washington DC: Institute for Education Sciences, US Department of Education.

National Center on Education Statistics. (2012). *National Indian Education Study 2011 (NCES 2011-466)*. Washington DC: Institute for Education Sciences, US Department of Education.

National Center on Education Statistics. (2013a). *The nation's report card: Reading 2013 Trial urban district snapshot report*. Washington DC: Institute for Education Sciences, US Department of Education.

National Center on Educational Statistics. (2013b). *The nation's report card: A first look: 2013 mathematics and reading (NCES-451)*. Washington, DC: Institute for Education Sciences, U.S. Department of Education. (See also Digest of Education Statistics, 2014, Tables and Figures, Table 221.10.)

National Early Literacy Panel. (2008). *Developing early literacy: Report of the National Early Literacy Panel*. Washington, DC: National Institute for Literacy.

National Indian Education Study. (2011). *The educational experiences of American Indian and Alaska Native students at grades 4 and 8.* Washington, DC: National Center for Education Statistics.

National Institute of Child Health and Human Development. (2000). Report of the National Reading Panel. *Teaching children to read: An evidence-based assessment of the scientific research literature on reading and its implications for reading instruction* (NIH Publication No. 00-4769). Washington, DC: Author.

Neuman, S. & Celano, D. (2006). The knowledge gap: Implications of leveling the playing field for low-income and middle-income children. *Reading Research Quarterly,* 41(2), 176–201.

Nguyen, M. (2011). Closing the education gap: A case for Aboriginal early childhood education in Canada, a look at the Aboriginal Head Start program. *Canadian Journal of Education,* 34(3), 229–248.

Niles, M., Byers, L., & Krueger, E. (2008). Best practice and evidence-based research in Indigenous early childhood intervention programs. *Canadian Journal of Native Education,* 30(1), 108–125.

Obama, B. (2011). *Executive Order 13592: Improving American Indian and Alaska Native educational opportunities and strengthening tribal colleges and universities* (2011-31624). Washington, DC: Office of the Federal Register.

Obama, B. (2014). *2014 Native Youth Report.* Washington, DC: Executive Office of the President.

Paulson, L., Kelly, K., Jepson, S., van den Pol, R., Ashmore, R., Farrier, M., & Guilfoyle, S. (2003). The effects of an early reading curriculum on language and literacy development of Head Start children. *Journal of Research in Childhood Education,* 18(3), 169–178.

Preston, J., Cottrell, M., Pelletier, T., & Pearce, J. (2011). Aboriginal early childhood education in Canada: Issues in context. *Journal of Early Childhood Research,* 10(1), 3–18.

Regional Educational Laboratory for the Central Region. (2011). *Compilation of abstracts: Effective teaching of American Indian students.* Centennial, CO: Author.

Reyhner, J. & Hurtado, D. (2008). Reading first, literacy and American Indian and Alaska Native students. *Journal of American Indian Education,* 47(1), 82–95.

Richards, H., Brown, A., & Forde, T. (2006). *Addressing diversity in schools: Culturally responsive pedagogy.* Tempe, AZ: National Center for Culturally Responsive Educational Systems.

Ritchie, S., Bates, T., & Plomin, R. (2015). Does learning to read improve intelligence? A longitudinal multivariate analysis in identical twins from age 7–16. *Child Development,* 86(1), 23–36.

Schoon, I., Parsons, S., Rush, R., & Kaw, J. (2010). Childhood language skills and adult literacy: A 29-year follow-up study. *Pediatrics,* 125(3), 459–466.

Schweinhart, L. (2004) *Lifetime effects: The High Scope Perry Preschool Study through age 40: Summary, conclusions, and frequently asked questions.* Ypsilanti, MI: High/Scope Educational Research Foundation. Retrieved February 1, 2007 from www.highscope.org/Research/PerryProject.perrymain.htm.

Smith, L. (1999/2006). *Decolonizing methodologies: Research and Indigenous peoples.* London: ZED Books (reprinted 2006).

Snow, C., Burns, M., & Griffin, P. (1998). *Preventing reading difficulties in young children.* Washington, DC: National Research Council, National Academy Press.

Sparks, R., Patton, J., & Murdoch, A. (2014). Early reading success and its relationship to reading achievement and reading volume: Replication of "10 years later". *Reading and Writing,* 27, 189–211.

Spicer. P., Bigfoot, D., Funderburk, B., & Novins, D. (2012). Evidence-based practice and early childhood interventions in Indigenous communities. *Zero to Three*, 32(4), 19–24.

Stanovich, K. (1986). Matthew effects in reading: Some consequences of individual differences in the acquisition of literacy. *Reading Research Quarterly*, 21, 360–407.

The White House, Office of the Press Secretary. (2014). *State of the Union address.* Washington, DC: Author.

Thompson, N., Hare, D., Sempier, T., & Grace, C. (2007). The development of a curriculum toolkit with Indigenous communities. *Early Childhood Education Journal*, 35, 397–404.

United National Children's Fund. (2012). *School readiness: A conceptual framework.* New York: United Nations Children's Fund, Education Section, Programme Section.

Vellutino, E. & Zhang, H. (2008). Preventing long-term reading difficulties through kindergarten and first grade intervention: The case for early intervention. *Perspectives on Language Learning and Education*, 15(1), 22–33.

Venn, E. & Frude, C. (2003). *Providing small group literacy instruction in preschool.* Paper presented at Velma E. Schmidt Early Childhood Conference at the University of Northern Texas (December 5–6).

Venn, E. & Jahn, M. (2004a). *Teaching and learning in preschool: Using individually appropriate practices in early childhood literacy instruction.* Newark, DE: International Reading Association.

Venn, E. & Jahn, M. (2004b) *Critical literacy competencies for young children within a preschool framework.* Iowa Reading Association, Iowa Association of School Libraries, and ESEA Title I Shared Conference (April 1–3).

Waldfogel, J. (2014, January 27). *Social Mobility Memos. Gaps in early childhood school readiness and school achievement: Policy Responses.* Washington, DC: Brookings Institution.

Weisleder, A., & Fernald, A. (2013). Talking to children matters. *Psychological Science*, 24(11), 2143–2152.

Williams, A. (2011). A call for change: Narrowing the achievement gap between white and minority children. *Clearing House*, 84(2), 65–71.

Wilson, S., Dickinson, D., & Rowe, D. (2013). Impact of an Early Reading First program on the language and literacy achievement of children from diverse language backgrounds. *Early Childhood Research Quarterly*, 29, 578–592.

Zucker, T., Cabell, S., Justice, L., Pentimonti, J., & Kaderavek, J. (2013). The role of frequent, interactive prekindergarten shared reading in the longitudinal development of language and literacy skills. *Developmental Psychology*, 49(8), 1425–1439.

PART II

Conceptualizing and Measuring the Achievement Gaps in Reading

6

WHY THE ACHIEVEMENT GAP?

Edmund W. Gordon and Paola C. Heincke

For the past 65 years several of us have been calling attention to the significant correlations between the social divisions by which populations are identified and the quality of academic achievement in members of those divisions. This gap between the general levels of academic achievement in Blacks as compared to Whites in the USA has been stuck at about one standard deviation for some time. We see comparable data when we compare low-income and high-income students. John Ogbu (1978) pointed to a similar phenomenon in comparisons between high caste and low caste students in several parts of the world.

I am not as troubled by these disturbing reports as by the fact that this is an issue with which our nation has struggled for most of my professional life. These reports remind us that the concern for the achievement gap is not a new concern. The College Board had been calling attention to the academic achievement gap even before the turn of the 21st century. Back in the 1950s Kenneth Clark (1954) called attention to this problem when he pointed to differences in the levels of achievement between students educated in segregated and integrated public schools. The Supreme Court case, *Brown vs. Board of Education of Topeka, Kansas*, which was decided in 1954, was about the academic achievement gap despite its focus on desegregation. In 1966 James Coleman called attention to the achievement gap in his "Report on Equality of Educational Opportunities," known as the "Coleman Report." Obviously this issue has received public attention for some time; however, its manifestations are still with us and while some progress has been made, it is not nearly enough and the gap persists. Why is this the case?

In the first instance we may have been in error in the way we conceptualized the problem. One of the problems has to do with the fact that for many years we have thought of the academic achievement gap as a primarily racial problem.

Too many people were comfortable explaining the gap as the result of differences that had to do with genetics. Others thought that the gap had to do with racism and racial discrimination. Some argued that the achievement gap is more related to socioeconomic status (SES) and the disproportionate number of people of color who suffer from low income; but as important as SES and income are, they are not a sufficient or adequate explanation of the problem. Data show that middle class status does not produce the same level of academic achievement as does middle class status for white students. James Coleman reported this anomaly 45 years ago in a much-neglected part of the 1966 Report. It may well be that middle class status has different meanings in this social division as we cross racial boundaries.

These differences that appear to be associated with race and SES are important, but they contributed to interventions that were misdirected at class and racial mix in public education and the neglect of a direct attack upon guaranteed access to education of high quality.

In the talk that I gave on the 50th anniversary of the 1954 Supreme Court decision concerning the desegregation of schools I suggested that as important as our attack on segregated schools was to the society, it may have been a setback for education because it prevented us from thinking more about the nature of education of high quality. In other words, the Supreme Court decision may have given the impression that solving the problem of racial separation would solve the problem of access to education of high quality. The reality that the data show is that even in the most racially integrated schools we are still having problems of an academic achievement gap. The opportunity to focus our attention on race may have taken us away from the opportunity to be multifocal in our attack and to direct attention to possible limitations in the appropriateness and quality of pedagogical practice.

Secondly, I think that we have concentrated on schooling to the neglect of the broad complex of educative forces that influence the development of intellective competence. John Dewey (1916), early in the 20th century, and Lawrence Cremin (1975/2007), later in that century, talked about what we now call comprehensive approaches to education, or thinking comprehensively about education. Weiss, Caspe, and Lopez (2006) prefer to call it complementary education and I edited a book in which I called it Supplementary Education (Gordon, Bridglall, & Meroe, 2005); but all of us are referring to the effective orchestration of the wide range of influences, opportunities, and resources by which teaching and learning are enabled and occur.

We are looking at the relationships of learning and teaching that occur out-of-school such as health, nutrition, childcare practices, cultural practices in the community and home, expectations, and other supports for academic development to the effectiveness of the teaching and learning that occur in school. Bourdieu (1986), a French social theorist, has referred to these resources as education relevant forms of capital that can be invested in education. These are forces that are not under the control of school. Despite this line of thought, throughout the 20th century and now in the 21st century with a radically different approach to national governance, the main focus of intervention addressed at the reduction of the academic achievement gap is focused on school reform.

We cannot afford to get too far away from quality of schooling and especially the quality of the teaching persons to whom students are exposed. Good schools and good teachers are tremendously important! But schooling, while necessary, may not be sufficient. Since school reform started in 1950 we have achieved some gains in access to schooling of higher quality. We cannot deny that we have seen some advances in the processes and technologies of instruction. Between 1950 and 1980 we even saw some gains in academic achievement, but we have not seen significant gains in the reduction of the academic achievement gap. Obviously there are limits to school reform as the solution or the reforms utilized may have covered too narrow a range.

As I read things today, there are things that happen in our society that enable schools to work and I think that those things are related to Bourdieu's education relevant forms of capital. I have referred to this position. In his use of this construct, Bourdieu goes beyond the specific forms of education relevant capital to talk about "habitus," which I translate to mean attitude, disposition, view of life, a way of thinking, a habit of mind. What he is suggesting is that when one has the privilege of access to those resources for education and living, one develops the disposition and capacity to use one's self in the disinterest of the self and in support of others. It is an approach to life that my colleague Bandura (1989) at Stanford University has called "agency." However, when the access to those kinds of resources is unequally distributed it gets in the way of the effectiveness of schooling. We have not addressed that issue in our efforts to close the achievement gap and we have certainly failed to address this issue in our efforts for school reform.

Education programs may have been too sharply focused on the improvement of schools. Again, I don't want to take anything away from that effort because I think that improving our schools is very important, but I believe that parallel to this effort there must be increased attention and support for better enabling families and communities to support the academic and personal development of their children. I have begun to talk of parent involvement not so much as parent involvement in the activities of the school but as parents' engagement in the active support of the academic and personal development of their children. This will be reflected in what parents do at home with respect to the distractions of TV; what they do in their faith-based institutions; what they do for summer vacation, or field trips, or travel of any sort; and more important, the kinds of conversations that they have at home; the way in which they feed their children; and the kind of people to which they expose their children.

Going back to the relationship of education to the civil rights struggle, I think that in a way we have focused on education of high quality as a civil right.

A democratic and humane society must ensure adequate education as a basic right of all citizens. But we have neglected the civil liberties with respect to education. We have taken education as a right of citizenship but it is also a liberty of citizenship. As I see the difference, education and learning as a civil right is something that the society does for and to people while education as a civil liberty is something that one does for one's self with the help of others. This means that learners exercise the liberty of becoming intellectively competent, while society must continue to protect and provide a safety net (right) under the existence of all children. But it must also provide scaffolds on which our children can climb, scaffolds that enable them to engage in the affairs of the society and that encourage them to learn, to explore, and to seek out for new answers to old and new questions. Jim Comer (1997) pointed in this direction when he wrote a very provocative little book *Waiting for a Miracle: Why Schools Cannot Solve Our Problems and How We Can.* Comer argues that we cannot wait for schools, working alone, to solve this problem. It is a problem of the people and we the people have to solve it.

A few years ago, my colleagues and I worked with a group of institutions in the New York area to try to give meaning and meaningful practice to this concern. We did some work with the Harlem Children's Zone, the Thurgood Marshall Academy, the Eagle Academy for Young Men, the New York Urban League, and SUNY Rockland Community College to open a Comprehensive Education Resource Center that had as its primary task the promotion of opportunities for teaching and learning that occur outside of school, to complement what happens inside of school. The idea was that the center would provide information and access to resources in areas such as health, nutrition, reading and talking to the children, modeling behavior for children, setting reasonable expectations and standards for children, and more important—teaching parents how to actively support the academic and personal development of their children. The core of the idea of the Resource Center was concerned with being a facility in low-income communities that teaches parents how to best use the schools and the other education resources available in their communities.

Back in the mid-70s my mentor Doxey Wilkerson (1979) found a group of mothers in Harlem with unrealistically high aspirations for their children's academic development. He concluded that they had high aspirations for their children's educational development but they had low levels of knowledge and skills with respect to how to translate those high aspirations into the activities that will support the high academic development of their children. When the Welfare Mothers of Philadelphia asked me to help them with a lawsuit against the Board of Education around the more effective use of Title I money, I discovered the same phenomenon. These low-income women had very high aspirations for their children, but had no notion of what they or their community had to do to enable those aspirations to be achieved. They began their children in school with great expectations that schooling would make a difference, but the longer their experience with school, the lower their expectation of schools and their willingness to sacrifice time in the agenda of the school.

Spotlight Recommendation

I would like to encourage teachers who have the privilege and the responsibility to influence the lives of children, their families, and their communities to work together with the parents and/or the adults responsible for children in their classrooms. The task is to teach these adults what they need to learn to become active supporters of the academic and personal development of their children; to help these parents to understand how to navigate our education system; and to show them the many resources that are available for them and how better to use them, and, yes, how to extract from us, professional educators, what they need to ensure that their children thrive.

If we really want to close the achievement gap, in addition to the safety nets we put under our children, we need to build the scaffolds that encourage and enable them to climb to the top.

References

Bandura, A. (1989). Human agency in social cognitive theory. *American Psychologist*, 44(9), 1175–1184.

Bourdieu, P. (1986). The forms of capital. In J. Richardson (Ed.), *Handbook of theory and research for the sociology of education* (pp. 241–258). Westport, CT: Greenwood Press.

Clark, K. B. (1954, April). *Segregated schools in New York City.* Paper presented at the Child Apart, Northside Center for Child Development, New Lincoln School, NY.

Coleman, J. S., Campbell, E. Q., Hobson, C. J., McPartland, J., Mood, A. M., Weinfeld, F. D., et al. (1966). *Equality of educational opportunity.* Washington, DC: US Government Printing Office.

Comer, J. P. (1997). *Waiting for a miracle: Why schools can't solve our problems and how we can.* New York: Dutton.

Cremin, L. (1975/2007). Public education and the education of the public. *Teachers College Record*, 109(7), 1545–1558.

Dewey, J. (1916). *Democracy and education: An introduction to the philosophy of education.* New York: Free Press.

Gordon, E. W., Bridglall, B. L., & Meroe, A. S. (2005). *Supplementary education: The hidden curriculum of high academic achievement.* Lanham, MD: Rowman & Littlefield

Ogbu, J. (1978). *Minority education and caste: The American system in cross-cultural perspective.* New York: Academic Press.

Weiss, H., Caspe, M., & Lopez, M. E. (2006). *Family involvement makes a difference: Family involvement in early childhood education.* Cambridge, MA: Harvard University, Harvard Family Research Project.

Wilkerson, D. E. (1979). *Educating all our children: An imperative for democracy.* Westport, CT: Mediax.

7

INCLUDING DIFFERENCES IN VARIABILITY IN ASSESSING THE ACHIEVEMENT GAP IN READING

Michael Harwell

The gap in reading achievement among certain groups of students has been a focus of educational research for several decades (Ladson-Billings, 2006), beginning with the large-scale study of Coleman et al. (1966). In this chapter the achievement gap will be understood as representing differences in reading achievement between Black and White students in grades K–12 (Magnuson & Waldfogel, 2008). However, it is important to recognize that achievement differences exist among other racial groups (e.g., Latinos and Whites), other student groups (e.g., English Language Learners and non-English Language Learners), and in other content areas such as mathematics (Lee, 2002).

This chapter argues that efforts to identify the antecedents of the achievement gap in reading and to assess the effectiveness of programs, policies, and practices that seek to reduce this gap can be enhanced by studying differences in variability alongside mean differences. For example, learning that the mean difference between Black and White high school students on a standardized reading test is three-quarters of a standard deviation provides information about students whose score is average; learning that the variability of scores about the mean is greater for Black students compared to White students provides different and potentially important information when assessing the achievement gap. Put simply, accounting for differences in variability among Black and White samples should enhance our understanding of differences in reading achievement. With the exception of Hedges and Nowell (1999) who included ratios of variances of the reading scores of Black and White samples in their analyses, assessments of the achievement gap have made little use of differences in variability.

Definitions

Race

There is substantial agreement that race and ethnicity are distinct but less agreement on definitions of these terms and their categories. In this chapter the definitions and categories used by the US Department of Education to regulate the collection and reporting of race and ethnicity data are used.

Ethnic and racial categories for the federal government were initially developed in 1997 by the US Office of Management and Budget (OMB), most recently updated in 2007 (see www2.ed.gov/policy/rschstat/guid/raceethnicity/index .html?exp=6), and appear on the standard form used by educational institutions, grantees, and federal agencies to collect this information. This form initially asks about a respondent's ethnicity (Hispanic or Latino, not Hispanic or Latino), and then race (American Indian or Alaska Native, Asian, Black or African American, Native Hawaiian or Other Pacific Islander, White). Definitions for these categories and a summary of the process used to generate them can be found at www .whitehouse.gov/omb/fedreg_race-ethnicity. This chapter uses the term race with five categories (American Indian or Alaska Native, Asian, Black or African American, Native Hawaiian or Other Pacific Islander, White), and uses Black to represent Black or African American.

Reading Achievement

Using descriptions employed by the National Assessment of Educational Progress (NAEP) (National Center for Education Statistics [NCES], 2010a, 2013a), reading achievement is tied to student performance on a test reflecting a range of text types and text difficulty and in response to a variety of assessment questions intended to elicit different cognitive processes and reading behaviors. These processes and behaviors are judged to be central to a student's successful comprehension of texts. Student test scores serve as a quantitative indicator of reading achievement.

Achievement Gap

The achievement gap typically refers to differing levels of average achievement via test scores between Black and White students (Jencks & Phillips, 1998; Lee, 2002; Magnuson & Waldfogel, 2008). However, it is important to emphasize that some scholars conceive of the achievement gap differently. For example, Ladson-Billings (2006) argued for looking at an "education debt" consisting of historical, economic, sociopolitical, and moral components, and Carpenter, Ramirez, and Severn (2006) argued for defining multiple achievement gaps based on differences between as well as within student groups. This chapter adopts the traditional definition of the achievement gap in reading as differences in test scores between Black and White students, but departs from tradition by adopting the Hedges and Nowell (1999) definition of the achievement gap as a difference in score distributions for Black and White students. Such differences could take the form of means but also includes variances.

Socioeconomic Status

The term socioeconomic status (SES), coined by the American sociologist Lester Ward (1883), does not have a single definition. However, a representative definition was provided by Hauser and Warren (1997) in which SES is "... a shorthand expression for variables that enable the placement of persons, families, households and aggregates such as statistical local areas, communities and cities in some hierarchical order, reflecting their ability to produce and consume the scarce and valued resources of society" (p. 178). The recommended measures of SES generally include household income, education, and occupation (e.g., American Psychological Association, 2007; Hauser & Warren, 1997).

Review of Relevant Literature

Race and Reading Achievement

The Coleman et al. (1966) study was the first large-scale examination of differences in reading achievement among racial groups. Although concerns about methodological aspects of this study arose (Jencks, 1972) the basic conclusions about differences in achievement between Black and White students have not been overturned. Coleman et al. has been followed by a vigorous and ongoing research effort to identify the antecedents of the achievement gap and its impact on a student's educational and occupational trajectory (e.g., Grissmer, Flanagan, & Williamson, 1998; Reardon, 2011; Reardon, Kalogrides, Shores, & Greenberg, 2013). Much of this work has followed the Coleman et al. model by analyzing nationally representative datasets such as NAEP and the Early Childhood Longitudinal Study Kindergarten Cohort (ECLS-K).

One of the most widely cited sources on the achievement gap is the book edited by Jencks and Phillips (1998) in which empirical results related to the gap are reported (e.g., Grissmer et al., 1998; Hedges & Nowell, 1998). More recent empirical evidence of the achievement gap is provided by US Department of Education reports in which NAEP results are summarized (e.g., NCES, 2009, 2010b, 2013b), as well as analyses of these data by scholars (e.g., Lee, 2002; Magnuson, Rosenbaum, & Waldfogel, 2008; Reardon et al., 2013). Results from analyses of data collected in particular regions of the US documenting the achievement gap in reading also continue to appear (e.g., Clotfelter, Ladd, & Vignor, 2009).

Collectively this literature shows that the achievement gap in reading narrowed in the 1970s through the mid-1980s, with scores of White students showing little change but those of Black students increasing on average. Then, for reasons still being studied and debated (Harris & Herrington, 2006), the gap once again began to increase (Lee, 2002). Although the achievement gap in reading today is smaller than that observed 40–50 years ago (Reardon et al., 2013), it is still about three-quarters of a standard deviation or the equivalent of about four years of learning in middle or high school (Reardon, 2011). Recent work also provides evidence that the gap in reading achievement varies considerably across US states (Reardon et al., 2013).

Most of the achievement gap literature has relied on cross-sectional data in large part because analyses are typically based on NAEP data, which are cross-sectional. Among studies using longitudinal data most have relied on the ECLS-K data, which provide information from kindergarten through eighth grade (Fryer & Levitt, 2004; Lee & Burkham, 2002). Patterns of results estimating the achievement gap in reading using cross-sectional NAEP data over time and longitudinal data have generally produced similar estimates (Reardon, 2008).

SES and Reading Achievement

Coleman et al. (1966) also provided evidence of the relationship between reading achievement and SES, concluding that, in effect, what happens outside school affects achievement at least as much as what happens in school. Among the most compelling findings in the literature involving SES is Reardon (2011), who reported that the achievement gap for SES was about twice as large as that for race. Remarkably, fifty years ago the achievement gap among Black and White students was one and one-half to two times as large as the gap based on SES, and various explanations of this change have appeared in the literature (Harris & Herrington, 2006). These results also provide evidence that while race and SES are related they also exert different effects on reading achievement.

Estimating the Achievement Gap In Reading

Mean Differences

Estimates of the achievement gap are frequently based on a simple mean difference $\overline{Y}_{Black} - \overline{Y}_{White}$, where $\overline{Y}_{Black}$ is the estimated reading mean for a sample of Black students that serves as an estimate of the corresponding population mean μ_{Black} (see Reardon, 2008, for an example of looking at Black–White differences across the entire test score distribution). Per recommended practice (Wilkinson & APA Task Force on Statistical Inference, 1999) a statistically significant mean difference should be followed by re-expressing this difference in ways that help to capture its magnitude, for example, by standardizing the difference using $d = \dfrac{\overline{Y}_{Black} - \overline{Y}_{White}}{S}$

(Cohen, 1988), where S is a standardizer (estimated standard deviation). For example, d = −0.75 would be interpreted to mean that, other things being equal, Black students on average scored 0.75 SDs lower on a test of reading than White students; if the assumptions of normality and homoscedasticity are added for the data then the −0.75 means that approximately 79 percent of Black students have a reading score less than the average reading score of White students.

Note that the choice of S can substantially impact d and its interpretation. Standard practice is to assume samples of Black and White students come from populations with a common variance, pool the sample variances, and take the square root of the pooled variance to generate S. However, unequal variances are fairly common in educational and psychological research (Ruscio & Roche, 2012) and using the square root of a pooled variance as a standardizer when population variances are unequal biases d. When unequal variances are suspected it is often wise to use the estimated standard deviation of one sample (e.g., Black students) as the standardizer.

Rigorous estimation of the achievement gap relies on regression methods to statistically control for the effects of student background variables that can confound (distort) the relationship between race and reading achievement such as SES. Confounders are likely because obtaining reading scores from Black and White samples represents an application of a quasi-experimental design which is subject to selection bias (Harwell, 2011), meaning that Black and White samples a priori differ on background variables that are correlated with reading achievement. Confounders represent a serious threat to the validity of inferences about the achievement gap because they can bias estimates of the Black–White difference in means and variances. Hedges and Nowell (1999), Yeung and Conley (2008), and Chatterji (2006) provide regression-based examples of controlling for background variables in estimating the achievement gap in reading.

Variance Differences

In randomized studies subjects are assigned at random to treatment or control groups and differences among sample means are often accompanied by differences among variances in the same direction (Bryk & Raudenbush, 1988). Variance heterogeneity then reflects a treatment × subject interaction with respect to an outcome variable meaning that whatever the effect of the treatment it is not uniform across subjects within the treatment group. This pattern also occurs in studies employing a quasi-experimental design albeit in a more complicated way (Kim & Seltzer, 2011), which includes studies of the achievement gap. Variance differences between Black and White samples represent a race × student interaction with respect to reading scores, meaning that the impact of race on reading scores varies across students of a common race.

Consider the hypothetical reading scores (overall mean of 250 based on NAEP) displayed in Figure 7.1a for two racial samples. Visually there is evidence

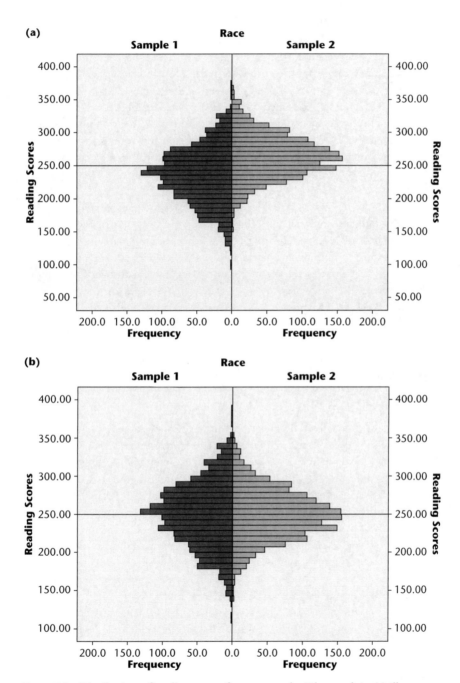

Figure 7.1 Distribution of reading scores for two samples. The graph in (a) illustrates samples with different means and variances, whereas (b) illustrates samples with the same mean but different variances. The horizontal line corresponds to the NAEP mean of 250.

that Sample 2 has a higher mean reading score based on increasing values on the vertical axis. But there is also evidence that a disproportionate number of (mostly low) scores in Sample 1 are further away from their sample mean compared to the pattern in Sample 2. Perhaps these students in Sample 1 are among the 48 percent nationally receiving a free or reduced price lunch (NCES, 2013c), the 25 percent who changed schools at least once since eighth grade (Rumberger, 2003), or are among the 41.4 percent of students living in a household with only the female parent present (NCES, 2010b), factors that have been shown to impact achievement. Identifying the variables that account for different patterns of variability in Samples 1 and 2 can reduce the achievement gap in reading and enhance understanding of its antecedents.

Now consider the case where the two samples have the same reading achievement mean but different variances (Figure 7.1b). If assessment of the achievement gap relied solely on means the conclusion would presumably be that there is no gap. However, following Hedges and Nowell (1999), a more appropriate conclusion is that there is still a gap because of different patterns of variability in the samples. Once again, identifying variables that account for these patterns can reduce Black–White differences and provide a deeper understanding of the achievement gap.

Methodology

Simulated Reading Scores

The process of using differences in variability in reading scores to complement information provided by mean differences is summarized next. Empirical examples are provided to facilitate interpretation. It is assumed that reading scores are independent and normally distributed which means that the mean and variance computed for the same data are independent of one other (Kendall & Stuart, 1977); thus using variability to study the achievement gap in reading applies even if Black and White sample means are equal as illustrated in Figure 7.1b.

To facilitate descriptions of using differences in variability to reduce the achievement gap, reading scores were simulated using SPSS (SPSS Inc., 2011). Using simulated (i.e., computer-generated) reading scores provided control of key data features not possible in datasets like NAEP or ECLS-K, such as specified differences in variability between samples, magnitude of the achievement gap, normality, and no missing data. Burton, Altman, Royston, and Holder (2006) provide a description of, and a rationale for, simulating data. Reading scores were simulated for two samples and in what follows it is understood that Sample 1 refers to (hypothetical) Black students and Sample 2 to (hypothetical) White students.

The parameter values used to guide the simulation of reading scores were from the 2013 NAEP fourth grade Reading Assessment, which consisted of test scores for approximately 33,000 Black students (17 percent of the total sample) and 114,000 White students (58 percent) out of a total sample of 196,400 (NCES, 2013b). NAEP reading scores are scaled to have a mean of 250 and a standard deviation of 50 but results for 2013 showed that the mean NAEP reading scale scores for Black and White students were 206 and 232, which were well below the mean of 250 (pooled SD = 33) (NCES, 2013b). The difference in 2013 NAEP reading means translates to $d = \dfrac{206 - 232}{33} = -0.78$, meaning that on average Black students scored more than three-quarters of a standard deviation below White students, which is consistent with other findings (Reardon, 2011).

The sample sizes for the simulated data maintained the percentages of 17 and 58 for Black and White students, respectively, but a smaller total sample of N = 10,000 was simulated. Thus 1,700 reading scores were simulated for Sample 1 and 5,800 reading scores for Sample 2 to show a difference of approximately d = −0.78.

Research in education and psychology frequently provides evidence of unequal variances (Ruscio & Roche, 2012) and NAEP reading scores are no exception. Variance ratios (e.g., $\dfrac{S^2_{Black}}{S^2_{White}}$) between 1 and 1.5 are fairly common with larger variances linked more or less equally to Black and White samples. Based on this information data for $\dfrac{\sigma^2_1}{\sigma^2_2} = 1.5$ were simulated where σ^2_1 is the population variance linked to Sample 1. Note that a variance ratio of 1.5 represents a substantial difference in variability between samples (i.e., Sample 1 scores are 50 percent more variable about their mean than Sample 2 scores about their mean).

Regression Model

Because rigorous estimation of the achievement gap requires controlling for the effects of background variables like SES, regression methods are needed. Subsequent descriptions rely on a single level regression framework employing ordinary least squares (OLS) to estimate parameters (Fox, 2008) but readily apply to multilevel (hierarchical) models like those illustrated in Raudenbush and Bryk (2002).

If race is the only predictor the model assumed to underlie reading scores can be written as

$$Y_i = \beta_0 + \beta_1 X_{Race_i} + \varepsilon_i \tag{1}$$

where Y_i is the (simulated) reading score of the ith student (i = 1, 2, ..., N), X_{Race_i} is a predictor representing race (Black, White), β_0 is the intercept and represents the mean reading score when X_{Race_i} has a value of zero, β_1 is a linear slope capturing the impact of race on reading scores, and ε_i is a residual representing the portion of Y_i not predicted by race. The fitted model is $\hat{Y}_i = \hat{\beta}_0 + \hat{\beta}_1 X_{Race_i}$, where $\hat{\beta}_0$ and $\hat{\beta}_1$ are the estimated intercept and slope, $\hat{Y}$ is a model-predicted reading score, and $\hat{\varepsilon}_i = Y_i - \hat{Y}_i$. In this model $\hat{\beta}_1$ is simply $\overline{Y}_{Black} - \overline{Y}_{White}$, i.e., the unadjusted mean difference estimating the achievement gap. Although not illustrated here, estimation of the achievement gap is often based on weighted scores that adjust for data issues such as sampling that produces over- or under-representation of racial groups, measurement error, and missing data (e.g., Chatterji, 2006; Reardon, 2008).

In practice the model in equation (1) is augmented to include predictors that control for student background variables like SES. For a single control variable SES the model assumed to underlie reading scores is

$$Y_i = \beta_0 + \beta_1 X_{Race_i} + \beta_2 X_{SES_i} + \varepsilon_i \tag{2}$$

Including X_{SES} removes its effects from Y, and, simultaneously, reduces the Black–White gap if X_{SES} accounts for variation in the residuals not accounted for by X_{Race}.

Equation (2) was used to simulate reading scores based on normally distributed residuals, a dichotomous predictor X_1 representing race (Black, White), and a dichotomous predictor X_2 representing a measure of SES frequently reported with NAEP scores: a student's eligibility for a free or reduced price lunch (NCES, 2009, 2010b). The X_2 predictor served as a background variable that could potentially reduce the variability between samples. Meta-analyses involving reading achievement, race, and SES (Gorey, 2009; Sirin, 2005) suggests that correlations of -0.30 between X_1 and Y, 0.45 between X_2 and Y, and 0.10 between X_1 and X_2 were reasonable and these values were used in simulating reading scores.

For unequal population variances the simulated data produced an estimated variance ratio of $\frac{S_1^2}{S_2^2} = 1.58$, which differed from 1.5 slightly because of sampling error. The achievement gap of the simulated data equaled d = -0.78. The net effect was that the simulated reading scores mimicked key features of the NAEP 2013 Reading Assessment results.

Examining Differences in Variability

Step 1. The first step in examining differences in variability is to estimate the variance of each sample and then test whether the variances are equal (see Hays, 1994). For the simulated reading scores $\frac{S_1^2}{S_2^2} = \frac{1643.12}{1037.34} = 1.58$, meaning that the variability in scores in Sample 1 about the mean was approximately 58 percent greater than that in Sample 2.

There are several tests of the statistical null hypothesis $H_0 : \frac{\sigma_1^2}{\sigma_2^2} = 1$. Assuming a Type I error rate of $\alpha = 0.05$ the Levene and Bartlett tests of equal variances each produced a statistically significant result (p < 0.001) for the simulated reading scores, providing evidence of differences in variability. These tests assume normality and are available in several statistical computing packages (e.g., R Development Core Team, 2012; SPSS Inc., 2011).

Another test of equal variances was described by Bryk and Raudenbush (1988):

$$\chi^2 = (\frac{1}{2})\sum_{j=1}^{2} v_j(c_j - \overline{c})^2 \sim \chi_1^2(1 - \alpha) \tag{3}$$

where $v_j = N_j - 1$, $c_j = \ln(S_j^2) + \dfrac{1}{v_j}$ (ln = natural log), $\overline{c} = \dfrac{\sum_{j=1}^{2} v_j c_j}{\sum_{j=1}^{2} v_j}$, and reading

scores are assumed to be normally distributed. For the simulated reading scores $c_1 = 7.405$, $c_2 = 6.944$, $v_1 = 1700 - 1 = 1699$, $v_2 = 5800 - 1 = 5799$, $\overline{c} = 7.048$, and the chi-square test was 139.6. Comparing this value to the critical chi-square value $\chi_1^2(0.95) = 3.84$ produced a statistically significant result and a conclusion that the population variances differ. If normality does not hold, the nonparametric Klotz test of equal variances can be performed (SAS Institute Inc., 2011).

Step 2. Results in Step 1 showed differences in variability for the simulated reading scores between Samples 1 and 2. The second step is to perform regression analyses that seek to explain why one sample has scores further away from their mean. The initial model fitted using SPSS was that in equation (1). In addition to graphing the resulting residuals as a function of X_1 to examine differences in variability, a useful strategy is to compute various percentiles for the residuals and the associated frequencies (see Hedges & Nowell, 1999 for a similar example of this strategy). The results are summarized in Table 7.1.

TABLE 7.1 Percentage of residuals exceeding selected percentiles based on a single predictor X_1

Percentile	Sample 1 (N = 1,700) (%)	Sample 2 (N = 5,800) (%)
5	11.8	5
10	17.6	10
15	22.2	15
20	26.2	20
80	27.6	20
85	23.8	15
90	18.2	10
95	11.6	5

Note: Residuals represent the portion of the simulated reading scores (Y) not predicted by race and are assumed to be normally distributed with both positive and negative values and to have a mean of zero.

For Sample 2 the percentage of residuals below the value corresponding to the 10th percentile equals 10, and so on for values at the lower end of the distribution. At the upper end the percentage of residuals above the value corresponding to the 90th percentile equals 10, and so on. The percentage of values corresponding to each percentile in Sample 2 equals the corresponding percentile because the values are normally distributed and are approximately equally distributed about the Sample 2 mean.

The residuals for Sample 1 are also normally distributed but are unequally distributed about their mean compared to Sample 2 and the impact is apparent in Table 7.1 (recall that the variance of Sample 1 is 1.58 times larger than that of Sample 2). Using the values corresponding to various percentiles for Sample 2, 17.6 percent of the residuals in Sample 1 were smaller (more negative) than the corresponding value for the 10th percentile for Sample 2. Because residuals are computed as $Y_i - \hat{Y}_i$, where $\hat{Y}_i$ in this instance is the model-predicted value in equation (1) and equals the mean of a student's sample (e.g., $\overline{Y}_1$), a large negative residual means the model over-predicted that reading score. Thus there were more over-predicted reading scores in Sample 1 compared to Sample 2 for the 10th percentile. For the 90th percentile 18.2 percent of the values in Sample 1 were larger than the corresponding residual in Sample 2 (a large positive residual means the model under-predicted that reading score). In fact, in every instance there are higher percentages in Sample 1 because of greater variability than in Sample 2.

Consider further what the difference in percentages between Samples 1 and 2 at the 10th percentile implies. If there were no differences in variability of residuals (which have had the effect of X_1 removed), both samples would have approximately the same percentage of cases in the bottom 10 percent of the distribution of residuals. However, $17.6 - 10 = 7.6$ percent more cases had over-predicted reading scores in Sample 1 compared to Sample 2, or, equivalently, the excess percentage of over-predicted scores in the bottom 10 percent in Sample 1 translates to $0.076 \times 1,700 = 129$ (hypothetical) students. It's likely that some and perhaps most of the greater variation in Sample 1 residuals is due to uncontrolled background variables such as SES.

Next the model in equation (2) was fitted in which X_2 was used to try to account for variability in the residuals beyond that accounted for by X_1. Dividing the Sample 1 variance of the residuals from the model fitted in equation (2) by that for Sample 2 produced 1.13. Recall that this variance ratio was 1.58 with only X_1 in the model, meaning that differences in variability in the two samples have been reduced $\dfrac{1.58 - 1.13}{1.58} = 0.28$ or 28 percent, a substantial reduction that suggests that a sizeable portion of the difference in variability between Samples 1 and 2 was attributable to X_2.

Variability was further examined by computing the frequencies associated with various percentiles for the residuals from equation (2), which are reported in Table 7.2. For Sample 2 the percentage of residuals above and below the specified

TABLE 7.2 Percentage of residuals exceeding selected percentiles based on two predictors X_1 and X_2

Percentile	Sample 1 (N = 1,700) (%)	Sample 2 (N = 5,800) (%)
5	8.6	5
10	14.2	10
15	19	15
20	24.9	20
80	24.9	20
85	20.6	15
90	15.5	10
95	8.6	5

Note: Residuals represent the portion of the simulated reading scores (Y) not predicted by race and are assumed to be normally distributed with both positive and negative values and to have a mean of zero.

percentiles once again equals that expected. However, in every case the percentages for Sample 1 are closer to those of Sample 2 than was true in Table 7.1. For example, the results in Table 7.2 show that the excess percentage linked to the 10th percentile shrank from 7.6 percent to 4.2 percent. Still, equation (2) needs to be augmented with additional predictors to try to produce approximately equal variation in the two samples and, thus, further reduce the achievement gap. Note that equal variances (homoscedasticity) are an assumption of OLS estimation in regression and that adding predictors to a model to reduce heteroscedasticity is an accepted strategy (Fox, 2008).

Other Methods for Examining Differences in Variability

Another method that can be used to study differences in variability in some settings relies on propensity scores (D'Agostino, 1998; Zanutto, 2006). Here a logistic (propensity) regression model is fitted in which race serves as the outcome variable and background variables as predictors (e.g., SES, whether a student changed schools at least once since eighth grade). A propensity is a model-predicted value for each student representing his/her probability of belonging to a given racial group conditional on the predictors in the propensity model. Propensities are often described as "balancing" scores because they take into account background variables that are related to group membership and in the process tend to balance out the effects of background variables. If the estimated propensity scores for all students equal 0.50 then, conditional on the propensity model, students are just as likely to be in either racial group, which mimics random assignment. Estimated propensity scores differing from 0.50 indicate a higher or lower propensity to be in a given racial group.

Using propensity scores in studies of differences in variability between Black and White samples begins by estimating these scores for each student and partitioning the distribution of estimated propensity scores into quintiles (or quartiles, deciles, etc.). Assuming the estimated propensity scores represent the likelihood of a student belonging to the Black sample (conditional on the propensity model), a ratio of variances of the two samples (e.g., $\frac{S_{Black}^2}{S_{White}^2}$) is computed for each quintile using the reading scores in that quintile. If the variance ratio in the middle of the propensity distribution (third quintile) is close to one, but the ratios for quintiles 1 and 2 (or 4 and 5) steadily decrease (or increase), the inference is that the predictors in the propensity model do a good job of controlling for background variables in the center of the propensity distribution but less so for students whose likelihood of being in the Black sample decreases (or increases). If additional predictors are added to the propensity model such that the resulting variance ratios are nearly one in every quintile, the inference is that these predictors account for differences in variability and, thus, provide information about the antecedents of the achievement gap in reading.

Another method to explore differences in variability can be used when data obtained from two-stage cluster sampling are available such as students within classrooms, and are analyzed using a multilevel model. Raudenbush and Bryk (2002) describe how cluster variances can be modeled as a function of background variables using the HLM (HLM7, 2011) software.

A third method is meta-analysis, which is appropriate when differences in variability between Black and White samples in a pool of studies of the achievement gap in reading are to be synthesized (e.g., Gorey, 2009). For example, a researcher may be interested in a meta-analysis of 30 studies of the achievement gap in reading. In addition to synthesizing d values for each study representing a standardized Black–White difference, differences in variability could be examined across studies by first computing within-study differences in coefficients of variation for Black and White samples.

The coefficient of variation for a Black sample in the kth study ($k = 1, 2, \ldots, K$) is estimated for outcome Y as $\hat{\zeta}_{Black} = \frac{S_{Black_k}}{\overline{Y}_{Black_k}}$, and for a White sample in the same study as $\hat{\zeta}_{White} = \frac{S_{White_k}}{\overline{Y}_{White_k}}$. The difference $\Delta_k = \hat{\zeta}_{Black_k} - \hat{\zeta}_{White}$ serves as an effect size for differences in variability for the kth study. Note that scale differences in reading outcomes across studies in a meta-analysis of reading achievement are easily handled by a within-study difference in coefficients of variation. Analyses of the Δ_k provide information about variation in differences in variability across studies and moderators of that variation. Computations for estimation and hypothesis testing are illustrated in Feltz and Miller (1996).

Conclusion

The tradition in assessing the achievement gap in reading is to treat a difference in means between Black and White student samples as evidence of a gap. This information provides evidence of the average difference but says nothing about reading scores for which averages do not apply. If the variation of reading scores of Black and White students is equal then inferences about an average difference in reading achievement are not likely to be distorted; if the variation differs then such inferences can be seriously distorted.

This chapter argued that including differences in variability in reading scores between Black and White students complements information provided by mean differences and provides a more thorough assessment of the achievement gap. After all, if samples of Black and White students had identical reading score means yet one sample had a variance that was noticeably larger than the other, it is hard to imagine a conclusion that there is no achievement gap. Various statistical procedures for estimating the variability between samples were illustrated using simulated reading scores. Regression models containing predictors that reduce differences in variability between samples of Black and White students were given special attention as these offer insights into the origins of that variability, which can provide a deeper understanding of the achievement gap in reading.

Spotlight Recommendation

Educational research continues to focus on group mean differences and to largely ignore group differences in variability, including studies of the Black–White achievement gap. Yet the insight that analyses of variability can provide speaks to the need for researchers to add statistical methods for studying variability to their research toolbox. For example, using statistical methods to identify students whose reading scores are well above or below the group mean, and to account for this variation via regression analyses, offers an important opportunity to more holistically explain such differences. A dual focus on mean and variability differences in reading achievement can also strengthen our understanding of the antecedents of these differences and of the effectiveness of programs, policies, and practices that seek to reduce them. In turn, research findings demonstrating the value of comprehensively studying differences between groups offers the best opportunity for convincing administrators, state officials, and federal offices that closing the achievement gap in reading must be driven by more than mean differences.

References

American Psychological Association. (2007). *Report of the APA task force on socioeconomic status.* Washington, DC: Author. Retrieved January 4, 2014 from http://www2.apa.org/pi/SES_task_force_report.pdf.

Bryk, A. S. & Raudenbush, S. J. (1988). Heterogeneity of variance in experimental studies: A challenge to convetional interpretations. *Psychological Bulletin, 104,* 396–404.

Burton, A., Altman, D. G., Royston, P., & Holder, R. L. (2006). The design of simulation studies in medical statistics. *Statistics in Medicine*, 25, 4279–4292. doi: 10.1002/sim.2673.

Carpenter, D. M., Ramirez, A., & Severn, L. (2006). Gap or gaps: Challenging the singular definition of the achievement gap. *Education and Urban Society*, 39(1), 113–127. doi: 10.1177/0013124506291792.

Chatterji, M. (2006). Reading achievement gaps, correlates, and moderators of early reading achievement: Evidence from the early childhood longitudinal study (ECLS) kindergarten to first grade sample. *Journal of Educational Psychology*, 98(3), 489–507. doi: 10.1037/0022-0663.98.3.489.

Clotfelter, C. T., Ladd, H. F., & Vigdor, J. L. (2009). The academic achievement gap in grades three to eight. *The Review of Economics and Statistics*, 91(2), 398–419. doi:10.1162/rest.91.2.398.

Cohen, J. (1988). *Statistical power analysis for the behavioral sciences* (2nd ed.). Hillsdale, NJ: Lawrence Erlbaum Associates.

Coleman, J. S., Campbell, E. Q., Hobson, C. J., McPartland, J., Mood, A. M., Weinfeld, F. D., & York, R. L. (1966). *Equality of educational opportunity*. Washington, DC: US Department of Health, Education, and Welfare, Office of Education.

D'Agostino, R. B. (1998). Propensity score methods for bias reduction in the comparison of a treatment to non-randomized control group. *Statistics in Medicine*, 17, 2265–2281.

Feltz, C. J., & Miller, G. E. (1996). An asymptotic test for the equality of coefficients of variation from k populations. *Statistics in Medicine,* 15, 647–658.

Fox, J. (2008). *Applied regression analysis and generalized linear models* (2nd ed.). Thousand Oaks, CA: Sage.

Fryer, R. G., & Levitt, S. D. (2004). Understanding the Black-White test score gap in the first two years of school. *Review of Economics and Statistics*, 86(2), 447–464. doi:10.1162/003465304323031049.

Gorey K. M. (2009). Comprehensive school reform: Meta-analytic evidence of Black-White achievement gap narrowing. *Education Policy Analysis Archives*, 17(25), 1–14.

Grissmer, D. W., Flanagan, A., & Williamson, S. (1998). Why did the Black-White score gap narrow in the 1970s and 1980s? In C. Jencks and M. Phillips (Eds.), *The Black-White test score gap* (pp. 182–226). Washington, DC: Brookings Institution Press.

Harris, D. N., & Herrington, C. D. (2006). Accountability, standards, and the growing achievement gap: Lessons from the last half-century. *American Journal of Education*, 112(2), 209–238. doi: 10.1097/DBP.0b013e3181ba0e64.

Harwell, M. R. (2011). Research design: Qualitative, quantitative, and mixed methods. In C. Conrad & R. C. Serlin (Eds.), *The Sage handbook for research in education: Pursuing ideas as the keystone of exemplary inquiry* (2nd Ed.) (pp. 147–164). Thousand Oaks, CA: Sage.

Hauser, R. M. & Warren, J. R. (1997). Sociological indexes for occupations: A review, update, and critique. *Sociological Methodology*, 27, 177–298.

Hays, W. L. (1994). *Statistics* (5th ed.). Fort Worth, TX: Harcourt College Publishers.

Hedges, L. V. & Nowell, A. (1998). Black-White test score convergence since 1965. In C. Jencks and M. Phillips (Eds.), *The Black-White test score gap* (pp. 149–181). Washington, DC: Brookings Institution Press.

Hedges, L. V., & Nowell, A. (1999). Changes in the Black-White gap in achievement test scores. *Sociology of Education*, 72(2), 111–135.

HLM. (2011). *Hierarchical linear and nonlinear modeling* (Version 7) [Computer software]. Lincolnwood, IL: Scientific Software International.

Jencks, C. F. (1972). The quality of the data collected by the Equality of Educational Opportunity Survey. In F. Mosteller and D. P. Moynihan (Eds.), *On equality of educational opportunity* (pp. 437–512). New York, NY: Random House.

Jencks, C. & Phillips, M. (1998). *The Black–White test score gap.* Washington, DC: Brookings Institution Press.

Kendall, M. & Stuart, A. (1977). *The advanced theory of statistics* (Vol. 1). New York, NY: Macmillan Publishing Co.

Kim, J., & Seltzer, M. (2011). Examining heterogeneity in residual variance to detect differential response to treatments. *Psychological Methods*, 16(2), 192–208. doi: 10.1037/a0022656.

Ladson-Billings, G. (2006). From the achievement gap to the education debt: Understanding achievement in U.S. schools. *Educational Researcher*, 35(7), 3–12. doi: 10.3102/0013189X035007003.

Lee, J. (2002). Racial and ethnic achievement gap trends: Reversing the progress toward equity? *Educational Researcher*, 31(1), 3–12. doi: 0.3102/0013189X031001003.

Lee, V. E. & Burkam, D. T. (2002). *Inequality at the starting gate: Social background differences in achievement as children begin school.* Washington, DC: Economic Policy Institute.

Magnuson, K. & Waldfogel, J. (2008). Introduction. In K. Magnuson & J. Waldfogel (Eds.), *Steady gains and stalled progress: Inequality and the Black-White test score gap* (pp. 1–29). New York, NY: Sage Foundation.

Magnuson, K., Rosenbaum, D., & Waldfogel, J. (2008). Inequality and Black-White achievement trends in the NAEP. In K. Magnuson & J. Waldfogel (Eds.), *Steady gains and stalled progress: Inequality and the Black-White test score gap* (pp. 33–65). New York, NY: Sage Foundation.

National Center for Education Statistics. (2009). *Achievement gaps: How Black and White students in public schools perform in mathematics and reading on the National Assessment of Educational Progress* (Rep. No. NCES 2009-455). Washington, DC: US Department of Education. Washington, DC. Retrieved January 6, 2014 from http://nces.ed.gov/pubsearch/pubsinfo.asp?pubid=2009455.

National Center for Education Statistics. (2010a). *An introduction to NAEP.* Washington, DC: US Department of Education. Retrieved January 20, 2014 from http://nces.ed.gov/nationsreportcard/pdf/parents/2010468.pdf.

National Center for Education Statistics. (2010b). *Status and trends in the education of racial and ethnic groups* (Rep. No. NCES 2010–015). Washington, DC: US Department of Education. Retrieved January 3, 2014 from http://nces.ed.gov/pubs2010/2010015.pdf.

National Center for Education Statistics. (2013a). *Reading framework for the 2013 National Assessment of Educational Progress* (Rep. No. ED–02–R–0007 by the American Institutes for Research). Washington, DC: US Department of Education. Retrieved January 11, 2014 from www.nagb.org/publications/frameworks/reading/2013-reading-framework.html/.

National Center for Education Statistics. (2013b). *A first look: 2013 mathematics and reading trial urban district assessment* (Rep. No. NCES 2014–466). Washington, DC: US Department of Education. Retrieved January 6, 2014 from http://nces.ed.gov/nationsreportcard/subject/publications/main2013/pdf/2014466.pdf.

National Center for Education Statistics (2013c). *The condition of education 2013* (NCES 2013-037). Washington, DC: US Department of Education. Retrieved January 25, 2014 from http://nces.ed.gov/pubsearch.

R Development Core Team. (2012). *R: A language and environment for statistical computing* (Version 2.12.2) [Computer software]. Vienna, Austria: R Foundation for Statistical Computing. Retrieved September 25, 2013 from www.R-project.org.

Raudenbush, S. W. & Bryk, A. S. (2002). *Hierarchical linear models: Applications and data analysis methods* (2nd ed.). Newbury Park, CA: Sage.

Reardon, S. F. (2008). Differential growth in the Black-White achievement gap during elementary school among initially high- and low-scoring students. Institute for Research on Education Policy & Practice, Stanford University. Retrieved January 10, 2014 from www.ccpr.ucla.edu/events/ccpr-seminars-previous-years/reardon_Differential%20 Growth.pdf.

Reardon, S. F. (2011). Whither opportunity? Rising inequality, schools, and children's life chances. In G. J. Duncan and R. J. Murnane (Eds.), *The widening academic achievement gap between the rich and the poor: New evidence and possible explanations* (pp. 91–116). Thousand Oaks, CA: Sage.

Reardon, S. F., Valentino, R. A., Kalogrides, D., Shores, K. A., & Greenberg, E. H. (2013). Patterns and trends in racial academic achievement gaps among states, 1999–2011. Retrieved January 6, 2014 from http://cepa.stanford.edu/sites/default/files/reardon%20et%20al% 20state%20achievement.

Rumberger, R. W. (2003). The causes and consequences of student mobility. *The Journal of Negro Education*, 72(1), 6–21.

Ruscio, J. & Roche, B. (2012). Variance heterogeneity in published psychological research: A review and a new index. *European Journal of Research Methods for the Behavioral and Social Sciences*, 8(1), 1–11. doi: 10.1027/1614-2241/a000034.

SAS Institute Inc. (2011). *Procedures Guide* (Version 9.3) [Computer software manual]. Cary, NC: SAS Institute Inc.

Sirin, S. R. (2005). Socioeconomic status and academic achievement: A meta-analytic review of research. *Review of Educational Research*, 75, 417–453.

SPSS Inc. (2011). *Command syntax reference* (Version 20.0) [Computer software manual]. Chicago, IL: SPSS, Inc.

Ward, L. F. (1883). *Dynamic sociology* (Vol. 1). New York: D. Appleton & Co.

Wilkinson, L. & APA Task Force on Statistical Inference. (1999). Statistical methods in psychology journals: Guidelines and explanations. *American Psychologist*, 54, 594–604. doi: 10.1037/0003-066X.54.8.594.

Yeung, W. J., & Conley, D. (2008). Black–White achievement gap and family wealth. *Child Development*, 79(2), 303–324. doi: 10.1111/j.1467-8624.2007.01127.x.

Zanutto, E. L. (2006). Comparison of propensity score and linear regression analysis of complex survey data. *Journal of Data Science*, 4, 67–91.

8

INTERNATIONAL BRAIN WARS

Adolescent Reading Proficiency, Performance, and Achievement from a Competitive Global Perspective

Rosalind Horowitz

Background

Student reading proficiency, performance, and achievement in the United States are being scrutinized from an international competitive framework. Historically, our nation's reading achievement has been based upon federal or state assessments as an index of student intellectual abilities, national stability, and the productivity of our nation. In the past 50 years, America has become increasingly data driven, and competitive, using routine quantitative assessments of students to inform school practices. More recently, worldwide big data has been collected by corporations and business sectors as evidence of reading performance and cognitive growth—moving beyond the states with comparisons across the world's geographic locations. In numerous instances, the prevalent rhetoric is such that policy developments are implicated, and they are beginning to take shape and follow, infiltrating the future of American education—and reading. But what is regarded as advancements in reading and learning depend on how one defines reading, and who designs the assessments, collects and reads the data, or uses it. Moreover, motivations for assessments cannot be ignored. Often missing from the dialogue are the cultural contexts and local attitudes or beliefs about reading and learning, held by a community and teachers, all critical elements and assets in any interpretation of assessments (Anagnostopoulos, Rutledge, & Jacobsen, 2013).

This chapter (a) describes international reports where the goal is to present comparisons of student ability to read with comprehension under a range of academic tasks; (b) addresses some of the changes in reading proficiency, performance, and achievement over time as evidenced in these reports with particular attention to Mexico and Latin America; and (c) provides a critique of findings with attention to achievement "gaps" in reading.

The international reports addressed in this chapter target adolescents. Throughout the world, after a century of attention to research on child development, there is growing use of data to investigate adolescent ability to read with critical thinking—analytically and interpretively—for real-world applications. In many instances, adolescents are perceived as limited in problem-solving abilities that are deemed essential for college success, the work world, and decision-making in everyday life. Claims about adolescent reading proficiency are heightened by those nations who treasure a democracy—and are striving to achieve and sustain a democratic way of life for all of its citizenry.

Proficiency in reading across a range of domains of knowledge is vital for the growth of a democratic nation; low literacy is sacrosanct. Further, advanced reading is the foundation of adolescent learning in all domains of knowledge—the sciences, mathematics, the social sciences, humanities, and the arts. But it is also high levels of reading—that create high levels of thinking, reasoning, and decision-making—that are extremely difficult to develop as many secondary schools are presently structured (Botstein, 1990).

It is these skills that can be used to generate solutions to a long list of complex problems of today's life—poverty and hunger; homelessness; violence, medical, political, familial, and neighborhood obstacles; mental and physical health; or development of morals, ethics, and serenity of mind. New directions have been proposed by the Organization for Economic Cooperation and Development (OECD) and the World Bank that show there is growing attention to low-income students and some of the culprits of poverty. More is needed.

Particularly in the United States, the fourth and ninth grades have been targeted as critical turning points in the development of academic reading. At these age-grades, texts used become linguistically, conceptually, and rhetorically more complex. Prior knowledge of different disciplines becomes of paramount importance in advancing reading comprehension. This is also recognized in international reports of fifteen-year-olds where there is a sense of urgency about building reasoning skills (Alexander, 2003; Alexander & Fox, 2011).

Adolescence is a rocky, tumultuous time. This makes assessing the adolescent's academic reading performance increasingly difficult and many times unreliable. The adolescent brain is easily subject to mood swings, tempered by risk-taking that may result in dangerous, life-threatening experimentation (Fantuzzo, LeBoeuf, & Rouse, 2014; Horowitz et al., 2012). Research across disciplines on adolescent experimentation, risk-taking, and logical reasoning suggests that teachers must be vigilant, more so than ever, in guiding teenage listening and reading—thinking and acting. However, in order for teachers to educate adolescents, teachers will need information about how to design reading instruction, how to help students achieve "high levels" of critical reasoning while reading (Horowitz, 2015a), flow in completing in-school tasks (Csikszentmihalyi, 1997) and, above all, help adolescents find purpose in life (Damon, 2008).

International Comparisons and Evaluations of Adolescent Reading

There is an international brain war raging that necessitates control and direction. A competition now exists between countries in school achievement from elementary to higher education. This is evident from official data-based documents circulating across business sectors and governments, resulting in global rather than local state-by-state comparisons and rankings (Horowitz, 2015b, 2015c). These rankings have been compared to the "Olympic Games," (by academics across the world, of late, Russia). These "Olympic Games" offer potential benefits of prestige and financial gains that will bring, supposedly, an intentional international visibility (Yudkevich, Altbach, & Rumbley, 2016). What becomes lost in the shuffle is regard for the highest forms of learning such as discourse synthesis or analysis, and innovation or creativity. Another loss is a description of and caring for the individual's human development (also noted in the final chapter of this volume, Horowitz & Samuels, 2017). With comparisons across nations through big data, unique needs and reading strengths of individuals are missing. While this essay focuses on globalization and big data, it must be combined with more local meta-analyses, descriptive studies, and cases of individual literate behaviors, reading proficiency, and performances, acquired in specific sociocultural contexts.

Finally, it must be noted that these international reports give attention to adolescent reading of primarily non-narrative text-sources—i.e., expository, informational extended continuous discourse, as well as non- or less-continuous sources—e.g., tables, diagrams, graphs—often embedded in continuous text. This consideration of the non-narrative is based on the intent to describe what adolescents can do on a practical level with reading activities. However, there are many genres of texts that adolescents encounter and use worldwide that have not been considered—but may have cognitive socio-cultural and practical merits as stepping stones at an adolescent stage of development—from Japanese graphic novels to autobiographies, historical diaries, adolescent fiction, poetry, and narratives through computer gaming.

Research Reports Briefly Examined: Accounts of Achievement Gaps in Reading

Three international research assessment efforts provide cross-national comparisons and are described below: *the IEA Study of Reading Literacy, PIRLS, and PISA.*

How in the world do students read? *The IEA Study of Reading Literacy*, authored by Warwick Elley (1992), although produced much earlier than the PISA reports, remains worthy of our close attention among international assessments. Elley's report was funded by research institutes acting as the national centers in each country, with funding amounting to $615,000. Additional funding was also provided by prestigious institutions known for their dedication to scholarly inquiry:

the MacArthur Foundation, the Mellon Foundation, the National Center for Educational Statistics, through the National Academy of Sciences, the European Community, the Maxwell Family Foundation, and UNESCO. Originally problems in conducting educational research were addressed by members of these groups, which led to comparisons across countries. This report by the International Association for the Evaluation of Educational Achievement (IEA) was conducted to produce valid international tests that could be used to compare countries' literacy development, to provide baseline data to monitor changes in literacy levels, and to identify policy and reading practice differences and how they relate to reading achievement.

Warwick Elley's study (1992) is impressive. It examined nine-year-olds and fourteen-year-olds in 32 systems and 27 countries across the world, totaling 210,000 students. Elley, of the University of Canterbury, New Zealand, has written extensively about literacy progress worldwide and although his study dates back to 1992, it gives us substantial information that can be used to examine trends and policy developments of the 21st century.

The Progress in International Reading Literacy Study (PIRLS) is a study of the reading of United States fourth graders, typically nine-year-olds and what is comparable by age-grade in other participating countries. The administration of PIRLS, coordinated by the IEA, has occurred in 2001, 2006, 2011, and 2016. This data is routinely collected to provide information on trends in reading achievement of fourth-grade students and to provide baseline data for new countries. PIRLS 2011 assesses reading comprehension and measures change since 2001. It includes surveys that examine experiences young children have at home and school in learning to read.

It is important to note that PIRLS addresses specifically fourth grade. It appears that many nations throughout the world concur that fourth grade or a comparable age-grade is a critical turning point in reading expository and argumentation text-sources and exercising the higher literacy skills needed for processing disciplines such as history and science or mathematics. Students who do not exhibit proficiency in reading at the fourth grade continue to plummet in school reading performance, and in many cases never recover at a level where they can succeed in completing high school reading tasks and graduate.

Ninth graders, 14- to 15-year-olds, with some overage students, in our research in a magnet school in South Texas, 100 miles from the Texas–Mexico border, reported in interviews that they wanted to drop out from United States schools at ninth grade, because they "cannot read the textbook" that was assigned in content areas in the school curriculum. Their preference was for teacher *oral reading of texts* so that they could comprehend through listening to the text, without the stressful work of decoding, with hope that this would facilitate their transition from oracy (listening and speaking) to literacy (reading and writing) (Horowitz, 1991).

The Programme for International Student Assessment (PISA) is an international survey where the goal is to evaluate education systems worldwide, every three years, and examine the skills and knowledge of 15-year-old students in reading, mathematics, and science. It is produced by the OECD, Paris, and is driven by *economies* of nations, and their financial growth and productivity. There are three OECD reports that are highlighted herein: *PISA 2009, PISA 2012,* and *PISA 2015 Executive Summary.* We are reminded by OECD that, to date, students representing more than *"70 economies"* have participated in the assessment, with the latest assessment in 2012, with a 2016 report due during the time this chapter is in press. PIRLS, a predecessor of PISA, reports that about 510,000 students in *"65 economies"* took part in the *PISA 2012* assessment of reading, mathematics, and science representing about 28 million 15-year-olds globally. Of those economies, 44 took part in an assessment of creative problem solving and 18 in an assessment of financial literacy (OECD 2013a, b).

PISA documents indicate the focus has been on applied tasks, what students can do, their understanding, uses, and reflection about texts (See OECD, 2014). In 2000, PISA's first cycle of testing, the majority of test items were devoted to reading tasks. Interestingly in 2003 and 2006, reading is given less priority, with precedence given to applications in science and mathematics. Text formats, reading processes, and situations—personal use, public use, occupational and educational uses of reading—were given priority in 2009. In *PISA 2000,* a reading scale was developed with an average of 500 and possible score of up to 1,000. Over 75 percent of the students tested fell between 400 and 600.

In *PISA 2009*, reading performance is reported for a *low literacy—access and retrieving information*—but also what is deemed *high literacy*—determined by *integrate and interpret, reflect, and evaluate skills.* Attention is also given to text formats, reading processes, and situations including personal, public, occupational, and educational use. The rhetorical structure of texts is valued in PISA reports but could use elaboration: There are descriptive, narrative, expository, argumentative, and transaction type texts which exchange information among interlocutors (OECD, 2010a, b, c, d).

In *PISA 2009*, the countries performing highest in *high literacy tasks* were Korea, Finland, and Shanghai-China, where there also was the smallest variability in performance. Top performing countries across all levels of literacy (*access to evaluate*) included Hong Kong-China, Singapore, Canada, New Zealand, Japan and Australia—also, the Netherlands, Belgium, Norway, Estonia, Switzerland, Poland, Iceland, and Liechtenstein.

In *PISA 2012*, countries which rated highest in reading among continuous texts in PISA were Shanghai-China, Hong Kong-China, Singapore, Japan, Korea, and Finland. Other top performers in 2012 were Canada, New Zealand, Australia, Netherlands, Norway, Belgium, Poland, and Iceland. These countries all had scores about the OECD average.

The lowest of performers in *PISA 2009* was Mexico, with additional Latin American countries worthy of attention, particularly by political officials and educational leadership here in my State of Texas. There is much migration, more than only immigration, to and from the Latin nations with returnees to Mexico increasing in numbers due to economic hardships in the United States (Lukes, 2015). The scale validity for PISA has been examined by researchers in Mexico (Tristan & Mendoza-Gonzalez, 2008) with growing reservations about the appropriateness of measures used for their specific cultures and economic groups.

The *PISA 2009* report goes on to say, "This means the gap between the highest country [e.g. Shanghai-China, Singapore, Japan] and lowest performing OECD countries [e.g. Mexico, Peru, Kazakhstan] is 114 points, the equivalent of more than two school years. And the gap between the highest and lowest performing partner country or economy is even larger, with 242 score points, or more than six years of formal schooling separating the mean performance of Shanghai-China and Kyrgyzstan (314)" (OECD, 2010a, p. 6). This *PISA 2009* report conveys that the populations studied are extremely diverse and have varying needs and expectations for reading. This diversity in performance is also visible in Southeast Asian countries (Thien, Razak, Keeves, & Darmawan, 2016).

In *PISA 2012*, a number of Latin American countries were consistently at the bottom of the assessments, including Mexico, Brazil, Colombia, Argentina, and Peru. The reader herein is directed to the *Latin America after PISA: Lessons learned about education in seven countries (2000-2015), Executive Summary* by Axel Rivas (2015) with calls for greater attention to the educational needs of this region and the slow pace of movement in literacy improvement. This project was developed by the Center for Implementation of Public Policies Promoting Equity and Growth with attention to the new century in Latin America. In this report, Latin America and its countries are characterized as "the most unequal continent on the planet" (p. 6) suffering from unemployment resulting in severe poverty, malnutrition and infant mortality. A positive is that all countries extended their years of compulsory education from 10 to 13 years from 2000 to 2015, with increasing attention to early adolescence. Mexico, in particular, brings the largest population of Latino immigrants to the United States and they function as transnational communities (Christiansen & Farr, 2013). Obvious is the need for more education among the upper-age adolescent population in Mexico and Latin America. The recent *Latin America after PISA* (2015) report conveys Latin American academics are expressing trends for more flexibility and divergent educational models in order to improve reading.

In sum, adolescent achievement accounts in Latin America and other countries across the world incorporate a focus on reading and are rank ordered by country in each of the above reports. But why do these reports concentrate on adolescence? At this juncture, there is an international alarm, followed by fear, that adolescents are declining in achievement, particularly literacy, science, and mathematics, which endangers the future of a nation's economic productivity.

But more than economics is at stake.

Multiple demographic trends that bear on literacy such as family, cultural traditions, turmoil, and poverty affect youth not only in the United States but around the world (see Brown, Larson, & Saraswathi, 2005). Since reading is the foundation for learning in content fields in school, a decline in reading signals a decline in acquiring and developing knowledge of numerous subject areas that bear on the future quality of one's life. Adolescent motivation is perceived as a serious problem in many locations in the world, not only the United States, and has been linked to student effort and performance on reading measures. But there are also different cultural expectations for literacy performance that the data do not convey (Snow & Biancarosa, 2003; Snow & Moje, 2010). Some students are low performing on certain types of reading (science), however, they may excel with other types of reading (history) or required reading styles (fast or slow). Finally, transnational youth who experience war and trauma have entered into the equation of demographics in school achievement, typically outside of the picture (Horowitz, 2014a; Sullivan & Simonson, 2016). Reading can be especially therapeutic and life-reaffirming in a time of turbulence when youth are traumatized by war or poverty. Reading may also build one's mental strength, resilience, and survival abilities.

Is There a Decline in Reading Achievement in Specific Locales of the World?

Some of the educational problems that we face in the United States are no longer unique to the United States, but problems that are encountered worldwide. The following questions are posed in the pages ahead in this chapter:

1. Have there been significant changes in adolescent *reading proficiency* (what students know and are capable of doing), *performance* (what they actually can do under specific well-defined reading tasks), and *achievement* (measures and scores that demonstrate what is achieved, acquired over time about a concept, on standardized tests) across the world, and, if so, in which countries is this substantial change the case?

    What are some of the changes in reading proficiency and performance that are identified in *PISA 2009*, and followed up on in *PISA 2012* and the *2015 summary* that convey trends? Which nations are excelling and which are dropping in reading performance?

2. What factors have contributed to student success or failure in reading achievement in specific nations? What can we learn from these nations? What must follow in our thinking about and design of global assessments and cross-national aspirations?

International Assessments of Achievement and Reading

International progress assessments are frequently used for high-stakes testing, to determine trends in student achievement, teacher effectiveness, and school stature. The reports that were consulted for this chapter provide data on numerous countries and the nature of their classrooms, student populations, language at home versus school language, teacher preparation, school resources, home environment, and benchmarks (PIRLS 2016).

PISA Rankings of Countries for Literacy Achievement

In PISA scores in reading in 2009, the US ranked 11th with a score of 500 and by 2012 ranked 24th with a score of 498. Relatedly, PISA scores dropped in math and science. In math, the US ranked 30th in 2009 with a score of 487 and 37th in 2012 with a score of 481. In science, the US ranked 18th in 2009 with a score of 502 and ranked 28th in 2012 with a score of 497. In summary, the United States appeared to drop in measures of reading performance from 2009 to 2012. Since reading is vital to performance in math and science, we should expect performance in these subject areas and other subject areas as well to decline when reading expertise is not developed or drops.

TABLE 8.1 Average Reading Scores of 15-year-old Students on PISA 2009 and 2012

	Consistently at the Top					
Country	*Reading*		*Math*		*Science*	
	2012	*2009*	*2012*	*2009*	*2012*	*2009*
Shanghai-China	570	556	613	600	580	575
Hong Kong-China	545	533	561	555	555	549
Singapore	542	526	573	562	551	542
Japan	538	520	536	529	547	539
Republic of Korea	536	539	554	546	538	538
Finland	524	536	519	541	545	554
Chinese Taipei	523	495	560	543	523	520
Canada	523	524	518	527	525	529
Estonia	516	501	521	512	541	528
Liechtenstein	516	499	535	536	525	520

Country	Consistently at the Top					
	Reading		Math		Science	
	2012	2009	2012	2009	2012	2009
Australia	512	515	504	514	521	527
New Zealand	512	521	500	519	516	532
Netherlands	511	508	523	526	522	522
Macoa-China	509	501	531	534	515	517
Belgium	509	506	515	515	505	507

Country	Consistently at the Bottom					
	Reading		Math		Science	
	2012	2009	2012	2009	2012	2009
Thailand	441	421	427	419	444	425
Mexico	424	425	413	419	415	416
Brazil	410	412	391	386	405	405
Tunisia	404	404	388	371	398	401
Colombia	403	413	376	381	399	402
Jordan	399	405	386	387	409	415
Malaysia	398	n/a	421	n/a	420	n/a
Argentina	396	398	388	388	406	401
Indonesia	396	402	375	371	382	383
Albania	394	385	394	377	397	391
Kazakhstan	393	390	432	405	425	400
Qatar	388	372	376	368	384	379
Peru	384	370	368	365	373	369

Increase of 15 or more mean points from 2009 to 2012. Decrease of 15 or more mean points from 2009 to 2012.

Note: "Consistently at the Top or Bottom" refers to those countries that were ranked in the top 20 countries or bottom 20 countries in both 2009 and 2012.

Finland was recognized by Elley (1992) as having the highest average score for narrative and expository reading among the 27 countries studied and has been repeatedly identified as being high performing. *PISA 2009* shows Finland excelled in reading performance in the *interpreting and integration of information* (see Figure 1.2.24 from the PISA 2009 OECD report, reading achievement for nine-year-olds and fourteen-year-olds). This high performance has been characterized as due to the homogeneous nature of the Finnish population, certainly more homogeneous than the United States population. However, this high reading performance also has been attributed to the highly regular letter-sound correspondence in Finland's writing system. This regularity in letter-sound relationships does not exist in many languages of the world including English. Data in Table 8.1 and the *PISA 2015* summary indicate that Finland scores in Reading, Math, and Science are dropping. Some argue that this is due to the growing heterogeneous population. See *Real Finnish Lessons: The True Story of an Education Superpower* and other sources that argue for a homogeneous population economically (Horowitz 2014a, 2014b; Sahlberg, 2011; Sinko, 2012).

The Strengths and Weaknesses of Countries Considering Different Kinds of Reading Processes: Continuous versus Non-Continuous Texts

The Progress in PISA 2009 OECD Report has presented important information examining reading performance on the basis of two categories of text: continuous versus non-continuous. *Continuous text* consists of texts which present a main argument or what is known as a thesis, with supporting information, such as evidence, examples, and arguments to convey a message. This text, if well designed, is cohesive, allows for flow in reading and creates integration of ideas, and ultimately analytical comprehension. In contrast, *non-continuous* text may consist of data, chunks of ideas, tables, graphs, and snippets/segments of information, and, in technology, may be text messages that depend on a reader's prior knowledge and ability to rapidly process and analyze different text formats.

According to *PISA 2009*, countries performing significantly better with continuous text on high literacy processes, i.e., *reflect* and *evaluate*, are English-speaking countries (Australia, New Zealand, United Kingdom, and the United States). Similarly Hong Kong-China and some Latin American countries such as Brazil, Colombia, Panama, Chile, Mexico, and Argentina are identified by *PISA 2009* as performing well on the *reflect* and *evaluate* category of high literacy. Students in these countries [Latin American] demonstrate strength in expressing views about texts and discerning the text structure and purpose, but a comparative limitation in attentive and accurate information-focused reading.

In addition to those countries successful with continuous text, success with non-continuous text includes Estonia, Liechtenstein, United Kingdom, Switzerland, the United States, and Chinese Taipei. Some countries rated first may have shifted, such as Korea, but not significantly (to second or third). Finland remained the same with a ranking of 535 points. Other Asian countries may have modified results in spite of other factors.

Plummeting Scores in Reading Performance Are Present across Multiple Countries

David R. Olson (2013, personal communication) laments what he and others in Canada view as a growing worldwide decline in reading achievement. PISA data show the reading scores in international assessments of 15-year-olds in 2012 have plummeted consistently across several reading achievement surveys. To the chagrin of many in Ontario, Olson targets, according to PISA research, Canada's decline in reading achievement is not unique but is accompanied by adolescent declining scores in the United Kingdom, New Zealand, Australia, Sweden, and the United States. Note these are all primarily English-speaking countries with a similar economic base and youth lifestyle. In the case of Sweden, in 2000, Olson reminds us that Sweden was at one time one of the top three nations in reading. By 2012, there was a significant drop in performance and achievement. "Finally, the United States, a pioneer in the strict accountability reform movement, has languished at a level below the international average in nearly every PISA Survey," Olson reported in 2013 (see Figure 8.1).

Warwick Elley (2012) concurs with Olson's declaration. Elley indicates New Zealand, like Finland, has intentionally avoided high stakes testing in the primary school years, conveying "A National Standards Policy is a threat to our high standing." He argues, like Olson, "...that those countries that have introduced similar system-wide policies with 'league tables,' [rating of students] are going backwards" (p. 3).

As the figure below demonstrates, it is not only reading scores that have plummeted but also those in mathematics and science, based on PISA means for the above five nations, looking at the years 2000 to 2012 (Olson, 2013). Of course, youth will not be able to perform in math and science if they do not possess those specialized reading skills needed for cognitive processing of the academic language of these disciplines. PISA data which demonstrates plummeting of scores has generated strong reactions, in turn causing educational reforms in many countries across the world—in Germany, Denmark, Japan, Finland, and additional European countries (see summary by Rutkowski & Rutkowski, 2016). Alarmist reactions have surfaced, with strong criticism of PISA intentions as well as methodologies, and they continue to be expressed in scholarly journals and books (see Alphonso, 2013).

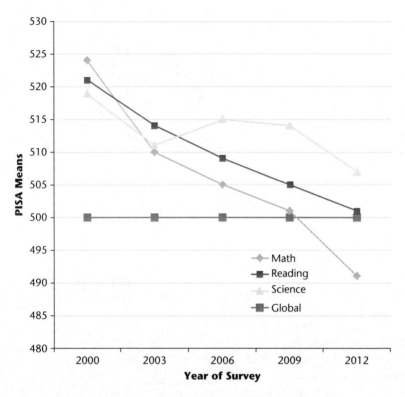

Figure 8.1 PISA Means for Five Nations Using Standards-Based Assessment

What Factors Have Contributed to Student Success or Failure in Reading Achievement in Specific Nations? What Can We Learn from These Nations? What Must Follow in Our Thinking about Assessments?

For over four decades, our focus on achievement in reading has been on cognitive and meta-cognitive strategies that teachers have been trained to address in reading instruction and assessments. Our attention has shifted, more recently, to broader considerations that are factors beyond the teacher, yet connected to a classroom context. These are social-cultural considerations—out-of-school cultural life of the student, with consideration of the family, community, and neighborhood; and personal interests and motivations that contribute to reader engagement and con-centration (Guthrie & McRae, 2017, in this volume; Renninger & Hidi, 2016).

The Role of the Family and Parent/Guardian in High Achievement and High Literacy

Immigrant mothers have historically been highly motivated and actively engaged in their children's achievement and reading practices in many cultures and loca-tions in the world where literacy is high. For one, the Japanese mother dedicates time for close monitoring of her child's achievement. The Japanese family has traditionally been considered one of the most important elements of society and school success. The mother and other immediate family members, including even more distant relatives, have been directly involved in adolescent development (Stevenson & Zusho, 2002) leading to the conclusion that parent training is paramount.

More specifically, the traditional Japanese mother has been characterized as active in requiring that their children complete homework and reading requirements posed by the school, and in guiding their children with high expectations as children prepare for tests. This work may not be in vain. Research has demonstrated that homework completion is a predictor of school grades and achievement. It is also an index of student commitment to the institution of schooling and personal commitment and identity as a student who will succeed (Frontera & Horowitz, 1995; Guthrie & McRae, 2017, in this volume). In contrast, in the western world, in the United States, homework and its completion is viewed as less of a critical factor for achievement in schools. This has resulted in United States parents often "overlooking" homework assignments, teachers finding grading cumbersome and reducing homework, and schools even choosing to eliminate homework all together. Evidence of the importance of homework in Japan and China can be demonstrated by the fact that not only is time devoted in the home for study, these parents actually purchase a desk—an elaborate and expensive one—for this purpose for their child (Stevenson & Stigler, 1992). In Beijing, China, parents intentionally devote a quiet space in their extremely tiny apartments for their children to read and finish homework. This is so their children can be competitive in school, nationally, and in competitions such as international brain wars.

In the book, *Battle Hymn of the Tiger Mother*, the author, Chua, a Chinese Yale University law professor (2011a, b) pinpoints her requirements as a *Chinese mother* and identifies other cultures where the model of the Chinese mother is evident: "I know some Korean, Indian, Jamaican, Irish, and Ghanaian parents who qualify too" (p. 4) and she adds South Dakota males might qualify as well in being Chinese mothers. This author portrays how the Chinese mother is not a constant in one culture but rather also exists even among Western parents who take on this role of monitoring the children's progress by overseeing schoolwork at home. However, Chua claims that the Western mother and father, even when resembling the Chinese mother, fall short of being as demanding as the Chinese mother. Chua gives the example of the Chinese mother supervising a child's practice with a musical instrument. Like learning to read, learning to play a musical instrument involves acquiring skills that will influence performance. It requires building good work habits—scheduling and persisting, even doggedness or what we call today "grit"—until a goal is reached. Thus, the Chinese mother requires constant practice in order to build stamina and achieve excellence. Chua (2011b) says:

> For example, my Western friends who consider themselves strict make their children practice their instruments 30 minutes every day. An hour at most.

For a Chinese mother, the first hour is the easy part. It's hours two and three that get tough. (p. 4)

But Chinese children and adolescents are required to go the extra mile, to the extent of forgoing television or computer games, and other desirable extracurricular activities. These denials are there when obtaining a grade of no less than an A is the pursuit. In the Sputnik era, excellence in science infiltrated schools and homes, so that we could win the battle with Russia. Schools took on what Barak Rosenshine called "time on task" for science, more academic activities, and more assessment time than occurred in previous years in schools in the United States. It was a different "time on task" than we encounter today.

While the pursuit of excellence reigns in China, there is quite a contrast of worrying about a child's self-esteem in the United States parent world, says Chua (2011a, b). Many American parents hesitate when it comes to being a Chinese mother for fear of damaging their child's self-esteem. Letting a child naturally become who they are or will become is the theme of Western parents but in a non-threatening way. The Chinese mother is insistent on excellent performance and the hours of practice which are necessary, while being less concerned about the self-esteem of their child. With practice, excellence will happen and, as a result, self-esteem, it is believed, is raised.

Note that child rearing was the responsibility of the entire community in a village as well as the responsibility of the adolescents' parents. Today, families have often relinquished control and relegated to teachers and schools the overseeing of adolescent behavior and studies. Japanese teachers, rather than parents, are at the forefront of disciplined study in many Japanese communities. While the Japanese mother is not addressed in the Elley (1992) study, the latter report shows that Hong Kong adolescents score in the upper category of reading achievement, despite low income, the complexity of the Chinese language, and other barriers to learning. The relation between socioeconomic status and academic achievement is worthy of greater attention worldwide (White, 1982). But it is not only completion of homework that is a critical factor in school achievement.

Parent Motivation and Engagement: Verbal Support as a Contribution to Education

We have little documentation of immigrant parental support of reading of the waves of immigrants of the 1920s, except in diary accounts or visual portraits. Yet, parent engagement in the school experiences of their adolescents, more recently, has been shown to be a significant factor in student achievement in schools and may be in some sectors increasing. According to an Educational Testing Service Study (ETS) (Barton & Coley, 2009, pp. 18–19), using a Chicago longitudinal data base, of 1,539 low-income learners over a 17-year period, with a pool of 93 percent African Americans, parent engagement was shown to be a significant factor in school success and a correlate of higher achievement, with parent-school-involved teenagers more likely to graduate high school than where there was no parental involvement.

Mexican immigrant parents have been shown to have definite literacy ideologies that they apply to school language practices, evidence they value school experiences. These ideologies are manifested in attitudes toward their child's reading habits and language use at home. Notable is that for some parents there is preference for the child's use of the English language at home for schooling, with ingenious language minority maintenance, so that children and adolescents become proficient in speaking and reading English in order to succeed in the English-based work world (Bayley & Schecter, 2007; Christiansen & Farr, 2013). While data from 1999–2003 by ETS shows increased parent involvement of racial/ethnic groups, many Mexican immigrant parents shy away from participating in school functions and there is little known about the kind of parent participation that holds the most payoff.

When children have rich opportunities to process oral language—i.e., listening to parent speech and oral readings of books found at home, they acquire vocabulary that later benefits their own reading practices. The Hart and Risley (1995) study showed that by the end of the first four years of life, children in professional families heard about 35 million more words than children in welfare families. This study showed that vocabulary acquired by children in these early years was related to the number of words heard from parents. We know that vocabulary knowledge is a powerful scientific predictor of reading comprehension across the grades. The Educational Testing Service (ETS) (2009) cites a *Child Development* 2006 study of 2,581 low-income mothers which showed that almost half of the welfare families had no alphabet books in their home, while only three percent of professional families lacked such books. PISA (2009) finds students from single-parent families score below student scores from "other" families. Parental talk about politics to children resulted in higher reading skills than where there was no or limited parental talk.

Another factor related to the mother's contribution to reading achievement is her own level of education and literacy. David Berliner (2017, in this volume) argues that the mother's education level is more important than the father's as a determinant of school achievement, a matter which has been given presence in research. He cites a study using Philadelphia schools, where he notes the most important determinant of student and school achievement was the educational level of the mother. This would suggest that continued investment in adult, parental education has the potential of making a significant difference in a child's success in school and reading proficiency (Fantuzzo, LeBoeuf, & Rouse, 2014, Horowitz, 2015c).

In another study, conducted in South Texas, we investigated intervention methods for parents and/or guardians of gang-affiliated adolescents. Our study showed that gang-affiliated teenagers had parents/guardians who did not know how to verbally interact with the school or how to interact with their teenager about the school and the teen's performance, homework, and school requirements. This study provided parents and/or guardians with dialogue patterns and questioning that they needed in order to communicate with the school officials, and were useful for talking with their teenager about school, in order to motivate them to succeed. In middle-class homes, and professional-based families, parents ask questions about their teenager's performance, school-required reading and projects, and expected output, but the parent and/or guardian of gang-affiliated teenagers did not talk about nor seem to know how to communicate about such school-related matters with their teenagers. Our interviews with these mothers revealed that they did not know how to initiate talk about school, or generate, persevere, or resolve queries about school requirements related to their teen's academic performance (Valdez, Cepeda, Parrish, Horowitz, & Kaplan, 2013).

Immigrant and Migrant Populations and Reading: Binationalism and Mobility Factors That May Contribute to Adolescent Reading Practices and Achievement

The reports of international literacy and reading per se cited in this chapter focus on single countries in the world but do not address the current-day adolescent binationalism, bilingualism, and cross-cultural mobility, more prevalent at this time than ever before, that may influence reading habits, practices, and achievement.

There is greater physical movement across borders than in the past and geo-spatial activities that expose students to varied written languages. The research reports referenced do not address this binational activity, which I argue may bear on reading activity, particularly outside of school. On the positive side, the OECD does have a report on migration (see discussion of migrant education in OECD, 2010b; Luke, 2011; Sirens & Van Avermaet, in press).

With e-mail communication, adolescents are linguistically navigating across new kinds of writing while accessing new reading styles. There is psychological mobility across more than one country's sources available for reading with varied text genres and multiple-text processing stratagems. They are also more physically mobile than any previous generation of teenagers, across all economic levels. For example, South Texas adolescents who are financially strapped often travel regularly across border towns to Mexico for extended periods of time to visit family and friends, and to pursue Mexico-based activities, where reading habits may alter and be influential as out-of-school reading that influences in-school reading (Horowitz, 2012a). Students from the United States secondary and post-secondary schools may be gone the entire summer to Mexico and lose some of the reading skills and abilities acquired in English in their United States schools, but advance in Spanish reading that could or may not contribute to their English reading. As Allington and McGill-Franzen (2017, in this volume) convey, summer reading loss is common among poverty populations and has a detrimental effect on school achievement and motivations. Our international data sets typically do not incorporate information about the quantity of reading in a second language and/or nation for physically mobile students or students who have frequent Internet activity with their families in another nation, although this has been reported for some United States Chinese adolescents (Lam & Warriner, 2012).

Shifts in Foci with Attention to Poverty and Low-Income Countries

A new *Executive Summary for PISA 2000-2015* calls for a cooperative rather than a competitive effort when globalizing educational accountabilities (Lingard, Martino, Rezal-Rashti, Goli, & Sellar, 2016). The OECD has apparently paid heed to some of the criticisms of the limitations of PISA. Thus, the goal is now to enhance PISA to make it more relevant to a wider range of countries, including low-income and middle-class ones. Wealthier countries have typically participated in PISA for a variety of reasons. Other economic groups have been found to be more complex to measure—as, for instance, low-income adolescents are unlikely to be in schools where and when assessment takes place. In some cases, there are locations where funds were not available for administering the PISA with some of the populations in a given locale.

The Executive Summary of 2015 report makes recommendations that the OECD should acknowledge differences between countries participating in PISA by "revising cognitive instruments, background questionnaires, and school questionnaires" to incorporate low-income population proficiencies and achievements (Lockheed, Prokic-Brue, Shadrova, 2015, p. 16).

Without doubt, PISA results have influenced educational system changes filtering into classroom instructional designs. Some argue that it has led to "massive and swift educational reforms" in several European countries. The United States, based on PISA data, has been categorized as "a picture of educational stagnation" by United States Secretary of Education Arne Duncan in 2013 (Rutkowski & Rutkowski, 2016, p. 252). But these observations may be questionable and premature.

PISA's Executive Summary (2015) now acknowledges the evolving nature of international comparisons. The goal is now to "better capture the diverse contexts" in which testing is done, to develop new instruments that are more sensitive to performance differences among diverse student contexts. PISA reports that there are over 70 million students without access to lower-secondary schooling so that "out of school" assessment needs to take place. There is a need for greater research ethics internationally, as recently surveyed by the European Conference on Educational Research, stemming from a 2015 meeting with the World Education Research Association (WERA) in Budapest.

Several chapters in the present volume underscore that poverty is a significant factor to be reckoned with in low reading achievement (Berliner, 2017, in this volume; Allington & McGill-Franzen, 2017, in this volume). Brief mention is made of poverty in PISA reports. However, discussion of the role of poverty in school achievement in the United States has resulted in increasing interventions in community and schools. How we might overcome the debilitating effect of poverty on adolescent cognition and reading habits remains one of the most challenging issues we face in overcoming reading achievement gaps worldwide.

Conclusions

A major strength of the PISA reports is that they have stimulated international examination of a select number of reading practices that contribute to academic achievements. They have generated dialogues and publications that may have valuable spin-offs for many countries, including those that require input and assistance. They elevate the goal of adolescents being able to "do" literacy acts in concrete terms. They have the potential to connect countries, in ways that we cannot yet determine or imagine.

In this discussion of countries across of the world, we have paid particular attention to Mexico and the Latin American countries that are gaining visibility after years of low attention to literacy across their various populaces and omission/diminished status in study of the Americas. The PISA reports have added to our understanding of ways these south of the border countries might progress, ultimately contributing to all of the Americas.

But the international community will need to expand and cooperatively define international goals, incorporating theories of reading, empirical studies, and the understanding of proficiency and high literacy—by the best minds. The PISA reports referred to herein have ignited what I am calling "International Brain Wars" concentrated around adolescent reading proficiency, performances, and achievements. This contestation of reading achievement identifies countries as top or low performers. It has provoked a dangerous competitiveness between countries that may be unjust with respect to the countries and the adolescent students tested. Collaborations should focus on the commonalities and differences of the 21st-century adolescent that influence the development of reading. Understanding adolescent uses of the oral and written within cultural groups is a prerequisite to developing their academic literacy (Horowitz, 1994, 2017a). Worldwide, there appear to be some commonalities in motivation and intellectual performance among urban adolescents that contribute to or compete with academic reading. Adolescents in rural communities should not be marginalized or left out of the examination of such reading performance in international large-scale assessments.

The good news is that the American Educational Research Association (AERA) has, at the time of my reviewing this chapter, called for a meeting with

13 countries and the OECD to address ethics and practices in country comparisons. The National Academy of Education (NAEd) has established a steering community to examine the methods and policy uses of international large-scale assessments (ILSA) from a variety of disciplinary perspectives. The goal is to provide suggestions for improving the design and reporting of international large-scale assessments and to give guidance on the appropriate interpretations of its data and policy applications. As emphatically argued by Stromquist & Monkman (2014), contestation across cultures is worthy of our close reconsideration. Rather than bringing countries together in a cooperative spirit where strengths in reading practices can be shared and utilized for specific well-informed purposes, the PISA reports have divided countries. Given the dangers of non-literacy or low literacy, particularly in financially strapped countries pursuing a democracy, a cooperative spirit where countries can learn from one another is most needed at this time, with identification of common goals and productive prospects for the world of the future.

Spotlight Recommendation

1. *Developing longitudinal study*. Research about adolescent reading habits and achievement would benefit from longitudinal studies that trace changes in the *same* learners over time. We have a sizeable body of research on the development of child speech. However, less is known about how adolescents develop over time as they transition to and process the complexities of written language and engage in literate behaviors. Yet, adolescence is a potent period of growth for enhancing intellectual, linguistic, and related psychological-social creativity. Growth in reading enhances these developments.

   Data reported in PISA 2009 and 2012 and the forthcoming 2016 report are not based on the same students. The data provided, thus far, do not represent true longitudinal accounts of the same students—across texts and tasks. Longitudinal data and analyses of that data would be helpful to educators and policy makers in designing reading instruction for academic purposes across the globe.

2. *Promoting positive perspectives*. The literature is replete with negative perspectives, incomplete representations, and counterproductive stereotypes of the present adolescent generation. Instead, what are the cognitive and affective strengths that talented adolescents, such as emerging artists, musicians, and the science-oriented, bring to literacy, through schooling and personally driven learning? How do these strengths help high-performing adolescents achieve reading proficiencies in academic fields?

3. *Advancing the production and use of argumentation in written language*. Knowledge of how rhetorical arguments are produced in a variety of modalities and accessed by teenagers, in spoken, written, or visual language, in various content domains should be assessed. Argumentation in writing, essential

for "getting things done," will most likely vary in communicative style and function in different countries and regions, under different economic, political, and social-cultural contexts and fields. Knowledge of these differences in persuasion can help build understanding among adolescents during international communication.

4. ***Preventing the Adolescent from "Being Took."*** Moreover, student knowledge of argumentation strategies prevent adolescents from "being took"—by social media, not to mention published work. Adolescence has been identified as a stage of development where there is unique vulnerability. With increased marketing of misguided messages, adolescents will require critical reading skills that have not been given sufficient attention in schools. International data can provide information about the nature of this vulnerability as well as the astute processing of information by smart, well-informed teenagers.

5. ***Recognizing different cultural habits in reading***, different ways of knowing, and socially interacting will influence performance and proficiency on assessment measures in reading across countries (Gutiérrez & Rogoff, 2003; Horowitz, 2012a, 2013). We have witnessed and recorded different styles of reading at different periods of time and in different geographic locations. For instance, at the turn of the century in Europe, and still today in many neighborhoods in the United States, reading of texts was/is performed in Jewish immigrant homes—in male groups, at long dining room tables, with the father at the head of the table for initiating and guiding interactive dialogue or commentaries that flow from multiple texts. On the other hand, female-led study groups and book clubs have been formed in many locations, such as parlor meetings, to explore interpretations of books with quite different defined rules of how to talk about books and share perceptions. Teenagers use chats or discussion boards, study groups on and off the computer, and SKYPE exchanges. More needs to be known about these social and culturally based book talks and their contribution to reading achievement for specifically adolescents.

6. ***Considering affective contributions to reading.*** Personal attributes such as adolescent curiosity about text topics and persistence in the pursuit of content, doggedness, related to aspirations or goals when reading, are being discussed in the research literature. These personal attributes and their manifestations within and between social-cultural groups propel students to pursue complex reading in different disciplines (See Duckworth & Yaeger, 2015; Tough, 2013). Ways of validly assessing these affective contributions to academic reading, however, have not been developed. In addition, the beliefs students hold about text topics, and the amount of effort the reader consciously exerts when reading and answering particular test items, warrant assessment (Durik, Vilda, & Eccles, 2006; Horowitz, 1994; Zipf, 1949). Further, shifts in motivation and cognitive engagement during an adolescent's reading of a text do occur. Research often operates as if all of the above considerations are

fixed but they are fluid and subject to shifting attention, interferences, or encouragements under particular social-situational contexts.

7. ***Exercising caution in interpreting PISA results***. Finally, I urge that comparisons across countries be exercised with great caution. Their implications for policy actions warrant careful evaluation. See Gaber et al. (2012) and Thien et al. (2016), who also advocate for a cautious stance, joining many others. While it is valuable to know how a particular country is performing on specific reading measures, the countries that appear to be high or low performers in reading may have preferences for oracy over literacy, a precious concern of mine, and may have very specialized views/functions of the nature of school literacy, its consequences, and benefits for their general populace, or for "advancements" of minority groups. Another concern is that the individual is lost in the nation-by-nation comparisons. Yet, we know from psychological studies that there are individual differences in the uses of acquired knowledge and beliefs about academic reading that are related to reading outcomes. In sum, there may be cultural, social or geopolitical factors that are relevant to measuring and interpreting achievement in reading within and across particular countries. Having said that, the attention to adolescents, and their higher order reading habits and development in reasoning, are worthy of the academy's international comparisons and for collaborative goal setting.

Acknowledgments

This chapter is based on a Keynote Address delivered by Rosalind Horowitz on *The Global State of Literacy*, at the American Educational Research Association Conference on April 19, 2015 in Chicago, Illinois. I thank Wayne H. Slater, The University of Maryland—College Park for his contributions at the Conference. The chapter was prepared with the research assistance of Lisa Griffith, M.A. Policy Studies and Administration, College of Public Policy; Traci Kelley, doctoral student in Interdisciplinary Learning and Teaching; Mingxia Zhi, doctoral student in Culture, Language, and Literacy; and Meliyara Vallej, Melba E. Ochoa, and Loren Torres-Cruz, undergraduate students, College of Education and Human Development at The University of Texas—San Antonio.

References

Alexander, P. A. (2003). The development of expertise: The journey of acclimation to proficiency. *Educational Researcher*. 32(8), 10–14.

Alexander, P. A. & Fox, E. (2011). Adolescents as readers. In M. L. Kamil, P. D. Pearson, E. Birr Moje, & P. P. P (Eds.). *Handbook of reading research*. Volume IV (pp. 157–76). New York & London: Routledge/Taylor & Francis.

Allington, R. L. & McGill-Franzen, A. (2017). Summer reading loss is the basis of almost all the rich/poor reading gap. In R. Horowitz & S. J. Samuels (Eds.). *The achievement gap in reading: Complex causes, persistent issues, possible solutions* (pp. 170–183). New York: Routledge/Taylor & Francis.

Alphonso, C. (2013, December 3). "National emergency" as Canadians fall out of the global top 10 in math. *Globe and Mail*. Available at: www.globeandmail.com/news/national/education/canadas-fall-in-math education-ranking-sets-off-redflags/article15730663/ (accessed November 14, 2014).

Anagnostopoulos, D., Rutledge, S. A., & Jacobsen, R. (Eds.) (2013). *The infrastructure of accountability. Data use and the transformation of American education*. Cambridge, MA: Harvard University Press.

Barton, P. E. & Coley, J. R. (2009, April). *Parsing the achievement gap II*. Policy Information Center. Princeton, NJ: Educational Testing Service.

Bayley, R. J. & Schecter, S. R. (2007). Doing school at home. Mexican American immigrant families interpret texts and instructional agendas. In R. Horowitz (Ed.), *Talking texts: How speech and writing interact in school learning* (pp. 159–183). London and New York: Routledge/Taylor & Francis.

Berliner, D. (2013). Effects of inequality and poverty versus teachers and schooling on America's youth. *Teachers College Record* 115. Available at: www.tcrecord.org.proxy 1.lib .nwo.ca/library.

Berliner, D. (2017). Poverty's powerful effects on reading achievement and the achievement gap. In R. Horowitz & S. J. J (Eds.). *The achievement gap in reading: Complex causes, persistent issues, possible solutions* (pp. 23–37). New York: Routledge/Taylor & Francis.

Botstein, L. (1990, Spring). Damaged literacy: Illiteracies and American democracy. Special issue: Literacy in America. *Daedalus*, 119(2), 55–84.

Brown, B. B., Larson, R. W., & Saraswathi, T. S., (2005). *The world's youth. Adolescence in eight regions of the globe* (pp. 344–372). Cambridge, UK & New York: Cambridge University Press.

Christiansen, M. S. & Farr, M. (2013). Learning English in Mexico: Transnational language ideologes and practices. In J. Kalman & B. Street (Eds.) *Literacy and numeracy in Latin America* (pp. 200–213). New York: Routledge/Taylor & Francis.

Chua, A. (2011a). *Battle hymn of the tiger mother*. New York: Penguin.

Chua, A. (2011b, January 8). Why Chinese mothers are superior. *The Wall Street Journal. The Saturday Essay*. Retrieved from http://online.wsj.com/news/articles/SB10001424052 748704311504576059713528698754.

Csikszentmihalyi, M. (1997). *Finding flow: The psychology of engagement with everyday life*. New New York: Basic Books.

Damon, W. (2008). *The path to purpose: Helping our children find their calling in life*. New York and London: Free Press.

Duckworth, A. L. & Yaeger, D. S. (2015, May). Measurement matters: Assessing personal qualities other than cognitive ability for educational purposes. *Educational Researcher*, 44(4), 237–251.

Durik, A. M., Vilda, M., & Eccles, J. (2006). Task values and ability beliefs as predictors of high school literacy choices: A developmental approach. *Journal of Educational Psychology*, 98(2), 382–393.

Elley, W. B. (1992, July). *How in the world do students read?* IEA Study of Reading Literacy. International Association for the Evaluation of Educational Achievement.

Elley, W. B. (2012, March 2). Education system's weak spot. *The New Zealand Herald*, p. 48.

Fantuzzo, J. W., LeBoeuf, W. A., & Rouse, H. L. (2014). An investigation of the relations between school concentrations of student risk factors and student educational well-being. *Educational Researcher*, 43(1), 25–36.

Frontera, L. & Horowitz, R. (1995, February). Reading and study behaviors of fourth grade Hispanics: Can teachers assess risk? *Hispanic Journal of Behavioral Sciences*, 17(1), 100–120.

Gaber, S., Cankar, G., Marjanovič Umek, L., & Veronika Tašner, V. (2012). The danger of inadequate conceptualization in PISA for education policy. *Compare: A Journal of Comparative and International Education*, 42(4): 647–663.

Gutiérrez, K. D. & Rogofff, B. (2003). Cultural ways of learning: Individual styles or repertoires of practice. *Educational Researcher*, 32(5) 19–25.

Guthrie, J. & McRae, A. (2017). Motivating and instructing African American adolescents through literacy engagement in classrooms. In R. Horowitz & S. J. J (Eds.), *The achievement gap in reading: Complex causes, persistent issues, possible solutions* (pp. 57–81). New York and London: Routledge/Taylor & Francis.

Hart, B. & Risley T. R. (1995). *Meaningful differences in the everyday experience of young American children*. Baltimore: Paul H. Brookes.

Horowitz, R. (1991). A reexamination of oral versus silent reading. *Text*, 11(1), 133–166.

Horowitz, R. (1994). Adolescent beliefs about oral and written language. In R. Garner & P Alexander (Eds.), *Beliefs about text and instruction with text* (pp. 1–24). Hillsdale, NJ: Erlbaum.

Horowitz, R. (2012a). Border crossing: Geographic space and cognitive shifts in adolescent language and literacy practices. In H. Romo & C. Garrido de la Caleja, & O. Lopez (Eds.), *A bilateral perspective on Mexico-United States migration* (pp. 147–164). XaLapa, Veracruz, Mexico. Universidad Veracruzana and The University of Texas at San Antonio, UTSA–Mexico Center.

Horowitz, R., Barea-Rodriguez, E, Le Monds, C., Gilbert, M., Wilson, T., Maurer, T., & Brietry, H. (2012b, February 2). *The teenage brain: Propensities to dangerous risk-taking versus healthy creative expression*. Symposium sponsored by the Secondary Education Committee, Department of Interdisciplinary Learning and Teaching, College of Education and Human Development, The University of Texas at San Antonio. CD.

Horowitz, R. (2013, November). *Crossing the border. How physical space and place contribute to adolescent realignment of language, loyalties, and life aspirations*. Border Language and Culture. Translingual, Transcultural, and Transnational Symposium. World Education Research Association (WERA) Meeting, XII National Congress for Education Research, sponsored by the Consejo Mexicano Investigacion Educativa (COMIE) Mexican Society for Educational Research and Guanajuato University, Guanajuato, Mexico.

Horowitz, R. (2014a, November 4). War and poverty: Building reading achievement in a time of turbulence. *Afikim Newsletter*. The Israeli Family Enrichment Association. Jerusalem, Israel.

Horowitz, R. (2014b, November 20). *Literacy and orality: The reconstitution of writing in technologically and culturally evolving contexts*. The Meadows Lecture of Educational Excellence, The University of North Texas, Denton.

Horowitz, R. (2015a). Oral language: The genesis and development of literacy for schooling and everyday life. In P. D. Pearson & E. Hiebert (Eds.), *Research based practices for teaching common core literacy* (pp. 57–75). New York: Columbia University and Newark, DE: International Literacy Association.

Horowitz, R. (2015b, April 19). *The global state of literacy*. Keynote Address presented at the American Educational Research Association Conference. Chicago, Illinois.

Horowitz, R. (2015c, September 9). *Adolescent achievement in high literacy: Consistent and competitive global perspectives*. Paper presented at the World Educational Research Association (WERA) Focal Meeting. Corvinus University. Budapest, Hungary.

Horowitz, R. (2016, August 23). *Characterizing adolescents, youth oral cultures, and literacies: A global perspective*. Presented at the Symposium on Global Issues of Language and Literacy. XVI World Congress of Comparative Education Societies. World Council of Comparative Education Societies (WCCES). Dialectics of Education: Comparative Perspectives. Beijing Normal University, Beijing, China.

Horowitz, R. & Samuels, S. J. (Eds.) (2017). The achievement gap in reading: Unique historical and future perspectives. In R. Horowitz & S. J. J (Eds.), *The achievement gap in reading: Complex causes, persistent issues, possible solutions* (pp. 1–19). New York and London: Routledge/Taylor & Francis.

Lam, W. S. E. & Warriner, D. S. (2012, April/May/June). Transnationalism and literacy: Investigating the mobility of people, languages, texts, and practices in contexts of migration. *Reading Research Quarterly*, 47(2): 191–215.

Lingard, B., Martino, W., Rezal-Rashti, Goli, & Sellar, S. (2016). *Globalizing educational accountabilities*. New York & London: Routledge/Taylor & Francis.

Lockheed, M., T. Prokic-Bruer, & A. Shadrova (2015), *The experience of middle-income countries participating in PISA* 2000-2015, PISA, World Bank, Washington, DC/OECD Publishing, Paris. http://dx.doi.org/10.1787/9789264246195-en

Luke, A. (2011). Generalizing across borders: Policy and the limits of educational science. *Educational Researcher*, 40(8): 367–377.

Lukes, M. (2015). *Latino immigrant youth and interrupted schooling: Dropouts, dreamers and alternative pathways to college*. Tonawanda, NY & Bristol, UK: Multilingual Matters.

OECD (2002). *PISA 2000 results*. Ministry of Education and Culture. Finland.

OECD (2010a). *PISA 2009 results: What students know and can do – Student performance in reading, mathematics and science* (Volume I). http://dx.doi.org/10.1787/9789264091450-en.

OECD (2010b). *PISA 2009 results. Executive Summary*. Paris.

OECD (2010c). *Closing the gap for immigrant students: Policies, practice and performance. OECD Reviews of Migrant Education*. Paris: OECD Publishing.

OECD (2013a). *PISA 2012 results: What students know and can do. Student performance in mathematics, reading and science* (Volume I), Revised edition, February 2014. *PISA, OECD* Publishing. http://dx.doi.org/10.1787/ 9789264201118-en.

OECD (2013b). *PISA 2012 results in focus: What 15-year-olds know and what they can do with what they know*. Paris. OECD Publishing.

OECD (2014). *PISA 2012 results: What students know and can do – Student performance in mathematics, reading and science* (Volume I, Revised edition, February 2014), PISA, OECD Publishing. http://dx.doi.org/10.1787/9789264201118-en.

Olson, D. R. (2013, December 31). Personal communication. *Ontario is not alone*. Unpublished document.

PIRLS (2016). *Progress in international reading literacy study*. International Association for the Evaluation for Educational Achievement (IEA). Progress in International Reading Literacy Study. Monitoring trends of achievement in five-year intervals across the world since 2011.

Renninger, A. & Hidi, S. (2016). *The power of interest for motivation and engagement*. New York: Routledge/Taylor & Francis.

Rivas, A. (2015). *Latin America after PISA: Lessons learned about education in seven countries. Executive Summary*. Buenos Aires: CIPPEC-Natura-Instituto Natura.

Rutkowski, L. & Rutkowski, D. (2016). A call for a more measured approach to reporting and interpreting PISA results. *Educational Researcher*, 45(4), 252–257.

Sahlberg, P. (2011). *Finish lessons. What can the world learn from educational change in Finland?* New York: Teachers College Press.

Sahlberg, P. (2014a). *Finnish lessons 2.0: What can the world learn from educational change in Finland?* (2nd ed.). New York, NY: Teachers College Press.

Sahlberg, P. (2014b, July 24). Five U.S. innovations that helped Finland's schools improve, but that American reformers now ignore. *Washington Post*.

Sinko, P. (2012, August 14). *Main factors behind the good PISA reading results in Finland*. Power Point Presentation. Finland National Board of Education, IFLA, Helsinki, Finland.

Sirens, S. & Van Avermaet, P. (forthcoming). Bilingual education in migrant languages in Western Europe. In O. Garcia, & A. Lin (Eds.), *Encyclopedia of language and education* (3rd ed., Vol. 5, Bilingual Education). New York: Springer.

Snow, C.E. & Biancarosa, G. (2003). Adolescent literacy and the achievement gap. What do we know and where do we go from here? (Adolescent Literacy Funders Meeting Report). New York: New York: Carnegie Corporation.

Snow, C. E. & Moje, E. (2010, March). Why is everyone talking about adolescent literacy? *Phi Delta Kappan*, 91(6), 66–69.

Stromquist, N. P. & Monkman, K. (Eds.) (2014). *Globalization and education: Integration and contestation across cultures*. Lanham, MD: Roman & Littlefield.

Stevens, M. (2011, July 29). Poverty, reading scores, and resilient schools. *New American Weekly*. New America Foundation.

Stevenson, H. W. & Stigler, J. W. (1992). *Learning gap: Why our schools are failing and what we can learn from Japanese and Chinese education*. New York: Simon and Schuster.

Stevenson, H. W. & Zusho, A. (2002). Adolescence in China and Japan: Adapting to a changing environment. In B. B. Brown,, R. W. Larson, & T. S. S (Eds.) *The world's youth: Adolescence in eight regions of the globe* (pp. 141–170). New York: Cambridge University Press.

Sullivan, A. L. & Simonson, G. R. (2016, June). A systematic review of school-based social-emotional interventions for refugee and war-traumatized youth. *Review of Educational Research*, 86(2), 503–530.

Thien, L., Razak, N. A., Keeves, J., & Darmawan, I. G. N. (Eds.). (2016). *What can PISA 2012 data tell us? Performance and challenges in five participating Southeast Asian countries*. Boston: Sense.

Tough, P. (2013). *How children succeed. Grit, curiosity, and the hidden power of character*. New York: Houghton, Mifflin, Harcourt.

Tristan, A. & Mendoza-Gonzalez L. (2008, September 19). *A contribution to the evidence of the scale validity of the PISA test*. Submitted to the International Meeting of the Evaluation in Higher Education, Veracruz, Mexico. Colegio de Bachilleres de Veracruz, Instituto de Evaluación e Ingenieria Avanzada, S.C. IEIA, Mexico.

Valdez, A., Cepeda, A., Parrish, D., Horowitz, R., & Kaplan, C. (2013, July). An adapted brief strategic family therapy for gang-affiliated Mexican American adolescents. *Research on Social Work Practice*. 23, 383–396.

White, K. R. (1982). The relation between socioeconomic status and academic achievement. *Psychological Bulletin*, 91, 461–481.

Yudkevich, M., Altbach, P. G., & Rumbley, L. E., (2016). *The global academic rankings game: Changing institutional policy, practice, and academic life*. New York & London: Routledge/ Taylor & Francis.

Zipf, G. K. (1949). *Human behavior and the principle of least effort*. Cambridge, MA: Addison-Wesley Press.

PART III

Explaining and Reducing the Achievement Gaps in Reading

9

THE TALK GAP

Terrance D. Paul and Jill Gilkerson

Nearly twenty years ago, two researchers at the University of Kansas—Betty Hart and Todd Risley—published a book, *Meaningful Differences in the Everyday Experience of Young American Children* (1995), in which they described their ground breaking study on parent–child talk. The study, which uncovered an important link between academic success and the volume of talk between parents and young children, captured the attention of the child development community and has since become renowned for its impact in the field. Voluminous research connects oral language and vocabulary to reading comprehension and academic success. Hart and Risley showed that talk is the foundation.

In the Hart and Risley (1995) study, a team of researchers observed 42 families in their homes and recorded all communication that took place between parents and children (aged 7 months to 3 years) for 1 hour each month for 30 months. At the end of the study, they transcribed more than 1,300 hours of recordings by hand and analyzed the data. What surfaced was a startling finding: from birth to 48 months, parents in professional families spoke 32 million more words to their children than did parents in welfare families, and this talk gap between the ages of 0 and 3 years—not parent education, socioeconomic status, or race—explains the vocabulary and language gap at age 3 and the reading and math achievement gap at age 10.

Although the Hart and Risley study has been heralded by educators, speech professionals, and others interested in child development, their contribution has had little effect on national or state policy or funding to close the achievement gap. Given the potentially far-reaching implications of the study, one might reasonably ask: Why have the findings of Hart and Risley not led to changes in early childhood development programs or the allocation of funding between schools and parent training programs? Why do we rely so heavily on preschools or schools to close the achievement gap when we know the value of parental talk in the first 3 years of a child's life?

Over the years, some have criticized the correlational nature of the Hart and Risley study and suggested that it was too small to warrant sweeping policy changes; however, these arguments are not valid. Indeed, their study is only small in terms of number of participants (42 families). It is a large study in terms of the richness of data collected and the years it covered (i.e., from 7 months of age to 10 years of age). Also, investigations prior and subsequent to Hart and Risley of smaller size and cross-sectional studies consistently confirm the connection between the early language experience and later vocabulary development, which seemingly negates the importance of sample size in the original work. And, in our opinion, the causation argument—essentially that nature, not nurture, could explain the talk gap—has always been a moot point. Nature provides a massive longitudinal experiment by randomly making some children born deaf and others born with classic autism. Children who are deaf are denied access to language because they can't hear, and children with autism are denied access to language because social impairment severely limits communicative interactions. Without early intervention, children who are deaf and children with classic autism have severe language and vocabulary limitations and may not learn to read, let alone achieve success in school. It's not nature or nurture. It's both, and we can do something about nurture.

We believe that it is neither study size nor type that explains the lack of impact of the Hart and Risley study. Rather, it has been difficult to test or implement their recommendations because measuring talk in the natural environment of children is time consuming and expensive. This last bottleneck to implementing effective and scalable intervention programs in children aged 0 to 3 years has been removed. There is now a practical and reliable replacement to the painstaking, lengthy, and costly method of hand transcription used by Hart and Risley. A newly developed technology—the language environment analysis (LENA) system—automatically counts the number of words that a parent (or other caregiver) speaks to their child and the number of conversations they have with them and generates instantaneous feedback reports.

Scientific advancement is the result of improvement in measurement technology. Without instruments to measure vocabulary and reading comprehension there would be no science of reading. Similarly there would be little known about astronomy without telescopes, biology without microscopes, or neuroscience without fMRI. Hart and Risley could not have done their study without the development of the handheld cassette recorder in the mid-70s. LENA is a breakthrough in the ability to automatically measure talk in the natural language environment of the child.

The LENA system was inspired by the work of Hart and Risley and developed by the LENA Research Foundation (LRF), a 501c3 public charity cofounded in 2009 by one of the authors of this chapter (Terrance Paul) and his wife Judith Paul.

The LRF mission is to accelerate language development to improve the cognitive, social, and emotional health of children from birth to the age of 5 years and to close achievement gaps.

The purpose of our chapter is to discuss research pertaining to the talk gap in a historical and contemporary context. In the following pages, we focus on these topics: (a) the natural language environment of young children; (b) the development of LENA; (c) LRF findings that confirm the Hart and Risley study; (d) new LFR findings; and (e) recommendations aimed at helping to close the talk and achievement gap.

Deciphering the Noisy Environment of Infants and Toddlers

The natural language environment of infants and toddlers is a messy place— extremely noisy and complex, often consisting of competing sounds. Indeed, in a given day, a young child is exposed to the speech of many people, including that of adults and other children, as well as a variety of non-speech sounds. Some of the speech may be directed at the young child (near speech), some of it may be intended for another person (far speech), and some of it may overlap with other speech or random environmental sounds (e.g., doorbell, air conditioner, wind, or truck). The vocalizations of the young child may also contribute to the complexity of the environment as he or she reacts to the speech of others or initiates communication. Such vocalizations, which often obscure the speech of others, can take the form of meaningful communicative sounds or vegetative sounds, such as coughing or gurgling.

The most obvious technology that one might think of to measure talk is automatic speech and speaker recognition technology; however, such technology is designed to measure only adult speech and is useless to measure infant vocalizations or adult speech in the uncontrolled noisy natural language environment of the child. To measure the talk that matters, we had to start from scratch. We knew that it was not technologically possible to measure all of the communication domains that Hart and Risley measured, so the first step was to define the most important variables that could possibly be automatically measured. We were fortunate in this regard because Todd Risley was an enthusiastic unpaid consultant for LENA development, which he called the "missing piece." With Todd's help, we narrowed the must-have variables to three: (a) adult words spoken to the key child; (b) conversational turns (the natural back and forth communicative exchanges between adults and children); and (c) child vocalizations. We later added a fourth variable: television and electronic sound.

One of the more difficult puzzles to solve was how to count words reliably in the natural language environment without the ability to decipher word boundaries (i.e., when a word starts and stops). The path to a solution started by realizing that we did not need a "dictionary." That is, the counts of words spoken to and near the child were more important than knowing actual words and word meanings. Readability formulas used in word processing programs to measure semantic difficulty provided an additional clue to the solution. Many of these formulas estimate semantic difficulty based on the number of syllables per word; the higher the number of syllables, the higher the semantic difficulty. Readability formulas use components of words. The components of adult words we believed we could count were phones, the audio equivalent of phonemes (the smallest unit of sound in a word). It was this insight that led to how we estimate word counts. Phone frequencies are converted to word count estimates by a relatively simple mathematical formula.

Yet, the challenges were enormous. With no roadmap to follow, we did not know how we would separate near from far speech, measure turns, identify the key child from other children and children from adults, distinguish vegetative gurgles from communicative babbles, or separate television speech from live human speech. We began by collecting and transcribing day-long recordings of children in the natural home environment. Along the way, we built a supercomputer to facilitate our experiments to develop the necessary algorithms and mathematical models. The end result was a product that has gained the respect of the child language research community.

What Is LENA and How Does It Work?

LENA is an easy-to-use system to measure talk in the natural language environment of the child composed of three parts: (a) a digital language processor (DLP); (b) specially designed children's clothing with a front pocket to hold the DLP; and (c) language environment analysis software. The DLP is a small device that records all of the sounds in a child's natural environment over the entire day. After recording, the data obtained on the DLP are downloaded to a computer for processing. LENA software segments audio into eight categories (adult male, adult female, key child, other child, overlapping speech, television and electronic sound, noise and silence) and provides reports estimating the number of adult words spoken to the child, conversational turns, child vocalizations, and television and electronic sounds.

The Development of LENA Algorithms

The magic of LENA lies in the algorithmic models that are embedded in the software. Algorithm development was a demanding endeavor that required the input and expertise of numerous professionals. To develop the algorithms, we first had to collect a large number of full-day recordings of children in their natural home environment, as well as measure the language development level of each child (Gilkerson & Richards, 2008a). The study sample was recruited from the Denver, Colorado, metropolitan area through newspaper ads and direct mail solicitations; more than 2,000 people expressed interest in participating. LRF eventually narrowed the group to match 2004 United States Census figures with respect to the attained education level of the participants' mothers.

Study participants were recorded in their natural home environment for at least 12 consecutive hours 1 day each month between January and June 2006. In Phase 1 of the study, we collected 18,000 hours of day-long recordings from 329 children who were equally distributed between the ages of 2 and 48 months. There were approximately eight children in each age-month interval through the age of 36 months. All of the children were evaluated by speech and language pathologists using standard language assessment tests, such as the Preschool Language Scale-4 (PLS-4), Receptive-Expressive Emergent Language-3 (REEL-3), Child Development Inventory (CDI), and Clinical Adaptive Test/Clinical Linguistic and Auditory Milestone Scale (CAT/CLAMS).

As the next step in algorithm development, a team of professionally trained transcribers listened to and transcribed a sample from the original 18,000 hours of recordings to identify speakers (i.e., adult male, adult female, child wearing the DLP), near and far sounds, speech, infant communicative sounds, infant cries and vegetative sounds, television and electronic sounds, and many other variables. Experts in signal processing, statistics, and speech and speaker recognition techniques then built mathematical models to segment sound automatically into the transcribed categories and identify other variables. These models were then optimized through repeated experimentation using a supercomputer and software and hardware designed by our engineers and scientists.

LENA has demonstrated a high degree of reliability and accuracy. Segmentation agreement between human transcribers and LENA software for four segmentation categories of adult, key child, television, and all other segments combined is about 80 percent, and adult word count correlation for 70 hours of transcribed recordings vs. LENA counts is $r = 0.92$ ($p < 0.01$), with a cumulative error of 2 percent.

The Growth and Success of LENA

The initial 18,000 hours of day-long recordings coupled with demographic information, language assessments, and the results of LENA processing constitute a large body of data on child and adult speech, which to our knowledge is the largest of its kind in the world. The LENA database—or natural language corpus (NLC), as we call it—has grown to more than 112,000 hours of recordings from more than 750 children.

Since its inception in 2007, LENA has become a staple in the child language research community. More than 300 university and clinical researchers have purchased the professional version of the LENA software, and over 300 journal articles, conference papers, and posters have been published either about or incorporating LENA. Notably, LENA has become an accepted tool worldwide for use in intervention programs for children who are deaf or hard of hearing to measure how much parents talk to their child and to provide feedback that will help boost talk (Wiggin et al., 2012; Yoshinaga-Itano et al., 2011). LENA is also increasingly being used in parent centers, home visitation programs, day care centers, and preschools to accelerate the language development of disadvantaged children.

Confirming Discoveries

Numerous non-LRF studies (Wells, 1985; Wagner, 1985; Hoff, 2003; Rowe, Pan, & Ayoub, 2005; Walker et al., 1994) have confirmed key findings of Hart and Risley, but it is not within the scope of this chapter to summarize the professional literature. In this section, we discuss several LRF studies that corroborate four important conclusions reached by Hart and Risley: (a) college-educated parents talk more to their children than do less educated parents; (b) talk correlates with language ability; (c) talkative parents have talkative children; and (d) early parent talk predicts later language ability (Gilkerson & Richards, 2008b).

College-Educated Parents Talk More to Their Children Than Do Less Educated Parents

Hart and Risley compared talk in welfare, working class, and professional or college-educated families and concluded that parents in college-educated families talk far more than do parents in welfare and working class families. They calculated that during the first 48 months, children in professional, working class, and welfare families hear 45, 26, and 13 million words, respectively. In addition, Hart and Risley found that although college-educated parents talked a lot more than less educated parents, there was extreme variation in the amount of talk within all three of the groups. Some parents in welfare and working class families talked a lot to their children, and their children had high vocabulary scores, whereas some parents in professional families did not talk very much to their children, and their children tended to have low vocabulary scores.

In LRF studies, we stratified families into four groups based on maternal education level (some high school, high school graduate, some college, and college degree or higher). In the initial 329 families in the NLC database, the mean daily adult word count in those with college-educated mothers was significantly higher than that in the three other groups. Substantial variation in adult word count was also observed within the four groups. In fact, as shown in Figure 9.1, the upper 50 percent of parents who did not complete high school had a significantly higher mean daily word count than did the lower 50 percent of parents who graduated from college. The talk gap is not just a low SES problem. The talk gap affects all SES groups.

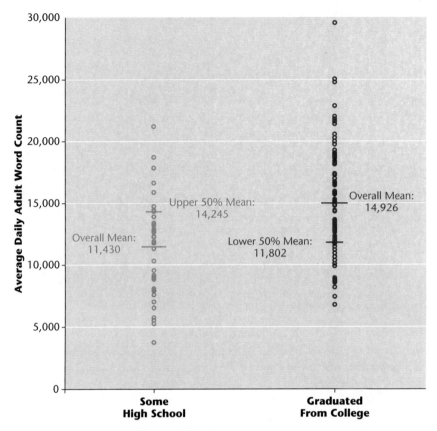

FIGURE 9.1 The variation in talk between families is substantial across maternal education strata. Although parents that include mothers who did not complete high school on average talk significantly less than parents that include mothers with college degrees, considerable variation exists within education levels, resulting in overlap between families at different levels. In fact, the average parents in the upper half of the less educated families talk significantly more than the average parents in the lower half of the more educated familes.

Talk Is Correlated with Language Ability

Hart and Risley found that the number of adult words spoken to a child between the ages of 0 and 3 years and the frequency of adult responses to child initiation of a conversational turn are significantly correlated with vocabulary use at 34 to 36 months of age ($r = 0.62$ and 0.63, respectively; both $p < 0.01$).

Similarly, our analysis of the initial 329 children in the NLC database showed that all measures of language development (based on CAT/CLAMS, PLS-4, REEL-3 assessment) correlated significantly with adult words and conversational turns ($p < 0.01$; Gilkerson & Richards, 2008b). In 87 children to whom both PLS-4 and

REEL-3 were administered, the correlation with adult words and conversational turns was $r = 0.42$ and 0.43, respectively ($p < 0.01$).

Talkative Parents Have Talkative Children

Hart and Risley showed that talkative parents have talkative children, a finding that we confirmed using data from NLC to compare average daily child vocalizations in children of parents in the highest and lowest 20th percentiles with regard to adult word count.

Our research showed that children with talkative and taciturn parents had similar child vocalization levels during the first 2 to 6 months of age; however, with time and cumulative experience with talk, child vocalization rates grew farther apart (Gilkerson & Richards, 2008b). Overall, from 2 to 48 months of age, children of talkative parents (top 20 percent) had average vocalization levels near the 67th percentile, whereas children of taciturn parents (bottom 20 percent) averaged below the 36th percentile ($t(326) = 5.33; p < 0.01$).

Early Parent Talk Predicts Later Language Ability

We examined the power of adult talk during the early months to predict later language ability in a longitudinal sample of 27 children (Gilkerson & Richards, 2008b). Average adult word counts and conversational turns from recordings of children between 2 and 6 months of age were compared with average PLS-4 language scores between 18 and 36 months. Our analysis showed that high language scores were correlated with high talk levels in the first 6 months; the correlations for words and turns were $r = 0.59$ and 0.51, respectively ($p < 0.01$ for both).

New Discoveries

As exciting as it has been to confirm the major findings of Hart and Risley, we have been equally excited to provide new insights about the talk gap and how to close it. Here we summarize some of our new discoveries.

Pattern of Talk during the Day

Unlike the recordings of Hart and Risley, which represent the level of talk in a single hour only (most often in the late afternoon), our recordings with the initial 329 families span the length of an entire day. The longer recording time has enabled us to compare changes in the pattern of talk over time, and importantly, has brought new findings to light (see Figure 9.2).

Our initial hypothesis—that the lunch hour would be a time of high talk—turned out to be incorrect. Indeed, we found that noon was one of the lowest talk times of the day. In listening to some of the recordings, we learned that most of

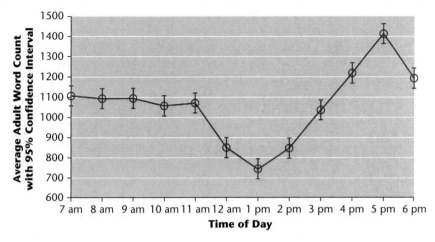

FIGURE 9.2 The rate of parent talk varies throughout a typical day. The cumulative sum of parent talk for a given day actually reflects a considerable degree of variation in the rate of talk over the course of that day. In our sample, parent talk was commonly stable in the hours after waking until nap time when it decreased before increasing again to peak around dinner time. Such patterns provide a potentially unexpected and deeper level perspective on family behavior and routines.

the talk during lunch time is "business talk" and that adults are busy controlling the child (or children), putting the food out, and cleaning up. An example of typical phrases used during this time included directives like "eat this," or "don't make a mess."

The time of highest talk in our study turned out to be in the late afternoon, findings that were subsequently confirmed in an independent study using LENA in 30 typically developing infants and toddlers from families of middle to high socio-economic status (Greenwood et al., 2011). Of particular interest is the fact that Hart and Risley typically recorded their participants in the late afternoon, suggesting that they may have overestimated the total amount of talk by as much as 20 percent.

Words, Turns, and Television

We knew from the Hart and Risley study that both words and the frequency that parents responded to child vocalizations were highly predictive of language scores. In LENA, the comparable variable to frequency of response is conversational turns. It was therefore natural to want to determine which of the variables— words or turns—is more relevant. The answer likely could be found in the NLC, so we enlisted economist Fred Zimmerman, Chair of the Department of Health Policy and Management at UCLA, to work with our scientists to analyze relevant NLC data.

Zimmerman cross-regressed words, turns, and television exposure and found that turns and words have a significant positive association with language development scores, whereas television exposure has a significant negative association. Each hour of television exposure was associated with a decline of 2.68 points in language standard score on the PLS-4 test (Zimmerman et al., 2009).When Zimmerman regressed all three factors together, words and television exposure were no longer significant, suggesting complete mediation by turns. Turns are more important than words.

Turn count is a powerful metric because it measures both communicative exchange and social engagement. High daily turn count is a marker for a positive social and emotional environment. Maternal responsiveness (Kaiser et al., 1996; Landry, Smith, & Swank, 2006; Landry et al., 2008; Tamis-LeMonda, Bornstein, & Baumwell, 2001;Warren & Brady, 2007) and brain research studies (Fox, Levitt, & Nelson III, 2010; Knudsen et al., 2006; Kuhl, 2004) confirm that social engagement is important for building language ability and for social and emotional health.

Book Reading Increases Talk and More

Numerous studies have documented the positive effect of reading books aloud with children for improved language, vocabulary, and reading achievement (Boschee & Knudson, 1997; Justice, Mashburn, & Petscher, 2013; Lee, 2011; LeVasseur, Macaruso, & Shankweiler, 2008; Ouellette, Dagostino, & Carifio, 1999; Saracho & Spodek, 2010). In addition to increasing talk, book reading facilitates close physical contact and increased social engagement. Furthermore, during book reading, word variety and sentence complexity increase which further improves vocabulary and language skills.

NLC includes information from hourly logs filled out by parents during recording days; book reading is one of the tracked categories. In a sample of 36 families with typically developing children, the rate of adult talk and turn-taking engagement increased on average by 148 percent and 64 percent, respectively, during book reading compared with the daily average, excluding reading time. We suspect that this finding may significantly understate the increase in talk as a result of book reading, given the potential for errors and/or lapses in parental reporting of activities.

Autism Research

Autism spectrum disorder (ASD) is characterized by impaired social interaction, which in turn, can lead to impaired language and reading development. In some cases, children with ASD never acquire language, and most children with classic autism have some language impairment even with intensive intervention. The issue of whether words are more important than turns or vice versa is particularly relevant in ASD research. ASD causes a *talk gap* because the child is unable to engage in typical levels of turn taking. Research based on the NLC shows that children with ASD engage in 1,000 fewer turns per week than do typically developing children and that turn counts are more predictive of language development than are word counts (Warren et al., 2010).

Preterm Infant Studies

Betty Vohr and neonatologists at the Brown University School of Medicine, use LENA to study the language environment of preterm infants in neonatal intensive care units. In one study, they showed that 8-week-old preterm infants participated in early conversational turns more frequently with their mothers than with nurses and that infant vocalizations and turns increased in response to increased talk by the mother. These infants were then followed longitudinally to investigate the relationship between very early language exposure and language development. Results from the Bayley Scales of Infant and Toddler Development (Bayley-III Screening Test), which was administered at 7 and 18 months, showed that increased parent talk was significantly correlated with language and cognitive development longitudinally (Caskey et al., 2014).

Seasonal Variation in the Talk Gap

We conducted a study with the Shanghai Children's Medical Center to measure the natural language environment in 22 Chinese families and to demonstrate that LENA feedback would help parents increase words and turns counts. Although words and turns increased initially, there was a decline during the summer months. We asked study participants to hypothesize as to the cause of the decline, and the response we received was that children played outside more in the summer than at other times of the year. We surmised therefore that children have more close contact with adults in winter than they do in summer, which led us to investigate whether the same seasonal variation existed in our initial NLC database. Indeed, we found a similar pattern. In a sample of 210 families with recordings that were made both in the summer and at other times of the year, there was a significant seasonal variation in talk, with peaks in the winter months and a drop in the summer months. During the summer months, adult words decreased 5.3 percent, and turns decreased 4.5 percent, compared with non-summer months (both $p < 0.001$).

Mothers Talk More Than Fathers, and They Talk More to Their Daughters Than to Their Sons

An important feature of LENA is its ability to distinguish between adult female and male words spoken to or near the key child. Although various adults may play a role in the life of the key child, most of the female talk is by the mother, and most of the male talk is by the father. We were not surprised that in our sample, mothers and fathers contributed 75 percent and 25 percent, respectively; however, we were surprised to learn that mothers talked 9 percent more to their daughters than to their sons, and that overall (from both adult male and female speakers), girls aged 0 to 3 years heard 5.8 percent more words than did their male counterparts (Gilkerson & Richards, 2008b).

Most Parents Think They Talk to Their Child More Than They Do

We asked parents from the initial 329 families in the NLC database to rate how much they talked to their child; of these, 239 parents responded. Parents were given five options to indicate how they believed the quantity of their talk compared with that of other parents: (1) much less than average; (2) less than average; (3) average; (4) more than average; or (5) much more than average. Virtually all of them—99 percent—thought that they talked to their child an average amount or an above average amount. Of the parents who thought that they talked more than average or much more than average, 40 percent of them were actually below the 50th percentile compared with our normative database in the number of words spoken.

LENA Feedback Narrows the Talk Gap

There have been many studies, including several experimental studies (Gilkerson, Richards, & Xu, 2013; Suskind et al., 2013; Pae, 2013; Xu, 2012; Zhang et al., 2015), showing that LENA feedback coupled with an instructional component helps parents increase the number of both words and turns.

To test the impact of feedback alone without instruction, we provided LENA home systems to 102 families in the US and United Kingdom and asked parents to record on a weekly basis and to try to improve the amount they talked to their children. No other instructions or coaching were provided. At week 13, the close of the study, parents in the lowest quintile at their first recording had increased their talk by 33 percent, whereas parents in the four other quintiles averaged a 17 percent increase. This is consistent with our other studies that generally show that the group performing the lowest initially improves the most and thus narrows the talk gap (Gilkerson & Richards, 2008b).

Discussion and Recommendations

One of the main goals of studying child development, talk, or reading achievement is to put relevant research findings into practice through informing the design of effective, replicable, and scalable intervention programs to do good—specifically, to improve reading and academic achievement. Though the talk gap impacts all economic and educational strata our primary concern is with regard to disadvantaged groups with the ultimate objective to close the poverty gap. Our discussion and recommendations are therefore focused on what can be done to reduce the talk gap in disadvantaged populations to in the long run improve reading comprehension and academic achievement.

There are many small-scale programs to improve language development, and a few of these have been shown to be effective by randomized controlled trials; however, we are aware of only one large-scale intervention program in the US—the Nurse-Family Partnership (NFP)—that has been proven to be effective by a randomized controlled trial and it does so only modestly in the realm of language. NFP, which was created to "empower first-time mothers living in poverty to successfully change their lives and the lives of their children through evidence-based nurse home visiting," currently serves about 32,000 first-time mothers (http://www .nursefamilypartnership.org/fact-sheets) nationwide. NFP nurses and paraprofessionals visit first-time pregnant mothers with continuing monthly visits until the child reaches 2 years of age. Even though improving vocabulary is not a focus of NFP, a large randomized experiment of 743 women and children in Memphis, Tennessee showed a significant though modest effect on receptive vocabulary measured at the age of 6 years, two years after the initial treatment (standard score of 84.32 for treatment vs. 82.13 for control; $p < 0.01$) (Olds et al., 2004).

Finding only one modest success story after spending many billions of dollars over the last 50 years to fight the War on Poverty ($200 billion on Head Start alone), we naturally approach our goals with trepidation. Nonetheless, we offer the following design recommendations to develop an effective, replicable, and scalable intervention program: (a) start early—birth is not too soon; (b) focus on talk, books, and television; (c) measure and provide feedback with LENA; and (d) reduce costs compared with existing intervention programs.

Start Early—Birth Is Not Too Soon

There are several reasons that an intervention should start early—preferably between the ages of 0 and 3 years. First, parents of young children are easier to motivate than those of older children. Second, the period between 0 and 3 years of age is the time of fastest brain development and one that creates the foundation on which all future development takes place. Notably, one study in children who were deaf or hard of hearing showed that the earlier an intervention was initiated, the greater the language development and vocabulary was later in life (Yoshinaga-Itano, 2003).

It is parental behavior toward the baby that we are most trying to change or improve. Hart and Risley showed that young children initiate turns five times more than adults, so encouraging adults to respond to a baby's communicative cues is even more important than getting a baby to respond to adult cues. Furthermore, studies show that preterm babies are born ready to learn to talk, and when mothers talk to them, they develop more quickly (Caskey et al., 2014). In addition, parents have more control over younger children and are also likely to have more face-to-face time to talk with them.

Focus on Talk, Books, and Television

Hart and Risley proposed closing the talk gap through large-scale government intervention programs aimed at children aged 0 to 3 years. They envisioned home visitation and quality child care centers, which on the surface are very similar to Early Head Start (EHS), a program that actually began the same year that the Hart and Risley findings were published. EHS, a program under the Head Start umbrella, currently serves about 100,000 children under 3 years of age at an estimated annual cost of about $9,000 to $12,000 per family. In total, Head Start (including EHS) reaches approximately 1.1 million children aged 0 to 5 years at an annual cost of $8 billion, or $7,500 per child per year (Early Childhood Learning & Knowledge Center 2012).

Despite the magnitude of resources being spent to support EHS, the findings from a large-scale experimental evaluation (n = 3,001) of the program are disappointing (Love, 2010). Although one of the stated goals of EHS is language development, there were only modest gains in vocabulary at age 3 years, and these gains were no longer evident at age 5 years. These findings are in contrast to those of the NFP program, which reported gains in vocabulary at age 6, four years after the program ended.

Large early childhood intervention programs that focus exclusively on increasing talk, shared book reading, and reducing screen time (i.e., time spent in front of a television, tablet, computer, or other electronic screen) have only recently emerged. The lack of attention to reducing screen time is particularly troubling, given our research showing the negative impact of television on language development and policy statements of the American Academy of Pediatrics, which recommends zero screen time for children under 18 months, except for live video chat (Reid Chassiakos et al., 2016).

A focus on closing the talk gap does not mean that the physical, social, and emotional environment of the child will be neglected. Indeed, counting conversational turns is a powerful proxy measure of the quality of the social and emotional environment. If turns are low, it means that the parent or caregiver is not responding to the child's effort to communicate; the lack of response could be explained by any number of reasons (e.g., the television is on, the mother is on her cell phone, depression, the caregiver does not know how important talk is for development, and so on). In most cases, however, our work with parents shows that they know why communication is lacking: all you need to do is ask the question. A focus on improving words and turns, shared book reading, and turning off electronic media is the best way to close the talk gap and may also be an efficient way to improve the social and emotional environment.

Measure Words and Turns and Obtain Feedback with LENA

We believe the inability to objectively measure words and turns has been the primary bottleneck to the development of effective programs to close the talk gap. Indeed, parents overestimate how much they talk to their children for the simple reason that in the past, they have had no way to measure the number of words spoken. Improving the talk gap is a critical challenge if the scope of the deficiency remains undefined.

Our work shows that when LENA is used and feedback is provided to those who can make a difference, improvement follows. The greatest endorsement of LENA's ability to automatically measure talk, however, came from Todd Risley himself, who wrote in the foreword to the first edition of LRF's Power of Talk, "Of course, it is critical that parents know they are talking enough with their children. And that's where LENA comes in. LENA makes it possible for parents to know exactly how much they talk with their child" (p. 2).

Reduce Costs

There are three primary intervention models (home visitation, child center, and parent center) that could serve as the structural basis for a program to increase talk. The models are associated with different cost profiles that must be taken into consideration. Cost, after all, is the primary impediment to scalability after effectiveness.

The cost of home visitation is directly proportional to the caseload. For NFP, the typical caseload is 20 to 24 families, with an average annual cost per family of $4,500. By regulation, the EHS–Home Visiting caseload is between 10 and 12 families; the average annual cost per family is between $9,000 and $12,000 (US Department of Health & Human Services, 2013). Developing and implementing a home visitation program to increase talk would likely be an effective—but expensive—endeavor.

The annual cost of full-time care at child care centers averages about $9,500 for infants and about $7,500 for 4-year-olds (Child Care Aware® of America, 2012). A program to increase talk in a child care center would focus on increasing the talk of the caregivers with respect to the children (i.e., children or their caregivers would wear the LENA DLP). Such an approach may be less effective than a home visitation program or parent center approach, however, as the child center caregiver attends to several children at any given time and therefore spends fewer hours with each individual child.

The parent center approach—one in which parents gather as a group (e.g. churches, libraries, etc.)—is potentially the least expensive of the three intervention models. One instructor could likely handle 10 to 20 parents, and the instructor could be contracted on a per meeting basis. Recruitment and time commitment would be the same as that for home-based programs. The main problem with a parent center approach is the likelihood of low attendance caused by issues like lack of transportation, low motivation, work schedule, disinterested spouse, and the need to care for other children. Conversely, the parent center approach could potentially be more effective for those who do attend because parents in a group can motivate and teach each other, building social capital.

If we want to improve the talk gap, all three primary intervention models need to be implemented. In the near term, the parent center approach seems to be the most attractive, but home visitation and child center approaches could be cost effective by adding the talk gap intervention on top of what is already in place. The issue, of course, is whether talk would get the attention it needs. LENA can help in this regard because, as the saying goes, "what gets measured gets done."

Setting performance standards for participation is another way to reduce costs while improving effectiveness and thus making programs more scalable. Unfortunately, current intervention programs rely on performance measures that are in many cases subjective, sometimes expensive and infrequent, and generally determined by the person delivering the service. In contrast, LENA provides an objective and unbiased measure of performance. We have already set performance standards in our parent center program (e.g., a parent must attend 75 percent of the sessions and complete 75 percent of the recordings in order to graduate) and strongly recommend that a progress requirement be implemented, especially for home visitation programs (if a parent does not show improvement in talk after a certain number of recordings, he or she will be dropped and referred to other programs). Finally, if a child comes from a home with high words and turns and has achieved high language ability, it only makes sense to graduate this child early from the program to make room for another child who is less fortunate. By having reasonable expectations, setting performance standards, and dropping non-performers from the program, the result will be lower costs and more effective and scalable programs that are able to serve a greater number of children and families.

Conclusion

Scientific advancement, indeed human progress, is driven by advancements in measurement. Hart and Risley uncovered an important link between reading achievement and academic success and the volume of talk between parents and young children. Their study was made possible by an advance in measurement technology, the handheld cassette recorder. LENA's ability to automatically measure talk in the natural language environment of the child advances the science of talk and potentially provides a means to help close the talk gap and improve reading comprehension and school achievement for all.

Spotlight Recommendation

Closing the talk gap is essential if we are to eliminate the achievement gap in reading. Children who enter kindergarten with a limited vocabulary face an uphill battle that they are unlikely to win. Early intervention is needed to circumvent the challenge, but it must embody four elements. First, the emphasis must be on infants and toddlers. The majority of brain development occurs in the first three years of life, and the environment created by the parent during these crucial first years cannot be underestimated. Second, caregiver coaching should focus on a small set of key behaviors that can maximally impact early development: improving words and especially turns, increasing shared book reading, and minimizing the distraction of electronic media. Providing caregivers with tangible goals for enhancing the early language environment will lead to more confident parenting and a closer family dynamic, as well as improved social and emotional development for the child. Third, give parents objective feedback on how much they are talking with their child so they can improve. The LENA system technology does just this and has been shown to influence parent behavior, resulting in positive changes in early language exposure and increases in child language ability. Finally, these components must be applied cost effectively through programs that integrate objective and unbiased performance measures. Such measures will drive resource deployment and allow intervention programs, whether they are parent center, home visitor, or child care models, to reach the greatest number of children and families.

References

Boschee, M.A. & Knudson, B.W. (1997). Preschool learning environments that promote or inhibit reading achievement. *Community Education Journal*, 25(3), 21–26.

Caskey, M., Stephens, B., Tucker, R., & Vohr, B. (2014). Adult talk in the NICU with preterm infants and developmental outcomes. *Pediatrics*, *133*(3), e578–e584. doi: 10.1542/ped.2013-0104

Child Care Aware® of America. (2012). *Parents and the high cost of child care: 2012 report.* Arlington, VA.

Early Childhood Learning & Knowledge Center. (2012). *Head Start program facts fiscal year 2012* [Fact sheet].

Fox, S. E., Levitt, P., & Nelson III, C.A. (2010). How the timing and quality of early experiences influence the development of brain architecture. *Child Development*, 81(1), 28–40. doi: 10.1111/j.1467-8624.2009.01380.x

Gilkerson, J., & Richards, J.A. (2008a). *The LENA natural language study* (Technical Report No. LTR-02-2). Boulder, CO: LENA Research Foundation.

Gilkerson, J., & Richards, J.A. (2008b). *The power of talk* (Technical Report No. LTR-01-2). Boulder, CO: LENA Research Foundation.

Gilkerson, J., Richards, J.A., & Xu, D. (2013, November). *The effectiveness of LENA technology for changing parent behavior and accelerating child language development.* Paper presented at the 2013 ASHA Convention, Chicago, IL.

Greenwood, C. R., Thiemann-Bourque, K., Walker, D., Buzhardt, J., & Gilkerson, J. (2011). Assessing children's home language environments using automatic speech recognition technology. *Communication Disorders Quarterly*, 32(2), 83–92. doi: 10.1177/1525740110367826

Hart, B., & Risley, T. R. (1995). *Meaningful differences in the everyday experience of young American children*. Baltimore, MD: Paul H. Brookes Publishing Co.

Hoff, E. (2003). The specificity of environmental influence: Socioeconomic status affects early vocabulary development via maternal speech. *Child Development*, 74(5), 1368–1378. doi: 10.1111/1467-8624.00612

Justice, L., Mashburn, A., & Petscher, Y. (2013). Very early language skills of fifth-grade poor comprehenders. *Journal of Research in Reading*, 36(2), 172–185. doi: 10.1111/j.1467-9817.2011.01498.x

Kaiser, A. P., Hemmeter, M. L., Ostrosky, M. M., Fischer, R., Yoder, P., & Keefer, M. (1996). The effects of teaching parents to use responsive interaction strategies. *Topics in Early Childhood Special Education*, 16(3), 375. doi: 10.1177/027112149601600307

Knudsen, E. I., Heckman, J. J., Cameron, J. L., & Shonkoff, J. P. (2006). Economic, neurobiological, and behavioral perspectives on building America's future workforce. *Proceedings of the National Academy of Sciences*, 103(27), 10155–10162. doi: 10.1073/pnas.0600888103

Kuhl, P. K. (2004). Early language acquisition: Cracking the speech code. *Nature Reviews Neuroscience*, 5(11), 831–843. doi: 10.1038/nrn1533

Landry, S. H., Smith, K. E., & Swank, P. R. (2006). Responsive parenting: Establishing early foundations for social, communication, and independent problem-solving skills. *Developmental Psychology*, 42(4), 627–642. doi: 10.1037/0012-1649.42.4.627

Landry, S. H., Smith, K. E., Swank, P. R., & Guttentag, C. (2008). A responsive parenting intervention: The optimal timing across early childhood for impacting maternal behaviors and child outcomes. *Developmental Psychology*, 44(5), 1335–1353. doi: 10.1037/a0013030

Lee, J. (2011). Size matters: Early vocabulary as a predictor of language and literacy competence. *Applied Psycholinguistics*, 32(1), 69–92. doi: 10.1017/S0142716410000299

LeVasseur, V. M., Macaruso, P., & Shankweiler, D. (2008). Promoting gains in reading fluency: A comparison of three approaches. *Reading and Writing*, 21(3), 205–230 doi: 10.1007/s1145-007-9070-1

Love, J. M. (2010). Effects of early head start prior to kindergarten entry: The importance of early experience. *Archives of General Psychiatry*, 53, 1033–1039.

Nurse-Family Partnership. (2011). Mission, vision and values. Retrieved February 17, 2014 from www.nursefamilypartnership.org/about/Mission-Vision-Values

Olds, D. L., Kitzman, H., Cole, R., Robinson, J., Sidora, K., Luckey, D. W., & Holmberg, J. (2004). Effects of nurse home-visiting on maternal life course and child development: Age 6 follow-up results of a randomized trial. *Pediatrics*, 114(6), 1550–1559. doi: 10.1542/peds.2004-0962

Ouellette, G., Dagostino, L., & Carifio, J. (1999). The effects of exposure to children's literature through read aloud and an inferencing strategy on low reading ability fifth graders' sense of story structure and reading comprehension. *Reading Improvement*, 36(2), 73–89.

Pae, S. (2013, April). *An investigation of the language environment of young Korea children and the impact of feedback on language development*. Paper presented at the LENA International Conference 2013, Denver, CO.

Reid Chassiakos, Y., Radesky, J., Christakis, D., Moreno, M. A., Cross, C., & Council on Communications and Media. (2016). Children and adolescents and digital media. *Pediatrics*, 138(5), e20162593.

Rowe, M. L., Pan, B. A., & Ayoub, C. (2005). Predictors of variation in maternal talk to children: A longitudinal study of low-income families. *Parenting: Science and Practice*, 5(3), 259–283. doi: 10.1207/s15327922par0503_3

Saracho, O. N., & Spodek, B. (2010). Parents and children engaging in storybook reading. *Early Child Development and Care*, 180(10), 1379–1389. doi:10.1080/03004430903135605

Suskind, D., Leffel, K. R., Hernandez, M. W., Sapolich, S. G., Suskind, E., Kirkham, E., & Meehan, P. (2013). An exploratory study of "quantitative linguistic feedback": Effect of LENA feedback on adult language production. *Communication Disorders Quarterly*, 34(4), 199–209. doi: 10.1177/1525740112473146

Tamis-LeMonda, C. S., Bornstein, M. H., & Baumwell, L. (2001). Maternal responsiveness and children's achievement of language milestones. *Child Development*, 72(3), 748–767. doi: 10.1111/1467-8624.00313

US Department of Health & Human Services. (2013, April 8). Estimated costs of implementation [Home visiting evidence of effectiveness: Implementing Early Head Start-Home Visiting (EHS-HV)]. Retrieved February 17, 2014 from http://homvee.acf.hhs.gov/document.aspx?rid=3&sid=8&mid=5

Wagner, K. R. (1985). How much do children say in a day? *Journal of Child Language*, 12, 475–487

Walker, D., Greenwood, C., Hart, B., & Carta, J. (1994). Prediction of school outcomes based on early language production and socioeconomic factors. *Child Development*, 65(2), 606–621. doi: 10.1111/j.1467-8624.1994.tb00771.x

Warren, S. F. & Brady, N. C. (2007). The role of maternal responsivity in the development of children with intellectual disabilities. *Mental Retardation and Developmental Disabilities Research Reviews*, 13(4), 330–338. doi: 10.1002/mrdd.20177

Warren, S. F., Gilkerson, J., Richards, J. A., Oller, D. K., Xu, D., Yapanel, U., & Gray, S. (2010). What automated vocal analysis reveals about the vocal production and language learning environment of young children with autism. *Journal of Autism and Developmental Disorders*, 40(5), 555–569. doi: 10.1007/s10803-009-0902-5

Wells, G. (1985). Language development in the preschool years. New York: Cambridge University Press.

Wiggin, M., Gabbard, S., Thompson, N., Goberis, D., & Yoshinaga-Itano, C. (2012). The school to home link: Summer preschool and parents. *Seminars in Speech and Language*, 33(04), 290–296. doi: 10.1055/s-0032-1326919

Xu, D., Zhang, Y., Mao, H., Xin, Y., & Xiao, L. (2012). The correlation of infants' and toddlers' responsiveness with language and cognitive development in Han-language families. *Chinese Journal of Evidence-Based Pediatrics*, 7(6), 435–439. doi: 10.3969

Yoshinaga-Itano, C. (2003). From screening to early identification and intervention: Discovering predictors to successful outcomes for children with significant hearing loss. *Journal of Deaf Studies and Deaf Education*, 8(1), 11–30. doi: 10.1093/deafed/8.1.11

Yoshinaga-Itano, C., Gilkerson, J., Moore, R. C., Uhler, K., Baca, R., & Wiggin, M. (2011, July). *LENA: Exploring novel approaches to language assessment and intervention.* Paper presented at the 2011 AG Bell Listening and Spoken Language Symposium, Washington, DC.

Zhang, Y., Xu, X., Jiang, F., Gilkerson, J., Xu, D., Richards, J. A., Harnsberger, J., & Topping, K. J. (2015). Effects of quantitative linguistic feedback to caregivers of young children: A pilot study in China. *Communication Disorders Quarterly*, 37(1), 16–24. doi: 10.1177/1525740115575771

Zimmerman, F. J., Gilkerson, J., Richards, J. A., Christakis, D. A., Xu, D., Gray, S., & Yapanel, U. (2009). Teaching by listening: The importance of adult-child conversations to language development. *Pediatrics*, 124(1), 342–349. doi: 10.1542/peds.2008-2267

10

SUMMER READING LOSS IS THE BASIS OF ALMOST ALL THE RICH/POOR READING GAP

Richard L. Allington and Anne McGill-Franzen

Although recent federal policy has focused on differences in teacher quality as the primary factor involved in creating the rich/poor reading achievement gap (IES, 2014), others have noted that children from low-income families gain as much reading growth as children from middle- and higher-income families during that part of the year when schools are open (Alexander, Entwisle, & Olson, 2001; Hayes & Grether, 1983; McCoach, O'Connell, Reis, & Levitt, 2006). These reports also provide evidence, as do others, that it is during the summer months, when schools are closed, that the rich/poor reading achievement gap is largely created.

In this chapter we first present the evidence on the size and nature of the rich/poor reading achievement gap. Then we evaluate the evidence on factors, such as teacher quality and summer reading activity, that contribute to the achievement gap. Finally we discuss the evidence on summer reading loss as well as the evidence that summer reading loss is primarily attributable to the limited access to books that poor children are likely to experience every summer. We close with a summary of several recent studies demonstrating that enhancing the access children from low-income families have to books during the summer months is a comparatively cost-effective approach to eliminating summer loss and narrowing the rich/poor reading achievement gap.

The Rich/Poor Reading Achievement Gap

Students from low-income families currently exhibit reading achievement that falls far below the achievement of students from middle-income families. The rich/poor reading achievement gap has been widening for quite a while. Over the past 30 years, the reading achievement gap between students from the 90th and 10th percentile income families grew from 0.9 SD to 1.25 SD, an increase of

40 percent (Reardon, 2013). In other words, schools today are less successful at educating poor students than schools were in the 1980s when *A Nation at Risk* was written. That report derided American education for its failure to educate both children from low-income families and children of color.

However, during the same time period that the rich/poor reading achievement gap was widening, the reading achievement gap between black and white students shrank from close to 1.25 SD to less than 0.75 SD (Reardon, 2013). Thus, American schools are doing better in developing readers within some subgroups but doing less well with other subgroups. There may be multiple explanations for just why American schools have been making progress with African American children while losing ground in educating the wider group of children of poverty, including increasing numbers of low-income immigrant families, but that is beyond the scope of the chapter. Nonetheless it is timely to readdress educating children from low-income families.

What we do know is the children from low-income families begin school already behind children from families with higher incomes. Two-thirds of all children, at kindergarten entry, know the names of the letters of the alphabet and one-third of the entrants know most of the consonant sounds (Pearson & Hiebert, 2010). Too often it is children from the low-income families who enter kindergarten ranking in the bottom third of their peers, knowing neither the letter names nor the sounds that those letters usually represent. At the same time, alphabet knowledge is one of those *constrained skills* that represent essential early literacy learning (Paris, 2005). Letter name knowledge is one of the print-related proficiencies that develop in print-rich home environments. But it is just those environments that are related to the mother's educational level and to family income (Piasta, Justice, McGinty, & Kaderavek, 2012). Children from low-income families arrive with far fewer experiences with books and with writing than do children from more economically advantaged families (McGill-Franzen, Lanford, & Adams, 2002). Thus, children from low-income families begin school behind their more economically advantages peers. Unfortunately, the gap that exists at kindergarten entry simply widens across the years these children attend school.

What seems even worse are the data on the quality of preschool print environments and lessons (McGill-Franzen & Lanford, 1994; McGill-Franzen et al., 2002; Neuman & Celano, 2001). These reports indicate that programs serving middle-class children are far more likely to provide print-rich learning environments than programs serving children from low-income families. It is the more economically advantaged children who are more likely to have easy access to books both at home and in preschool and have more contact with print and language-rich experiences and lessons. Additionally, more economically advantaged children are more likely to attend preschool and to attend preschool longer than children from low-income families.

So children from low-income families arrive at school with fewer, and in some cases far fewer, print experiences than children from middle-income families.

Although attending school will narrow that achievement gap modestly during the school year, during the following summer the gap again widens between children from low- and middle-income families. As Reardon (2013) notes, "The data show the gap narrowing between fall and spring of kindergarten and 1st grade years—periods when students were in school—and widening in the summer between kindergarten and 1st grade—when they were not in school" (p. 13). Burkam, Ready, Lee, and LoGerto (2004) provide further evidence that children from low-income families learn less during the summer months than do middle-class children. They also note that parents of children in low-income families were less likely to read a book to their child during the summer months, as well as less likely to take their child to a bookstore or a library than were middle-class parents.

Downey, vonHippel, and Broh (2004) also report that schools play a part in slowly narrowing the achievement gap, but that the achievement gap then widened the during the summer months. We could go on but suffice it to say that while policy makers have largely ignored summer academic loss, the research community has written about summer loss for more than a century (Aason, 1959; Allington & McGill-Franzen, 2003; Borman & D'Agostino, 1996; Carter, 1984; Cooper, Nye, Charlton, Lindsay & Greathouse, 1996; Elder, 1927; Hayes & Grether, 1983; Heyns, 1978; Kim & Quinn, 2013; White, 1906). What we know is that children from low-income families begin school behind their more economically advantaged peers and fall further behind every year (Allington & McGill-Franzen, 2013b).

In a classic study of summer reading loss, Heyns (1978) documented the rich/poor reading achievement gap in the Atlanta schools nearly forty years ago. She reported that children from middle-class families generally gained more reading proficiency during the summer than children from low-income families. In fact, this latter group actually lost reading proficiency during the summer months. However, academic growth during the school year was roughly comparable for both groups. It was during the summer months that poor students lagged behind their financially better-off peers. During those summer months children were not attending school and had to rely on family and community resources in developing reading proficiencies.

Cooper et al. (1996) report a meta-analysis of studies of summer reading (as well as mathematics) loss. Their findings stated that summer reading loss was related to family income levels. Quoting the authors, "Middle-class students appeared to gain on grade-level equivalent reading recognition tests over summer while lower-class students lost on them. There were no moderating effects for gender or race…" (p. 227). In other words, children from low-income families were observed to lose some of their academic proficiencies related to reading over the summer vacation months while middle class children actually added reading proficiency over those same months. The data analyzed indicated that, "On average, summer vacations created a gap of about 3 months between middle- and lower-class students" (p. 261). They hypothesized that this reading loss might be related to differential access to books experienced by the two, rich and poor, groups of children, "The income differences may be related to differences in opportunities to practice and learn (with more books and reading opportunities available to middle-class students)" (p. 265).

In a long-term study Alexander, Entwisle, and Olson (2007) reported that for adolescents from higher-income families enrolled in the college track, compared to students from lower-income families enrolled in the non-college track, the reading achievement difference at ninth grade was 124 raw score points on the California Achievement Test-Reading. However, 40 points of that difference were present at the beginning of first grade. An 8-point raw test score disadvantage accrued during the school years from first grade to ninth grade for the students from low-income families and there was the 76 raw score point disadvantage that accrued over the summer elementary school months for poor kids. Their data illustrated that during the first five years of school the amount of annual reading growth of low-SES students was not appreciably less than high-SES students during the months that school was in session. When school was not in session, the summer months, the achievement gap between rich and poor students significantly widened. When CAT-R tests were administered after the summer break, students from low-income families showed negative or no cumulative gains, while the more economically advantaged students showed positive cumulative reading achievement gains.

They go on to suggest that:

> Poor children in Baltimore may be progressing in parallel with better-off children during the school year, but that does not mean they are performing at the same level at year's end. To the contrary, at the end of elementary school they lag far behind, which we attribute to two sources: they start school already behind, a deficit that their good school years gains do not erase; and during the summer, when they are cut off from the school's resources, they lose ground relative to higher-SES children. (Alexander et al., 2007, p. 19)

In this study, economically better-off kids gained 52 raw score points on CAT-R during the summer months, while children from low-income families lost raw score points on the CAT-R during the summer months. By ninth grade the reading achievement of children from low-income families stood at 75 points behind middle class students' scores on the CAT-R. About a third of this difference (26.5 points) was present when these students began first grade but the largest contributor to the gap (48.5 points) was what happened (or didn't happen) during the summer months when the children were not enrolled in schools.[1]

Examining the reading achievement gathered through the National Assessment of Educational Progress one can see that by fourth grade children from low-income families are a bit more than a year behind other children. By eighth grade this gap has widened to over two and one-half years and by twelfth grade the gap is four years wide. That is, twelfth graders from low-income families read at the same level as the typical non-poor eighth grader (National Assessment of Educational Progress, 2013). The size of the reading gap on the NAEP assessment matches quite well with the Cooper et al. (1996) findings of a three-month difference in reading achievement that accrues every summer. That three-month difference is roughly one-third of a school year and suggests that children from low-income families will fall another year behind their middle-class peers roughly every three years. The four-year rich/poor reading achievement gap on the NAEP assessment at twelfth grade fits that projection quite nicely. This rich/poor reading achievement gap was primarily a summer months phenomena. The annual losses that were documented as occurring every summer accumulated into the substantial rich/poor reading achievement gap reported on NAEP.

We find the evidence available quite convincing that summer reading loss is both real and the major factor in the substantial rich/poor reading achievement gap that exists today. We also find the evidence on the source of the rich/poor reading gap is equally compelling. We turn to that topic now.

The Gap Is Not Primarily Attributable to Ineffective Schools or Teachers

It is not true that ineffective teachers are over-represented in high-poverty schools; nor is it true that high-poverty schools have created the achievement gap. In fact, evidence suggests that the opposite is true. Rather than schools that enroll many children from low-income families being *less effective* than other schools, the data available indicate that reading growth during the months that school is in session is *comparable* in schools with many poor children and schools with few poor children. Of course, all schools employ some teachers who are neither very expert nor very effective at teaching children to read (Bohn, Roehrig, & Pressley, 2004; Stuhlman & Pianta, 2009; Valli, Croninger, & Buese, 2012). However, it is not the case that high-poverty schools are filled with ineffective teachers producing reading achievement that falls short of the achievement attained in schools where most students are not economically disadvantaged (Alexander et al., 2007; Burkam et al., 2004: Downey et al, 2004; Hayes & Grether, 1983; McCoach et al., 2006).

The findings of Hayes and Grether (1983), thirty years ago, asserted that summer reading loss was the major contributor to the rich/poor reading achievement gap. They reported that achievement growth during the school year was remarkably consistent regardless of whether the school enrolled economically disadvantaged or more economically advantaged children. As Hayes and Grether noted, "The differential progress made during the four summers between 2nd and 6th grade accounts for upwards of 80 percent of the difference between economically advantaged all-white schools and the all-black and Puerto Rican ghetto schools" (p. 64). Again, most of the remainder of the rich/poor reading achievement gap was found in the differences that existed between children from families of differing economic status when the children began school.

Likewise, Entwisle, Alexander, and Olson (1997) noted that the cumulative gains in reading comprehension in elementary grades, as measured on the CAT-R, was 191 raw score points for children from low-income families and 193 raw score point gains for children who were financially better off. They note that, "Such parity hardly accords with popular (and some professional) depictions of poor children's schooling…" (p. 18). In other words, the identification of high-poverty schools as failing schools and the identification of the teachers in these buildings as failing teachers, based on student reading achievement, are fundamentally inaccurate. The schools children from low-income families attend produce just as much growth in reading achievement each year as do those award-winning higher-wealth elementary schools. Entwisle and her colleagues also note that their data is not unique but mirrors the achievement patterns reported by others (Hayes & Grether, 1983; Heyns, 1978; 1987).

Given these reports, it seems safe to conclude that while teachers and schools may contribute, in a small measure, to the rich/poor reading achievement gap, the evidence also demonstrates that it is the time during the summer months, when children are not attending school, that contribute most of the difference in reading achievement between rich and poor students. In other words, it is the contributions (or the lack of them) of families and communities during the summer months, when school is not in session, that carries the weight of the evidence on the cause of the rich/poor reading achievement gap.

Why Do Children from Low-Income Families Consistently Experience Summer Reading Loss?

Why do summer vacation months play such a different role in the reading development of children from families at different income levels? In our opinion it is the more restricted access to books and other reading material that children from low-income families experience that lies at the root of this problem.

Our opinion is based on the evidence available. Neuman and Celano (2001) found that in low-income neighborhoods, fewer books were available in stores, childcare centers, and local elementary school and public libraries. Also, in low-income neighborhoods, the books that were available were both older and of lower quality than the books available in middle-class communities. Similar findings are reported by Allington, Guice, Baker, Michaelson, and Li (1995), Constantino (2005), Fryer and Levitt (2002), McGill-Franzen et al. (2002), and Smith, Constantino, and Krashen (1997). Additionally, the numbers of books available in the homes of children vary by ethnicity with white children living in homes with two and a half times as many books as black children (Fryer & Levitt, 2002). Children from low-income families live in neighborhoods that offer fewer locations to buy or borrow books, attend schools where the numbers of books available are more limited, and live in homes where few books are found. Minority children live in homes with less than half the number of books found in white homes.

All this leads to some children spending summers with restricted access to books that could be read. This lack of access means that these children are less likely to read during the summer months. This lack of reading activity leads to a decrease in reading proficiencies just as the absence of practice leads to a decrease in almost any proficiency (think of ice skating activity and playing hockey here). What we do know is that there is positive correlation between volume of reading activity and reading proficiency (Anderson, Wilson, & Fielding, 1988; Cunningham & Stanovich, 1991) and that reading activity is related to ease of access to books and other reading material (McQuillan & Au, 2001; Waples, 1937/1972). This relationship was also reported by Heyns (1978) who suggested, "The unique contribution of reading to summer learning suggests that increasing access to books and encouraging reading may well have a substantial impact on achievement" (p. 172).

Recently, Lindsay (2013) established the relationship of access to books and increased reading behavior in a meta-analysis of research on book distribution programs. He reported that when examining the outcomes of rigorous experimental studies, where access was manipulated amongst populations of randomly assigned subjects, the impact of increasing book access on reading achievement produced an effect size of d = 0.435. This finding led Lindsay to conclude:

> Interventions that facilitate children's access to print material produce impacts that are one to four times as large as those in the average intervention (depending on the outcome category being examined). The more policy relevant outcomes—reading performance—showed impacts that are about twice as large as the average impact found in elementary schools. (p. 34)

The various forms of evidence just reviewed on ease of access to books, especially during the summer vacation months, led us to conclude that summer reading loss might be eliminated by enhancing access, of children from low-income families, to books.

Ameliorating the Rich/Poor Reading Achievement Gap

We developed an experimental test of this hypothesis by employing a three-year longitudinal summer books intervention (Allington, McGill-Franzen et al., 2010). In that study we randomly selected first- and second-grade children enrolled in high-poverty schools for either the treatment group, so that books for summer reading were provided, or to the control group where no books were provided for summer reading. Each year we provided a book fair in each of the 17 targeted elementary schools. Most children attending these schools were poor (from 66 percent to 98 percent of the students were eligible for free or reduced price meals) and most of the students were minority students (89 percent were Black or Hispanic).

The book fairs we provided for treatment children allowed each student the opportunity to select 12–15 books for voluntary summer reading from a collection of roughly 500 books each year. The books each treatment child selected were then distributed to treatment children on their final day of school. After completing the three-year voluntary summer book reading project the treatment children earned scores roughly 0.40 of a standard deviation above those of the control children. The difference in reading achievement at the end of study was statistically significant with a small effect size (ES=0.14, for the full sample and ES=0.21 for the free-lunch children). While the effect was, technically, small, it was as large as the effect size for attending summer school (Cooper, Charleton, Valentine, & Muhlenbruck, 2000) and as large, or larger, as the effect size on reading achievement reported for schools adopting one of the approved federal models of educational reform (Borman, Hewes, Overman, & Brown, 2003).

Kim (2007) also provided summer books to students in first through fifth grade. The books given to the treatment students were selected for them using an interest and reading difficulty procedure. Treatment group students reported reading three more books than did the children in the control group, but no significant differences in reading achievement were found between groups at the end of the one summer intervention study. Kim and White (2008) added a classroom scaffolding component and provided third-, fourth-, and fifth-grade students with summer books. They found that the classroom scaffolding produced significant differences in reading achievement at the end of this one-year summer intervention. They reported an effect size of ES=0.14, identical to that reported by Allington, McGill-Franzen, et al. (2010).

Similarly, Wilkens et al. (2012) compared providing eight books for summer reading to third-grade students with low-reading ability. However, children in the treatment group read only one more book than did children in the control group and no significant differences were observed in reading achievement at the end of the study. Again, however, student self-selection of the books they received was not an aspect of this research project nor were the participants necessarily children from low-income families.

White, Kim, Kingston, and Foster (2014) replicated the 2008 Kim and White study with students from 19 elementary schools in grades kindergarten through fifth grade. The overall comparison found no significant differences in reading achievement following the summer reading intervention. However, White et al. (2014) report that the reading achievement of treatment students in schools where more than 75 percent of the students were eligible for free lunch did differ from the reading achievement of control students. In other words, it was only children from low-income families who benefited from books for summer reading.

In Allington and McGill-Franzen (2013a) we suggest that there may be a number of reasons some scholars have not found the same positive effects of providing children with books to read during the summer months as we did. First, the Allington, McGill-Franzen et al. (2010) study was designed to ensure that children were given books that they actually wanted to read by allowing self-selection of the texts. Second, each child was provided 12 to 15 self-selected books each year. Fewer books seemed simply not a substantial enough number of books to have any great impact on the reading development of beginning readers. Third, the study was a longitudinally designed study (three consecutive summers) because the potential impact in any given summer can be expected to be small and difficult to capture on current standardized reading achievement tests.

Finally, the study targeted beginning readers (grades 1 and 2) in the first year because the impact of early reading experiences seems so potentially powerful (Torgeson, 2002; Vellutino, Scanlon, & Tanzman, 1998). Our study, then, provided more books, books that were self-selected, to younger students from low-income families for a longer period of time than did those who have published other reports of summer book distribution.

We have argued (McGill-Franzen & Allington, 2013) that self-selection is a powerful factor in supporting summer voluntary reading activity. Lindsay (2010) found that the effect size on reading achievement for access when individual choice was involved was $d = 0.766$ but substantially smaller ($d = 0.402$) when students did not choose the texts they were given. Additionally, Lindsay (2010) found that giving children books, as opposed to lending children books, for summer reading also produced larger effects on achievement.

No other studies, to date, have allowed children to self-select the texts they receive for summer voluntary reading, most studies did not target only children from low-income families to receive summer books, no other study has lasted longer than a single summer, and no other study has distributed summer books to primary grade students only. Thus, all four factors make the Allington, McGill-Franzen et al. (2010) study unique. We are unsure whether a single factor or multiple factors are influential in obtaining the outcome we reported. What our study did demonstrate is that providing primary grade students from low-income families with the opportunity to self-select books for summer reading did, in fact, substantially improve their reading achievement when compared to the control group children (Allington & McGill-Franzen, 2013).

Conclusion

Summer reading loss has been determined to be the major component of the existing rich/poor reading achievement gap. It now seems clear that children from low-income families have far more restricted access to books during the summer months than do more economically advantaged children. By expanding summer access to books for children from low-income families, several studies (Allington, McGill-Franzen et al., 2010; Kim, 2006; White et al., 2014) have demonstrated that summer reading loss can be at least ameliorated if not eliminated. The effect size (d = 0.14) of improving poor children's access to self-selected books during the summer months in our study equaled the effect size (d = 0.14) that Cooper et al. (2000) reported for attending summer school. However, our annual cost per student was substantially lower than the cost of attending summer school. The annual cost of the books we distributed was roughly $50 per child and because the summer book distribution was our only intervention it appears that distributing self-selected books to children from low-income families is a potentially powerful option that state education agencies and school districts should seriously consider.

Further support for providing books for summer reading comes from the meta-analysis of 41 recent studies of summer interventions completed by Kim and Quinn (2013) who report comparable effects for school-based and home-based summer reading interventions. As the authors noted:

> The magnitude of the effect size across the five outcome measures was similar for classroom and home interventions. More precisely, there was no significant difference in the mean effects of classroom and home interventions on each of the five outcome measures. (p. 400)

In other words, two meta-analyses (Cooper et al., 2000; Kim & Quinn, 2013) both report that it is possible to positively impact reading growth during the summer months with home-based interventions. The most common and least expensive home-based reading intervention has simply been to distribute books to children for summer voluntary reading.

Eliminating summer reading loss would substantially narrow the rich/poor reading achievement gap that currently undercuts school and life success. Distributing books that children from low-income families want to read, especially distributing such books to poor children enrolled in the early elementary grades, is a documented research-based intervention that should receive renewed attention from both policy makers and practitioners.

Spotlight Recommendation

1. Distribute summer books to children and especially children from low-income families. Our spring book fair model allowed children from low-income families to self-select 12–15 books from roughly 500 different books. This low-cost intervention effectively eliminated summer reading loss among the children from low-income families who had been randomly selected to participate in the spring book fairs. The books they selected were given to them on their final day of school.

2. Open the school library one or two days a week over the summer. We developed a model whereby school librarians worked a four-day week year around (with two weeks off in August). Thus, the school library was kept open four

days each week during summer vacation. A library that is closed for the summer months in a high-poverty neighborhood is an underused library.

3. Distribute three or four self-selected books on the final day of school and then schedule a book exchange at the school three or four weeks later. If children return the books they received earlier (say on the final day of school) they can select the same number of new books to replace the books they just returned. This option seems to work best when most children walk to school from their homes although we have worked with a district that scheduled buses to run on book swap days enabling children in rural areas to come to school and swap for new books.

4. Schedule a book bus to travel to low-income neighborhoods. Children then simply walk to the book bus to check out books for summer voluntary reading. Remove some of the seats on a regular bus to create the space for book racks or book bins filled with books. Children simply walk onto the bus and select the books they want to read.

Note

1   One criticism of studies of summer reading loss is that the testing that has been used typically occurred in the spring, often weeks before summer vacation periods began, and fall testing typically a few weeks after children returned to school. In some cases the test dates indicate that children had as many weeks of schooling between the testing periods as they had weeks of summer vacation. However, Burkam et al. (2004) used exact testing days as well as opening and closing of school dates to calculate summer losses more specifically. In their analysis the pattern of differential effects of summer vacation periods on reading achievement was robust, indicating the rich/poor achievement gap effects even after their adjustment for earlier measurement inaccuracies.

References

Aason, H. (1959). A summer's growth in reading. *Elementary School Journal*, 60(1), 70–74.

Alexander, C. L., Entwisle, D. R., & Olson, L. S. (2001). Schools, achievement, and inequality: A seasonal perspective. *Educational Evaluation and Policy Analysis*, 23(2), 171–191.

Alexander, K. L., Entwisle, D. R., & Olson, L. S. (2007). Summer learning and its implications: Insights from the Beginning School Study. In R. Fairchild & G. C. Noam (Eds.), *Summertime: Confronting risks, exploring solutions.* (Vol. 114, pp. 11–32). San Francisco: Jossey-Bass.

Allington, R. L., Guice, S., Baker, K., Michelson, N., & Li, S. (1995). Access to books: Variations in schools and classrooms. *Language and Literacy Spectrum*, 5(Spring), 23–25.

Allington, R. L. & McGill-Franzen, A. M. (2003). The impact of summer loss on the reading achievement gap. *Phi Delta Kappan*, 85(1), 68–75.

Allington, R. L. & McGill-Franzen, A. (2013a). *Summer reading: Closing the rich/poor reading achievement gap.* New York: Teachers College Press.

Allington, R. L. & McGill-Franzen, A. (2013b). The summer reading setback. *Better: Evidence-Based Education*, 5(2), 10–11.

Allington, R. L., McGill-Franzen, A. M., Camilli, G., Williams, L., Graff, J., Zeig, J., Zmach, C., Nowak, R. (2010). Addressing summer reading setback among economically disadvantaged elementary students. *Reading Psychology*, 31(5), 411–427.

Anderson, R. C., Wilson, P. T., & Fielding, L. G. (1988). Growth in reading and how children spend their time outside of school. *Reading Research Quarterly*, 23, 285–303.

Bohn, C. M., Roehrig, A. D., & Pressley, M. (2004). The first days of school in the classrooms of two more effective and four less effective primary grades teachers. *Elementary School Journal*, 104(4), 269–288.

Borman, G. D. & D'Agostino, J. V. (1996). Title 1 and student achievement: A meta-analysis of federal results. *Educational Evaluation and Policy Analysis*, 18(4), 309–326.

Borman, G. D., Hewes, G. M., Overman, L. T., & Brown, S. (2003). Comprehensive school reform and achievement: A meta-analysis. *Review of Educational Research*, 73(1), 125–139.

Burkam, D. T., Ready, D. D., Lee, V. E., & LoGerfo, L. F. (2004). Social class differences in summer learning between kindergarten and first grade: Model specification and estimation. *Sociology of Education*, 77(1), 1–31.

Carter, L. (1984). The sustaining effects study of compensatory and elementary education. *Educational Researcher*, 13(1), 4–13.

Constantino, R. (2005). Print environments between high and low socioeconomic status communities. *Teacher Librarian*, 32(3), 22–25.

Cooper, H., Charleton, K., Valentine, J. C., & Muhlenbruck, L. (2000). Making the most of summer school: A meta-analytic and narrative review. *Monographs of the Society for Research in Child Development, Vol. 65*(Serial number 260), 1–118.

Cooper, H., Nye, B., Charlton, K., Lindsay, J., & Greathouse, S. (1996). The effects of summer vacation on achievement test scores: A narrative and meta-analytic review. *Review of Educational Research*, 66(3), 227–268.

Cunningham, A. E. & Stanovich, K. E. (1991). Tracking the unique effects of print exposure in children: Associations with vocabulary, general knowledge, and spelling. *Journal of Educational Psychology*, 83(2), 264–274.

Downey, D. B., von Hippel, P. T. & Broh, B. A. (2004). Are schools the great equalizer? Cognitive inequality during the summer months and the school year. *American Sociological Review*, 69(5): 613–635.

Elder, H. E. (1927). The effect of summer vacation on silent reading ability in the intermediate grades. *Elementary School Journal*, 27, 541–546.

Entwisle, D. R., Alexander, K. L., & Olson, L. S. (1997). *Children, schools, and inequality*. Boulder, CO: Westview Press.

Fryer, R. G. & Levitt, S. D. (2002). *Understanding the black-white test score gap in the first two years of school*. Cambridge, MA: National Bureau of Economic Research.

Hayes, D. P. & Grether, J. (1983). The school year and vacations: When do students learn? *Cornell Journal of Social Relations*, 17(1), 56–71.

Heyns, B. (1978). *Summer learning and the effects of schooling*. New York: Academic Press.

Heyns, B. (1987). Schooling and cognitive development: Is there a season for learning? *Child Development*, 58(5), 1151–1160.

Institute for Education Sciences (2014). *Do disadvantaged students get less effective teaching?* Report no. NCEE 2014-4010. National Center for Educational Evaluation: Washington, DC.

Kim, J. S. (2006). Effects of a voluntary summer reading intervention on reading achievement: Results from a randomized field trial. *Educational Evaluation and Policy Analysis*, 28(4), 335–355.

Kim, J. S. (2007). The effects of a voluntary summer reading intervention on reading activities and achievement. *Journal of Educational Psychology*, 99(3): 505–515.

Kim, J. S. & Quinn, D. M. (2013). The effects of summer reading on low-income children's literacy achievement from kindergarten to grade 8: A meta-analysis of classroom and home interventions. *Review of Educational Research*, 83(3), 386–431.

Kim, J. S. & White, T. G. (2008). Scaffolding voluntary summer reading for children in grades 3 to 5: An experimental study. *Scientific Studies of Reading*, 12(1), 1–23.

Lindsay, J. J. (2010). *Children's access to print material and education-related outcomes: Findings from a meta-analytic review*. Naperville, IL: Learning Point Associates.

Lindsay, J. J. (2013). Impacts of interventions that increase children's access to print material. In R. L. Allington & A. McGill-Franzen (Eds.), *Summer reading: Closing the rich/poor reading achievement gap* (pp. 20–38). New York: Teachers College Press.

McCoach, D. B., O'Connell, A. A., Reis, S. M., & Levitt, H. A. (2006). Growing readers: A hierarchical linear model of children's reading growth during the first 2 years of school. *Journal of Educational Psychology*, 98(1), 14–28.

McGill-Franzen, A. & Allington, R. L. (2013). Children will read during the summer if we provide access, choice, and support. In C. Cahill, K. Horvath, A. McGill-Franzen & R. L. Allington (Eds.), *No more summer reading loss* (pp. 15–42). Portsmouth, NH: Heinemann.

McGill-Franzen, A. M. & Lanford, C. (1994). Exposing the edge of the preschool curriculum: Teachers' talk about text and children's literary understandings. *Language Arts*, 71, 264–273.

McGill-Franzen, A. M., Lanford, C., & Adams, E. (2002). Learning to be literate: A comparison of five urban early childhood programs. *Journal of Educational Psychology*, 94(3), 443–464.

McQuillan, J. & Au, J. (2001). The effect of print access on reading frequency. *Reading Psychology*, 22(3), 225–248.

National Assessment of Educational Progress (2013). *2013 Reading Assessment*. Washington, DC: US Department of Education, Institute of Education Sciences, National Center for Education Statistics. Retrieved on January 22, 2014 from http://nces.ed.gov/nationsreportcard/reading/

Neuman, S. & Celano, D. (2001). Access to print in low-income and middle-income communities. *Reading Research Quarterly*, 36(1), 8–26.

Paris, S. G. (2005). Reinterpreting the development of reading skills. *Reading Research Quarterly*, 40(2), 184–202.

Pearson, P. D. & Hiebert, E. H. (2010). National reports in literacy: Building a scientific base for practice and policy. *Educational Researcher*, 39(4), 286–294.

Piasta, S. B., Justice, L. M., McGinty, A. S., & Kaderavek, J. N. (2012). Increasing young children's contact with print during shared reading: Longitudinal effects on literacy achievement. *Child Development*, 83(3), 810–820.

Reardon, S. F. (2013). The widening income achievement gap. *Phi Delta Kappan*, 70(8), 10–16.

Smith, C., Constantino, R., & Krashen, S. (1997). Differences in print environment: Children in Beverly Hills, Compton and Watts. *Emergency Librarian*, 24(4), 8–9.

Stuhlman, M. W. & Pianta, R. C. (2009). Profiles of educational quality in first grade. *Elementary School Journal*, 109(4), 323–342.

Torgeson, J. K. (2002). The prevention of reading difficulties. *Journal of School Psychology*, 40(1), 7–26.

Valli, L., Croninger, R. G., & Buese, D. (2012). Studying high-quality teaching in a highly charged policy environment. *Teachers College Record* 114(4), 1–33.

Vellutino, F. R., Scanlon, D. M., & Tanzman, M. S. (1998). The case for early intervention in learning disability. *Journal of School Psychology*, 12(1), 29–39.

Waples, D. (1937). *Research memorandum on social aspects of reading in the depression* (No. Bulletin # 37. Reprinted by the Arno Press, New York, NY 1972): NY: Social Science Research Council.

White, T. G., Kim, J. S., Kingston, H. C., & Foster, L. (2014). Replicating the effects of a teacher-scaffolded voluntary summer reading program: The role of poverty. *Reading Research Quarterly*, 49(1), 5–30.

White, W. F. (1906). Reviews before and after school vacation. *American Education*, 10, 185–188.

PART IV

Contradictory Efforts and Commonalities in Attempts to Close the Gaps in Reading Achievement

11

THE FEDERAL EFFORT

How Five Different and Sometimes Contradictory Efforts Have Been Made to Close the Achievement Gap

Richard Long and Alan Farstrup

The 1964 War on Poverty launched a significant federal effort to bring fairness and equity to all Americans. There were many dimensions to this effort, including housing, voting, health, and education. The Elementary and Secondary Education Act (ESEA) of 1965 was a part of the greater goal of eliminating poverty (Elementary and Secondary Education Act, 1965). Since its original enactment ESEA has been rewritten eight times and it has been augmented by many other federal initiatives and programs (New York State Department of Education, 2006).

These revisions of ESEA and related changes, such as the addition of specialized reading programs, were further altered when President Barack Obama assumed office. And a new funding program, generated by the American Recovery and Reinvestment Act, pumped new funds into compensatory education. This chapter will highlight the many twists and turns in federal education policy, as it was being crafted and revised to close the achievement gap. Part of what will be reviewed is how major changes to the federal Title I program has moved it from being a program designed to simply provide funds to school districts to becoming one with many requirements and procedures designed to close the achievement gap that exists between historically disadvantaged groups of American children and those more privileged. This chapter will explore five major policy trends affecting the federal government's efforts to close the achievement gap.

These trends cover a wide range of ideas. The first of these policy efforts was to improve student access to quality, effective instruction. A second policy area was to address the effects of the culture of poverty. A third set of reforms addressed the culture of schooling itself and the importance of raising expectations for all students. These three trends ran, sometimes in parallel, from 1965 to 2002. In 2002, while still a part of ESEA, the policy known as *No Child Left Behind* significantly changed federal interventions into schooling. These were again changed in 2009 as President Obama's administration focused on ideas of how best to focus on schools that were historically failing.

Trend 1: Equity and Access to Effective Instruction

The ESEA, with its flagship program, Title I, or compensatory education, as it became known, was intended to close the achievement gap by providing funds so schools serving minority students could hire expert reading teachers and specialists. Title I provided books and other essential classroom materials. The initial Title I effort was based on the importance of providing access to quality education. The definitions and assessments of education quality and results were left to the discretion of state and district officials. As Senator Wayne Morris (R-OR) said shortly after ESEA's passage in 1965, "… we thought the only thing that was needed was money, once provided with the funds, the school districts knew what to do" (Cross, 2010). This idea that additional funding was the main need was quickly changed, as the program was rewritten in 1966 and 1968. This set in motion a series of changes to Title I programs and policies that have been incorporated in all of the subsequent iterations of ESEA.

Trend 2: Federal Reading Programs and Research—Demonstrating Success

The federal government has made reading a centerpiece of several education initiatives with the aim of demonstrating the type of program that could be effective. In 1974 the National Reading Program was enacted during the Nixon Administration (Education Amendments of 1974). This policy created the National Right-to-Read program (which later became the Office of Basic Skills when President Carter took office). The program provided funds to schools seeking grants to improve reading instruction and to demonstrate a specific program's effectiveness. The federal Office of Education funded programs based on applications submitted by states and schools. It, based on Congressional input, could not command any state or school district to follow specific instructional practices. It could, however, encourage evidence-based programs by providing demonstration grants with the expectation that such programs would be widely emulated. In addition, the federal government also provided funding for research on reading that could be used to disseminate information on effective practice, thus fueling the process of changing how reading was being taught. As P. David Pearson pointed out, "at that time, we believed that, if teachers and educational leaders had access to good information on reading instruction that the information alone would change practice" (Long & Selden, 2011, p. 452).

During the 70s and 80s, the US government funded grants that supported research and dissemination about reading conducted by The Center for the Study of Reading at the University of Illinois. Among the Center's many efforts, it convened a panel of experts to develop the influential report, Becoming a Nation of Readers (Anderson, Hiebert, Scott, & Wilkenson, 1984). This report provided research-based strategies recommended to close the reading achievement gap.

While not mandating specific methods it did provide a wide range of information on effective reading instruction and attempted to put key issues about beginning reading instruction into a perspective.

Then in the 1990s interpretation of the power of the federal government shifted. It moved away from providing funds for reading demonstration programs to being much more explicit. The 1998 Reading Excellence Act now called for the use of scientifically based reading instruction for high-need children, as defined by the Act. This program was succeeded by the Reading First program. Reading First was part of the No Child Left Behind Act (2002), and featured specific requirements for program selection, teacher training, and student assessment. Reading First had an additional required element that Reading Excellence did not. Schools were now called upon to apply the findings of the National Reading Panel (NRP) report published in 2000. The NRP produced one of the most influential reports on effective reading instruction that a government funded body had yet produced. These findings were used by Reading First staff as the touchstone for what they would fund in many states in order to improve beginning reading instruction and student achievement.

By the early 2000s, in spite of numerous federal, state, and local efforts at improving reading instruction, National Assessment of Educational Progress (NAEP) scores failed to show significant progress in eliminating the achievement gap in reading (National Center for Educational Statistics, 2012). While the NAEP (see Table 11.1) has reported a narrowing of the achievement gap between black and

TABLE 11.1 Changes in NAEP Reading Average Scores and Score Gaps for 9-, 13-, and 17-year-old Students, by Selected Characteristics: Various Years

Characteristics	Subgroups	Score Changes from 1973			Score Changes from 2008		
		Age 9	Age 13	Age 17	Age 9	Age 13	Age 17
All Students	All Students	⇑13	⇑8	⇔	⇔	⇑3	⇔
Race/ Ethnicity	White	⇑15	⇑9	⇑4	⇔	⇔	⇔
	Black	⇑36	⇑24	⇑30	⇔	⇔	⇔
	Hispanic	⇑25	⇑17	⇑21	⇔	⇑7	⇔
Gender	Male	⇑17	⇑9	⇑4	⇔	⇔	⇔
	Female	⇑10	⇑6	⇔	⇔	⇑3	⇔
Score gaps	White – Black	Narrowed	Narrowed	Narrowed	⇔	⇔	⇔
	White – Hispanic	Narrowed	Narrowed	Narrowed	⇔	Narrowed	⇔
	Male – Female	Narrowed	⇔	⇔	⇔	⇔	⇔

⇑ Number in box indicates score was higher in 2012
⇔ No number in box indicates no significant change in 2012 (National Center for Educational Statistics, 2012)

white students since federal education policies were implemented in 1965 (Kober, 2001), the gap has not been significantly reduced. More recent data from NAEP has continued to show little overall improvement in total scores and that the gap is only modestly closing. The emphasis on equity of access to quality schools and instruction seemed to have had little effect and progress seemed to have hit a wall.

Trend 3: A Focus on the Culture of Poverty

While the federal government was focusing on education equity and instruction, other ideas were being developed and slowly explored. As Title I priorities were again revised in the 1970s, research findings were reported that suggested this program was not effective in closing the achievement gap (Jencks et. al., 1972). Information was collected that challenged the widely held belief that schooling itself could positively impact poverty. With the observed lack of significant progress in closing the achievement gap between black and white, rich and poor, Title I and related federal programs were called into question. Researchers were finding that the emphasis on raising achievement scores by funding Title I education programs was resulting in little or no progress.

Policies during the decades of the 1960s through the 1980s were largely based on a belief that access to quality education was the most important metric. The reality was that there was little agreement among states and local school districts about the most effective way to teach all children to read and what results could be expected (Jacobsen, personal interview, 2012). What this meant specifically was that while the federal government was focused on an effort to improve equity of funding and thereby improve instruction, how this was being done differed widely from state to state. Title I wasn't seen then as a national program, it was seen as a funding program that varied considerably from state to state. One tool the federal government was trying to use to influence what states and localities were doing was through the definition of reading and how progress was assessed. The tool of choice to do this was the NAEP. In addition high profile reports such as *Becoming a Nation of Readers* (Anderson et al., 1985) and others were issued. During this period, however, the federal government wasn't seen by many to be holding states or localities accountable for educational outcomes; they were primarily evaluating results based on whether Title I money was equitably spent on instruction for all minority, at-risk student groups.

Research was showing that there were other factors to be emphasized. One factor that needed to be taken into account, as Jencks et al. (1972) reported, was the conditions surrounding poverty. They believed that poverty itself created a set of conditions inhibiting the development of extensive prior knowledge, knowledge essential for all children to be effective learners. These, and other non-school factors, were found to be negatively affecting student success, self-confidence, motivation, and achievement.

The belief emerged that in order to improve instruction the role of poverty and how it impacted learning had to be addressed. This now became a major theme of school reform and change for the next forty years. In some regard, it led to changes in Title I programs from those emphasizing instruction and individual learning in 1988 to emphasizing school wide programs for Title I (Augustus F. Hawkins-Robert T. Stafford Elementary and Secondary School Improvement Amendments of 1988, 1988). The focus on school-wide programs was taken up in the Obama administration, details of which will be discussed later in this chapter.

The school-wide approach encompassed the entire school curriculum, including the arts, physical education, and content subject classes. The belief was that if the entire school effort was emphasized, a positive result would be reflected in outcomes of reading classes and in reading test scores. By the close of the 1980s the school-wide model had become widely accepted and used as a basis for how Title I programs were structured, funded, and evaluated.

There were other efforts to change how federal programs were crafted and implemented. The Charlottesville summit, held in 1989, gathered 48 of the 50 state governors with the President of the United States and the Secretary of Education to meet and to establish a set of education goals that were to be implemented during the 1990s. A main idea was for states to adopt consistent content standards and criteria (Cross, 2010).

Until this time state education standards were often believed by many to reflect varied and too often minimum expectations. During the decade of the 1990s efforts to establish education standards that were national in scope emerged. Among the arguments in favor of national standards was the notion that expectations varied greatly across states and so where a student went to school largely determined the quality of instruction and what they were expected to learn. This inequity of expectation fueled the perception that some students had little hope of receiving what was then being called a "world-class education." The federal government began funding the development of content area standards meant to define broad goals, not specific curricula in major subject areas. The National Council of Teachers of Mathematics was a leader and had developed national content standards in the late 1980s stressing principles that could be used to solve essential, increasingly complex mathematics problems. The National Council of Teachers of English and the International Reading Association (1996), for example, developed standards for the teaching of the English language arts. During this period many other content area organizations developed and published their own national standards. Very often, in their effort to be broad without establishing instructional dictates and preferred approaches, such standards documents were widely criticized as being not specific about content or methods of instruction. Many of these standards were, however, used by many states to create their own related standards. Many such state-developed standards still resulted in children attending schools governed with a variety of different standards-based programs of instruction.

Trend 4: *No Child Left Behind* and IDEA Accountability as Policy Tools

The structure of *No Child Left Behind* (NCLB), the eighth revision of ESEA, was designed in reaction to experiences gained in previous versions of ESEA (NCLB, 2002). Among previous goals of ESEA was providing students with access to basic education. By 1992 success was defined and assessed by means of state-by-state NAEP frameworks and results (interview with Gordon Ambach, 2011). NCLB now shifted and broadened federal policy to focus also on the quality of programs, not only upon equity of access. It also altered the goals of federal education programs, from closing the achievement gap and providing all a basic education to one of assuring a high quality of education to all. In enacting a revised NCLB the federal government took the position that providing access to a basic education was not enough. Proficiency, as defined by NAEP, was now a major, quality-related purpose of federal compensatory programs. Proficiency now meant that students should be able to read effectively, to understand, and to apply information from complex text (National Center for Education Statistics, 2012).

The federal role in education has traditionally focused on providing funds to schools serving high need groups, including those living in poverty, the disabled, and language minority children. There was an evolution in how schools should identify and work with disabled children. Data describing student outcomes in federal programs were often inconsistent. Since the enactment of ESEA in 1965 some schools excluded low-performing students from assessments reporting overall achievement results. Excluding students receiving special education, and under individualized education plans (IEPs), from assessments resulted in achievement scores for entire schools that were inappropriate and inflated. As this problem became obvious ESEA was again revised and enacted as NCLB to require these results to also be reported. The 2004 revision of the Individuals with Disabilities Education Act (IDEA) also addressed the problem (President's Commission on Excellence in Special Education, 2002). Officials now questioned the increasing number of children being identified as disabled. Furthermore, the 2004 amendments to IDEA also changed how special education and Title I impacted students. The findings that built IDEA 2004 cited that too many minority children were being placed in special education and not in compensatory programs such as Title I. The suspicion was that children who were low-performing on NAEP were being systematically excluded from testing. Their now-required inclusion would result in overall lower test scores for individual schools. It was believed that schools excluding low-performing children, otherwise Title I eligible, were subverting the original intent of both Title I and of IDEA.

2004 amendments to IDEA incorporated a new tool, Response to Intervention (RTI). RTI is a philosophical concept more than a model or specific program. Key elements of RTI include universal screening, progress monitoring, and use of evidence-based instructional methods (created 2008 [RTI Action Network, n. d.]).

It was expected that classroom instruction would be altered according to RTI principles before assignment of a student to an IEP. RTI also addresses behavioral issues, providing appropriate interventions. It was based on a belief that if appropriate and concentrated changes in how students were taught were undertaken, and if students responded well, there would be no need for an IEP and for enrollment in special education. RTI was seen to change and refine how students were identified for special education services. It led to an over-identification of students as learning disabled.

While RTI has become widely accepted it has also been a subject of controversy. Some parents saw RTI as a delaying process. Special education was seen by many parents as one of the few ways to receive more individual instructional attention. However, the purpose of RTI is to reduce the number of referrals to special education and increase the success of students by changing the nature of instruction they are receiving in the classroom. It was hoped this would also reduce the number of students of low income (frequently African American and/or Hispanic) being referred for special education, a form of racial discrimination. RTI was also viewed as moving away from the existing deficit model where students had to first fail before they were evaluated.

As noted before, the *I* in RTI stands for *intervention*, including the importance of working with children having behavioral issues. While there has always been a behavioral element to programs like EHA and IDEA, implementation of RTI was now seen as blurring the lines separating programs of special education from those of general education. As RTI became more widely established, use of federal Title I funds for behavioral issues became more acceptable. This represents a change in federal policy and, as such, has an impact on how funds are used and programs structured. The understanding, in federal policy circles, that behavior and mental health have a direct bearing on instruction and learning, was only widely accepted and fully utilized beginning in 2012. This change in attitude resulted in the US Department of Education pointing out which sections of NCLB could be used to address behavior and mental health issues in schools (NCLB, 2002).

Trend 5: President Obama's Policy Initiatives—The Child and School Environment

The Obama Administration's policies focused heavily on the role of what many policy makers and academics saw as the self-fulfilling cycle of low expectations, especially for at-risk children. Low expectations encompassed several elements, including schools, teachers, families, communities, and the educational system itself. For example, if teachers excuse struggling learners because they come from poverty these students may not be sufficiently challenged. If the family is unable to demonstrate curiosity and persistence in problem solving the child may not be motivated to learn. Low expectations may also lead to lower standards defining successful school achievement. In short, the corrosive impact of low expectations was seen to be reaching too many aspects of teaching and learning.

The importance of establishing broad, yet clear standards was increasingly recognized by political- and policy-oriented leaders and groups. By 2007 the executive director of the Council of Chief State School Officers (CCSSO), Gene Wilhoit, a former chief state school officer in Kentucky, began advocating for new national, not federal, standards. Such common standards would consist of "fewer and clearer" elements (Rothman, 2011) than previous efforts had produced. A key principle was that learners should be encouraged to think critically and to solve real-world problems. Such standards would challenge students to succeed in an increasingly global economy where using information, not simply rote knowledge, was essential.

The Obama Administration assumed office in January of 2009, bringing with it a set of ideas on how to make a difference in closing the achievement gap. Many in the new administration believed that the US was "program rich, but systems poor" in social program areas including education. They felt there were too many small programs for improvement but little focus on low-performing schools where students were not significantly improving. The newly appointed US Secretary of Education, Arne Duncan (2009), announced a strong focus of funding for the bottom performing 5 percent of schools. His express intention was to concentrate federal resources in order to affect rapid and sustained change to address the achievement gap more effectively.

The School Improvement Grants (SIG) program (an element of Title I project funding for low-achieving schools) was refocused. Available funds were relatively small (less than $150 million) and fragmented across states. Each state followed its own counsel and standards varied. By 2009, and with added stimulus money, schools that had been repeatedly failing to make adequate yearly progress (AYP) were now eligible for added funding (American Recovery and Reinvestment Act of 2009). However, to be funded schools had to change how they were managed and how instruction was delivered. The federal government would now require that schools follow one of four approved models. These models of change, as of 2009, were:

1. Turnaround: District replaces the principal and rehires no more than 50 percent of staff;
2. Restart: District converts, or closes and reopens, a school as a charter school under public or private management;
3. Closure: District closes a school completely, enrolling students in higher achieving schools in the District; and
4. Transformational: District replaces principals, reviews and trains staff, institutes instructional reform, and applies community-oriented strategies. (Federal Register, 2009)

Over 70 percent of participating SIG schools opted for the Transformational model. They did so for several reasons. Firing 50 percent of staff in many low-performing schools would not necessarily result in hiring of "better" teachers. Many observers believed that teachers let go from such schools would simply be transferred elsewhere or that Turnaround, Restart, or Closure model impacts would be superficial at best. Other concerns arose. The number of schools receiving SIG funding varied from state to state. Total available SIG funding was not adequate and if a state identified too many schools it would be unable to concentrate sufficient funds to make a positive achievement improvement.

With a new and significant influx of federal stimulus money—resulting from the 2009 American Recovery and Reinvestment Act (ARRA)—some schools received additional funding. There existed disparities for how effectively districts might be able to efficiently use added funding, especially given differing realities faced by urban and rural schools. Federal education policy retained a high priority for the reduction or elimination of the achievement gap as called for by NCLB and by Title I.

Another new program, initially funded by the AARA, Race to the Top (R2T), was among new policy initiatives undertaken by the Obama Administration. R2T differed in many ways from existing programs. It was not a formula-driven program (where money went automatically to states and districts if specific criteria were met) like Title I or IDEA. To get R2T money, states had to apply for funds and only receive them if the US Department of Education accepted their policy decisions. R2T was a competitively funded program. While the policy concepts used by the Department of Education were essentially the same as those used for the SIG program, they would then be applied to many more schools in the state judged as low-performing (USED, 2009).

By 2011, the Administration concluded that NCLB was not going to be changed through the normal congressional reauthorization process. Four years had passed since ESEA and NCLB were to have been rewritten. Many states were desperate to be free of NCLB requirements to identify failing schools and to move 20 percent of federal funding to support private tutoring and/or public school choice provisions. States were then offered a waiver of requirements in exchange for agreeing to adopt the US Department of Education's plans for school change to accelerate closing the achievement gap. This process was intended to give states more flexibility.

The requirements for the states to receive this flexibility (relief from many of the NCLB requirements) was now that they had to adopt national career and college readiness standards and assessments, use those assessments as part of teacher and principal evaluations, make more decisions using data, and other required changes that were sweeping in scope (Announcement of flexibility for *No Child Left Behind* n. d.).

In contrast to programs such as SIG and R2T, the Administration also created a small demonstration program, Promise Neighborhoods (2010). According to the US Department of Education, the Promise Neighborhoods program is aimed at improving education and reducing the achievement gap by having communities focus on:

1. Identifying and increasing the capacity of eligible entities focused on achieving results throughout an entire neighborhood;
2. Building a continuum of solutions within educational, family and community support programs centering on excellent schools;
3. Integrating programs and breaking down agency "silos" so solutions are implemented effectively and efficiently across agencies;
4. Developing a local systems and resources infrastructure needed to sustain and scale up effective solutions across the region beyond the initial neighborhood focus; and
5. Learning about overall impact through rigorous evaluation of the program. (www2.ed.gov/programs/promiseneighborhoods/index.html?exp=0)

Another major emphasis has been placed on early childhood education. From the beginning of the Obama Administration there has been a major push to create and fully implement funding for all children to have access to quality Pre-K education. An initial set of programs aimed at children living in high-poverty areas was developed as part of the 2004 revision of Head Start. The Obama Administration expanded Head Start's coordination with existing federal programs, including all programs in USED and Health and Human Services (HSS) having an early childhood emphasis, to also include an education component.

In December 2012 the Administration announced a competitive grant program intended to support a limited number of states to develop alternative early childhood programs (USED, 2012). Such alternatives sought to close the achievement gap by providing more extensive early childhood programs. Influential research by Hart and Risley (1995), and others, showed that children from disadvantaged environments entered school with vocabularies of fewer than 6,000 words while middle class children entered school with more than 30,000. This vocabulary deficit was seen to be a major impediment to school success and that early childhood education was critical as well.

Conclusion

In the fifty years since the 1962 enactment of the first version of the ESEA, long-term NAEP trend lines show only a small improvement in achievement for at-risk students. While it can be argued that far too little effort and money may have been spent on low-achieving schools with high numbers of minority students living in poverty, it can also be argued that federal policy frequently changes far too quickly for success to be achieved. As Milton Goldberg, the former head of the commission that wrote *A Nation At Risk* (National Commission for Excellence in Education, 1983), has said (personal interview, 2010), "the American people thinks schools are never changing; the fact is that they are always changing, and that could well be the problem."

In the time since Congress passed the ESEA, one fact is clear: the federal government has tried many different education policies. Originally it was focused on equity and access to instruction; then policy moved towards an emphasis on quality with the use of standards. This was followed by a focus on accountability. Along the way policy programs tried to demonstrate what worked, and demanded the use of research-based practices and specific types of assessments. It has proven to be a dizzying set of ideas, with a confusing array of policies. All of this change is also *prima facie* proof of what Michael Fullan (2006) has taught: "the time line for implementation (of any educational change) is nearly always no longer than the next election" (p. 211).

Federal education policy has tried, and is still trying, to make a big difference in the lives of disadvantaged, disabled, and language minority students. Has it made a difference? The answer is yes, because simply without the federal government there would have been no effort to improve teaching and learning. Any modest gains would likely have been eliminated or reduced and replaced with an even larger, growing achievement gap. Without the ongoing focus on improving education for at-risk learners there likely would have been far less widespread and active concern for the well-being and improvement of outcomes for high need students (disadvantaged, language minority, and disabled). Perhaps the current system of federal involvement and policy is not enough to make the needed positive difference. Perhaps now it is time to ask what more needs to be done in order to make changes that apply all of the positive lessons that have been learned from excellent teachers and administrators found in successful, high-performing schools.

Spotlight Recommendation

Based on some 50 years of experience the federal government has been effective at providing funds, setting goals, and influencing program priorities and program content as well as strategic approaches in education programs. For reading instruction, federal policies have encouraged states to expend funds to benefit children living in poverty, those whose first language is not English, and those who are disabled. One significant feature of these policies has been the establishment of a national goal to close the achievement results gap that exists between children who are at risk and those who are not. The good news is that this gap is closing. However, the achievement gap isn't closing quickly enough for it to be eliminated in the near future.

To be effective federal policies must:

1. Be based on sufficient funding so that children in poverty have access to quality early childhood education programs and to elementary and secondary classrooms with teachers who have the time and training needed to meet the needs of at-risk students.
2. Support effective teacher education programs that produce large numbers of well-educated teachers essential for progress for schools and communities

where high-risk students are found. Community colleges should also be included.

3. Provide expanded federal research programs on effective instruction for high-risk students.
4. Encourage changes in the policy research agenda, focusing greater attention on the range of effective policy options used by states and local education agencies.
5. Support change in the dissemination of research to include more on how to share findings over a multi-year period, using professional societies, social media, professional publications, and other means.

One additional, needed policy change stands out. The federal government needs to stop paying mere lip service to the idea that teachers are important and then building systems, programs, and policies that short-change instruction and teachers. Good teachers are created and encouraged by strong professional education, by mentoring, and by access to relevant current information. It is an essential and ongoing process. All of these recommendations need to be implemented and supported for an extended period of time to become effective.

References

American Recovery and Reinvestment Act of 2009, 123 STAT. U.S.C. § 115 (2009), www .gpo.gov/fdsys/pkg/PLAW-111publ5/pdf/PLAW-111publ5.pdf. Accessed January 20, 2017.

Anderson, R. C., Hiebert, E. H., Scott, J. A., & Wilkenson, I. A. (1984). *Becoming a nation of readers: The Report of the Commission on Reading* (Monograph). Washington, DC: National Institute of Education.

Announcement of flexibility for No Child Left Behind. (n. d.). Retrieved June 17, 2014, from US Department of Education website: www.ed.gov/news/ press-releases/ obama-administration-sets-high-bar-flexibility-no-child-left-behind-order-advanc. Accessed January 20, 2017.

Augustus F. Hawkins-Robert T. Stafford Elementary and Secondary School Improvement Amendments of 1988, 20 U.S.C. § 2940 (1988).

Cross, C. T. (2010). *Political education: National policy comes of age* (updated edition). New York: Teachers College Press.

Duncan, A. (2009, June 14). *States lead the way toward reform* [speech]. Retrieved from US Department of Education website: www2.ed.gov/news/speeches/2009/06/06142009 .html. Accessed January 20, 2017.

Education Amendments of 1974, 20 U.S.C. § 821 (1974).

Elementary and Secondary Education Act, P.L. 89-10, 20 U.S.C. § 205-6 (1965).

Fullan, M. (2016). The New Meaning of Education Change, (fifth edition). New York: Teachers College Press.

Federal Register (2009). Guidance for School Improvement Grants 1003(g) Elementary and Secondary Education Act, 74 Fed. Reg. 65618 (2009).

Hart, B. & Risley, T. R. (1995). *The early catastrophe: The 30 million word gap by age 3.* Retrieved from www.unitedwayracine.org/sites/default/files/imce/files/SOH%20Th

Early Catastrophe -The 30 Million Word Gap by Age 3- Risley and Hart-summary.pdf. Accessed January 20, 2017.

Individuals with Disabilities Education Improvement Act of 2004, 20 U.S.C. § 1400 (2004), http://idea.ed.gov/download/statute.html. Accessed January 20, 2017.

International Reading Association & National Council of Teachers of English. (1996). *Standards for the English Language Arts*. Retrieved from http://www.reading.org/ Libraries/reports-and-standards/bk889.pdf. Accessed January 19, 2017.

Jencks, C., Smith, M., Bane, M. J., Cohen, D., Gintis, H., Heyns, B., & Michelson, S. (1972). *Inequality: A reassessment of the effect of family and schooling in America*. New York: Basic Books, Inc.

Kober, N. (2001, April). *It takes more than testing: Closing the achievement gap*. Retrieved from Center for Education Policy website: www.cep-dc.org/publications/index .cfm?selectedYear=2001. Accessed January 20, 2017.

Long, R. & Selden, R. (2011). How reading research and federal policy on reading instruction have interrelated over the past 38 years. In S. Jay Samuels and Alan E. Farstrup (Eds.). *What research has to say about reading instruction* (pp. 448–462). Newark, DE: International Reading Association.

National Center for Education Statistics. (2012). *National Assessment of Educational Progress Long Term Assessment*. Retrieved from US Department of Education website: http:// nces.ed.gov/nationsreportcard/ltt/. Accessed January 20, 2017.

National Commission for Excellence in Education. (1983, April). *A nation at risk: The imperative for education reform*. Retrieved from United States Department of Education website: www2.ed.gov/pubs/NatAtRisk/index.html

National Reading Panel. (2000). *Teaching children to read: An evidence-based assessment of the scientific research literature on reading and its implications for reading instruction*. Retrieved from National Institutes of Health website: www.nichd.nih.gov/publications/pubs/ nrp/documents/report.pdf. Accessed January 20, 2017.

New York State Department of Education. (2006). *Federal-state education policy chronology 1944-2002* (Monograph). Retrieved from www.archives.nysed.gov/edpolicy/ altformats/ed_research_chronology.pdf

No Child Left Behind, 115 Stat. 1425 U.S.C. § Title I (2002).

President's Commission on Excellence in Special Education. (2002). *A new era: Revitalizing special education for children and their families*. Washington, DC: US Department of Education.

Promise Neighborhoods [Description of promised neighborhoods discretionary grants program]. (n. d.). Retrieved 2010 from US Department of Education website: www2.ed.gov/programs/promiseneighborhoods/index.html?exp=0. Accessed January 20, 2017.

Reading Excellence Act, 115 U.S.C. § 2940 (1998).

Rothman, R. (2011). Touching the third rail: The standards take shape. In *Something in Common: The Common Core Standards and the Next Chapter in American Education* (pp. 53–76). Cambridge, MA: Harvard Education Press.

RTI Action Network. (n. d.). Retrieved June 17, 2014, from National Center on Learning Disabilities website: www.rtinetwork.org/

USED (Ed.). (2009, November). *Race to the Top executive summary*. Retrieved from www .ed.gov website: www2.ed.gov/programs/racetothetop/executive-summary.pdf

USED (Ed.). (2012). *We can't wait: nine states awarded early childhood grants* [White House announcement of early childhood education grants]. (2012, December 16). Retrieved from US Department of Education website: http://www.ed.gov/news/press-releases/ we-cant-wait-nine-states-awarded-race-top-early-learning-challenge-grants-awards

12

SYNTHESIS, DISCUSSION, AND RECOMMENDATIONS

What We Can Do to Advance Reading Achievement

Rosalind Horowitz and S. Jay Samuels

Although closing the reading achievement gap is a worthwhile endeavor, it is not what we are trying to accomplish by means of the ideas presented in this volume. One reason the gap does not close even when the quality of instruction improves is that both groups, the good readers and less effective readers, benefit from the improved instruction—but the gap remains. The critical question we are addressing is what approaches inside or outside classrooms that lead to a proficient level of reading and positive reading-related attitudes and behaviors teachers must focus on so that all students can develop to their potential in the 21st century. Our discussion of the chapters in this book, combined with additional research, lead us to believe that developing a nation of proficient readers seems to be a more realistic attainable goal than closing the achievement gap in reading.

Thus, the key question that we raise in this book is: What must educators do so that all of our students can become proficient readers, capable of acquiring the level of literacy and learning needed for the work world and a good life in the 21st century? The chapters in this book and the *Spotlight Recommendations* proposed by the authors contain a variety of suggestions as solutions to the problems our nation faces. There is commonality among chapters as well as some differences of opinion in how to proceed. In this chapter, we synthesize the approaches, with particular reference to *Spotlight Recommendations*, in order to better understand the difficulties we face and possible ways of overcoming them.

A Root Cause of the Reading Problem is Poverty

First and foremost, the problem in reading achievement does not reside strictly within the schools. Contrary to persisting viewpoints, reading problems or obstacles cannot be resolved strictly by teachers with teaching in the schools.

Chapter 2 by David Berliner is important because he takes a well-reasoned position that the root cause of the reading problem does not reside in the schools themselves, but in poverty, which is a problem that is external to the schools. At the same time, however, he does not rule out what the power of a good teacher may mean nor what a teacher can accomplish. It is just unrealistic, he claims, that one can find a substantial number of teachers who have this high degree of excellence to overcome the pernicious effects of poverty on reading achievement. He acknowledges that the correlation between poverty and academic achievement is not impressive. But it is the combined effects of low-income children, all put in the same school, often with the least experienced teachers, where—due to a smaller amount of parent–child talk and resources—the child comes to school with less vocabulary, less turn-taking speaking practice, and is less well prepared for school interaction and the reading of school texts than the child who comes from a middle or upper class home. In these cases, poverty exerts its pull and effects.

To support his thesis that the major cause of poor performance in reading is not faulty pedagogy, Berliner proposes the concept of what he calls *cohort characteristics*. By this he means that when students are lumped together, the group characteristics, their attitudes, skills, and aspirations for academic achievement, seem to get transferred to those individuals in the group. So, for example, if a student from a poverty family is transferred to a group having a higher income, the student from a poverty family may find improvement in academic achievement. This finding, which seems to be replicated in a number of studies, suggests a simple way to raise reading achievement among children in poverty.

The simple way to raise reading achievement among children experiencing poverty is to bus them to schools where the students at the school come from wealthier families where the level of school achievement is usually higher. Unfortunately, this simple straightforward solution does not work for a number of reasons. One of the reasons it does not work is that there is parental opposition to busing poverty children to schools where middle or upper class children are in attendance. Some parents have moved to particular neighborhoods precisely because they have learned that certain schools do well academically, but bringing in low-performing poverty children may actually lower the school's performance level.

Although busing is not a solution to the achievement problems of children suffering from poverty, there are still other options available that we should try. For example, the schools can increase instruction that may be limited or nonexistent in some homes due to the debilitating effects of poverty—on physical health, mental functioning, hunger, motivation, and energy needed for developing expert skill in various fields of study. For instance, the schools can insert a summer program to elevate learning, as Richard Allington and Anne McGill-Franzen (2017, in this volume) might advocate. Or there may be after-school programs added to the curriculum. Or, the federal government might give prenatal medical care and nutrition to poverty mothers-to-be so their children are not underweight and can begin life with good health. These same mothers might be taught how to interact with their infants so they enter school with a rich vocabulary, discourse styles and forms, and relatedly the concepts that will allow their children to prosper academically. Educators are increasingly aware that reading failure may actually be due to preschool conditions that jeopardize the student's future (see Blanchard & Atwill, 2017, Chapter 5 in this volume) but are reversible.

The strength to Berliner's article is the forceful way he argues that the route one takes to a destination may be wrong! He argues that the solution to underachievement in reading is not due to poor teaching but to poverty, although he acknowledges that a superb teacher can overcome the effects of poverty. But teachers of this quality are in short supply and there are not enough teachers of this quality to solve the problem for the large number of children in poverty across the nation today. Further, we know that high-quality teachers may not stay for long in schools with children in poverty and that these teachers suffer from various forms of "burnout" coupled with low pay and limited support structures.

Berliner is not alone. Allington & McGill-Franzen (2017, in this book), concur with Berliner. They indicate unequivocally, "The gap is not primarily attributable to ineffective schools or teachers." (p. 174). Later, they argue "In other words the identification of high poverty schools as failing schools and the identification of teachers in these buildings as failing teachers … are fundamentally inaccurate" (p. 175). The strict focus on schools and school reforms are examples of pervasive myths and the multiple inaccuracies associated with children and youth experiencing poverty and failing to succeed in literacy or in schools at-large that have not been sufficiently recognized as myths and reversed (see Berliner & Glass, 2014).

We have all heard the saying that goes something like this: "I do not have to be a millionaire, I just want to live like one." If we apply the underlying idea of this saying to Berliner's thesis that poverty is the root cause of the achievement differences between the children of the poor and children of the rich, we can come up with a clue as to how we can help the children of the poor to higher reading achievement. It is obvious that the government will not simply hand over money to poor to raise their income, but the federal government can, nevertheless, help them to live like the rich by providing food for their children, health care for the mother during pregnancy, summer school, and training on how to increase the amount and quality of talk the mother has with her child so that the child is ready for school communications. When the government provides these services that the poverty family does not have, i.e., the actual wealth of the richer families, the poverty family is able to live like the richer families.

While Berliner presents convincing arguments in his chapter that it is poverty that is the detrimental force causing the reading achievement gap that exists between the children who live in poverty and their more affluent fellow students, it is at the point of the role of education that we take a small but important step away from agreeing completely with Berliner's position. His position is that the classroom teacher can have a significant positive impact on reading achievement but it takes a highly skilled teacher, knowledgeable about the obstacles of poverty, to do that, and we have too few of them to make a meaningful impact. Our position is captured to a small degree by the automobile bumper sticker on cars that says, "If you can read this, thank a teacher." Our position is that teachers can have a value-added effect on what children learn. And our goal is to raise the level of all students, the poor as well as the rich, to where they are competent readers. Each of the chapters in this book has something important to say about how educators can indeed achieve this goal. And we believe this is a real possibility, doable if we set this as our goal.

Edmund Gordon and Paola Heincke, astutely advances a broader perspective than typically has been taken when addressing the achievement gap. They alerts us that the lack of achievement in particular social groups has been an issue that has been visible for 65 years, most of Edmund Gordon's professional life! It is an issue that James Coleman addressed in *The Coleman Report* (1966), which described the reading gap as due to teacher expectations and a self-fulfilling prophecy. Gordon reminds us that we have made errors in the ways in which we have tackled this problem in the United States. It is disheartening that socioeconomic status is highly associated with reading proficiency in the United States, more so than in many other nations in the world, as Guthrie and McRae convey.

Preschool Education Can Make a Difference

Preschool education also can make a world of difference in preparing students to succeed in reading performance in school. It can influence the knowledge children bring and attitude a child holds about reading for a lifetime. In some cities, preschool education has been substantially increased in order to prepare children in poverty for the education that they will encounter in schools. Rural and remote areas historically neglected in educational reform in the United States have not had, for the most part, the opportunity of preschool education. Nor have many locations in the southernmost part of the United States been offered this opportunity.

Allington and McGill-Franzen report from numerous studies (Reardon, 2013) that there has been progress with African American children in reading, reducing the gap between White children, however, we have actually been less effective with children of poverty. Low-income children enter school at a great disadvantage ranking at the bottom-third of their peers. They do not know letter names or the sounds of the letters (Chapter 10 in this volume). This teaches children vital learning skills such as the act of discrimination, developed through recognizing significant features of letters and sounds. Low-income children's preschool life with literacy may be minimal, as Berliner, Blanchard and Atwill, Horowitz and Samuels, Long and Farstrup, and others have argued in this volume—with fewer experiences with reading and writing, and listening to and talking about books, than children from more affluent homes.

Chapter 5 in this volume by Jay Blanchard and Kim Atwill incorporates knowledge gained from work with a preschool group of Indigenous reservation Indians. Their chapter contains a sad message conveying that for many Indian children reading failure starts well before they ever enter school because many of these children lack the prerequisite skills and oral vocabulary that are paramount for a successful start in school. For some children, even the motivation to learn to read may be missing. Jay Samuels reports that one preschool Zuni youngster told his classroom teacher he did not have to learn to read because it was not necessary, as he was planning to make jewelry when he became old enough and reading would not be required for that. As Blanchard and Atwill point out, if a poor attitude about learning to read is not enough of an obstacle to overcome, some of the native children live in remote areas of reservation where getting to the school bus on time, after battling the snow drifts, may be a huge problem. Missing the bus has important consequences because it leads to a lost day of instruction at school. Catching up is hard to do and reading books as part of homework after dinner may be impossible because the homes that are remote lack electricity. For some of the Indigenous students who live in remote areas the tribal language may be language used at home. Some of the children may have a culturally unique vocabulary so that understanding the teacher or the language used in their school-based books presents a real problem. Or they may have been taught to treasure silence over talk or believe that they should not speak out to elders. These are all factors that may not be considered by European American classroom teachers as they design curriculum and prepare for daily instruction but may prove to be a significant challenge to reading in schools.

The need for vocabulary development, specifically, that will enhance school learning is addressed by Blanchard and Atwill, but we wish here to call your attention to a vocabulary need that is instrumental for classroom learning, but is not addressed often in texts in teacher training dealing with learning to read. The important omitted topic is referred to as *the language of instruction*. The language of instruction is critical because it contains the key words that teachers use when teaching children to read. It contains key words like *letter, word, paragraph, uppercase* and *lowercase, letter sound, vowel* and *consonant*, and dozens of other words used in instruction. One reason these critical words are not taught as vocabulary is that teachers mistakenly assume the students know these words. Failure to know these words can lead to early school failure. If a teacher tells the students to count five words over, what does the student need to know in order to do the task? The student must know what a *word* is. For many children, this is acquired at a very young age, even before school (Horner & Olson, 1999), but in other instances these words are unknown. A word in the context of what the teacher wants has nothing to do with meaning. A word for purposes of counting simply means "a letter, or group of letters," surrounded by a space.

As important as the language of instruction is, and we think all students should know what the terms mean, what we do not know is what the earliest and best ages are for teaching some of these vocabulary terms. Could most students learn what a *word* is during preschool or at home from parents? Then, by all means they should be taught its meaning, early on, as it is used in language instruction.

Although closing the achievement gap in reading is not the specific goal of this book, Blanchard and Atwill cleverly give an explanation of how it occurs and how to avoid the learning gap. To do so they evoke Keith Stanovich's (1986) *Mathew Effects in Learning*. It is not a difficult concept to grasp but it is important. If Native American children, or other children in poverty, experience difficulty learning to read, they will tend to avoid reading-related activities and fail to practice reading. This is also discussed at length by John Guthrie and McRae with African American adolescents in Chapter 3. Getting off to a bad start and avoiding reading, according to research, means the children do not develop in reading through the elementary and secondary grades, even extending into adulthood, which ultimately affects the likelihood of the adult being employed. On the other hand, students who have success in learning to read, early on, will read more and through greater practice will get better. This tendency for the rich to get richer and the poor to get poorer is characterized as the underlying process of the achievement gap. The trick is to avoid early reading failure and for all students to find pleasure and have success in the early phases of the learning process, and that is the underlying reason for the preschool training.

Blanchard and Atwill draw heavily from the *Pump Up the Volume in Preschool* (PVIP) and the *Montana RBC Indigenous Project* to illustrate how the staff made their programs culturally responsive so the payoff was that the students did well with a successful start in kindergarten. Note that Blanchard tells us that these interventions for indigenous populations with a research base are relatively new and, for the most part, did not exist until 2003. Cultural artifacts, tribal languages, and culturally responsive books were used. A reasonable concern that we have is, will we be able to bring high quality preschool education to all indigenous children? Of great concern are the indigenous children who are hard to reach because they live in rural and remote areas.

A kindergarten through eighth-grade student who is a proficient reader should possess ability with speed and accuracy in word recognition. Also, and this is important, by definition, the ability to construct a meaning can come at any grade level. So, a first grader who is reading a first-grade text and who constructs meaning is proficient for that level of text. A second point to be emphasized is that no one is proficient on all topics and in all content or styles of reading. For example, a person may be highly trained reading psychology texts but prove to be inadequate reading a chemistry text with understanding and memory. The final point to be made is that when we think of proficiency in reading we think of a good reader;

the *No Child Left Behind* assessments sought to achieve success in reading for all children but this was not achieved.

English Language Learners Should Master the Language within the Context of Domains of Knowledge such as Mathematics, Science, Social Studies, and the Humanities and Arts

In Chapter 3 by Robert Jiménez, Sam David, Mark Pacheco, Victoria Risko, Lisa Pray, Keenan Fagan and Mark Gonzales, the authors pursue the extremely difficult task of helping English language learners [ELL] master the English language while at the same time helping them to learn the content of math, science, and social studies by a teacher who in many cases cannot speak the same language that the students speak at home. What makes this task so important and arduous is that we have a large and growing number of ELL students in American classrooms faced with this situation in which the text is written in English, and while the students may be able to decode the text, they do not understand its contents.

Under ideal conditions both the students and the teacher can speak the same language. To illustrate how the teacher can help students when they all share a common language, the chapter starts out with a Spanish speaking instructor working with Hispanic students and the task facing the students is to learn the meaning of the word "league," as in Little League. The teacher skillfully guides the students to realize there is a Spanish cognate *liga* that is similar in meaning to the English word. The lesson goes well and there are strengths in the teaching, in that the students learn there are many English words that have Spanish cognates, and the students seem motivated to cooperate and learn.

Considerable instructional difficulty arises when the teacher and students do not share a common language, and this is frequently the problem faced by students and their teacher, alike, particularly in urban schools. To add to this difficulty, teachers face the fact that in addition to helping the students learn how to translate the ideas in the English text into their own vocabulary, the instructor must at the same time help the students master the content of mathematics, science, and the other subjects that are part of the curriculum. As the authors of this important article point out, over much of the 20th century, teacher training colleges did not, and we find still do not, address this issue by training teachers to work with ELL students. On the plus side, the Jiménez et al. article explicates a brief scenario of how a talented teacher, who does not speak the home language of the students, manages to get across the concepts embedded in the English text; more examples of this practice are occurring in colleges of education, with practice in actual school classrooms needed. It would be helpful if videos could be taken to show how successful teachers who do not speak the home language of the students manage to help students understand the English texts that they commonly encounter in school and, thereby, bridge the family language and culture with the school academic languages and cultures. (Noguera, Wing, & Yonemura, 2006).

Addressing Language and Cultural Differences Requires Understanding of Diversity *within* a Given Culture and *across* Cultures

Early on in Chapter 4 by John Guthrie and Angela McRae, there is reference to the diversity within the African American population, a matter often overlooked in academic journals and national reports of school data. These groups include what Guthrie and McRae refer to as (a) *a transcendent group*—with economic wealth, power and influence, (b) *a mainstream group*—the middle group, a majority group with full stake in American society, (c) *an emerging group*—with mixed race and heritage, and Black immigrants, and (d) *an abandoned minority*—with less hope of escape from poverty, with educational difficulties. Many academic reports do not specify the particular group within the African American population to which they are referring, making discussions incomplete and less applicable for solving problems in schools, and making it difficult for transportable/comparable results to different contexts or situational settings usable across the United States.

Although they distinguish among African American populations, Guthrie and McRae early on in their contribution tell us that they depart from an emphasis prevalent in the literature on the structural and cultural elements of society that may influence African American school achievement. While Guthrie and McRae refer to the obstacles in the environment such as poverty, limited skills, joblessness, and limitations of opportunities for advancing education, incorporating many of Berliner's obstructions found in a life of poverty, these researchers depart from the sociologically oriented literature to an emphasis on factors inside the mind of the student, namely motivational factors transmitted to active engagement behaviors that are vital to school reading and reading achievement (Guthrie, 2016). They identify prominent African American figures who spent many years of disciplined learning, sometimes up to 10 years, to acquire expertise in a field; they were voracious readers and are now highly visible luminaries. For example, the surgeon Ben Carson had a passion for "learning through literacy." The successful examples of high literacy achievement remain missing from the school accounts of success. There is limited research to which to turn that describes voracious readers and their reading practices other than Victor Nell's (1988) *Lost in a Book*, which is a behavioral research study of hundreds of adults on two continents who read voraciously. Examples of children and youth who are voracious readers are limited and research should consider how they became engrossed in books and sustained their passion for reading under a range of settings.

Expanding Oral Language and Discourse Opportunities (in Listening) and Uses (in Speaking) Will Contribute to Language Processing in Reading (and Writing)

Speech (and its counterpart listening) has been identified as central to the development of language and literacy (reading, writing, and learning) (Horowitz, 2007; Horowitz & Samuels, 1985), yet remains neglected in research and teacher training in literacy education—whether it be reading education, writing development, training of reading specialists, or special education teachers. Oral language achievements begin with astute perceptions of prosodic features of language (e.g., pitch, rhythm, pauses), oral vocabulary knowledge, macrostructural knowledge, syntax, or discourse processes such as listening, retelling, and remembering, in a range of genres such as descriptive explanations, following procedures, giving an opinion, or arguing persuasively for a change or new idea (Horowitz, 2007; 2015; Kim, 2015; 2016; Searle, 1975; Spiro & Tirre, 1980; Weisleder & Fernald, 2013).

The contributions of parent–child interaction are identified as central to a child's achievement in school and discussed in Chapter 9 by Paul and Gilkerson. They refer to the Hart and Risley (1995) study that interestingly, 20 years later, has been resurrected and cited extensively to show some children hear far more words in parent–child exchanges (mostly mothers talking with children) than welfare low-income children, as revealed in audiotapes of family interactions.

Paul and Gilkerson emphasize that "Voluminous research connects oral language and vocabulary to reading comprehension and academic success. Hart and Risley showed that talk is the foundation" (pp. 151). Hart and Risley argued that their study of 7-month to 3-year-olds interacting with parents, including 1,300 hours of recordings, explains the reading and mathematics achievement gap years later, at age 10. Paul and Gilkerson describe the value and use of their new technology, the *Language Environment Analysis System* (LENA), developed to more efficiently record words of a parent or caregiver and number of conversations. The recordings are transferred to a computer that segments the oral expressions of a child, adult, and even television and other electronic sounds, which also produce speech that children regularly encounter but usually are not incorporated as speech in home environment studies. Their new technology has the potential for increasing child–adult speech research—that may be used, as noted, with a variety of special populations such as the deaf or autistic.

Paul and Gilkerson report that mother talk plays an important role in achievement, also referred to by other researchers in our book, although father talk is neglected in child and linguistic research sources in this book and elsewhere. They convey a Chinese study showed important seasonal variation as a factor in talk, with summer parent–child talk less than winter parent–child talk. Also noteworthy is that mothers talk more to their daughters than sons, although why this may be the case is not clear.

A somewhat similar claim about the quantity of talk and its effects of learning also were associated with Basil Bernstein in the 1970s and 1980s, as he characterized an *elaborated code*, more word use in some mother–child interaction, in contrast to a *restricted code*, limited language use said to be found in lower-income homes in the United Kingdom. Bernstein's attention to a class manifested in oral codes, years ago, gained attention by linguists, sociologists, anthropologists, psychologists, and educators, across the world, as it was met with intense controversy. While Bernstein received heavy criticism, today his work is being re-evaluated, and in some educational circles deemed important research for developing language styles and competence in language relevant to schooling. The view given today is that some language may be working in a restricting manner and other language forms as elaborating concepts and building relationships among ideas and agents of expression. Moore (2013) has recently argued that Bernstein's elaborated code promoted a universalistic meaning, as opposed to the restricted code which promoted a circumscribed, contextually limited language and meaning—which he argues was subjected to misinterpretations.

In the case of Hart and Risley, their work has of late received strong criticism as well, like Bernstein, from anthropologists and linguists who argue that there are cultural differences in patterns of talk and more words may not always mean better. For instance, in some cultures a short-lived gaze or body-tilt, a fast-paced expression or an increase or decrease in voice volume, elevated pitch from a parent signals a negative remark, inferences, and interpretations. Thus, although not verbally stated, or quantifiable in word counts, culturally-based expressions are understood by the receiving interlocutor in the context of use. On the other hand, we know increased knowledge of vocabulary and uses of words are a high scientific predictor of performance in reading comprehension and success in test-taking about reading as well. The more words a child hears and speaks, the more words the child will be able to process when reading (or listening) and use when writing or in some instances thinking through a problem or argument.

Paul and Gilkerson recommend we close the achievement gap by not only increasing parent–child talk, but also improving on talk turn-taking—a feature of healthy conversations. Talk turns are part of the social-interactive process of communication, where one speaker builds on and comments upon topics introduced by the previous speaker, with new input. They offer several recommendations for parent education. But they are not the first. In 1966, Gina Ortar, a child development researcher in Israel, called for training mothers in strategies for speaking to and with one's children. In 1971, Ortar articulated the importance of parent training in talk with one's child, for child development outside of school, and as central to advancing achievement in school and language production and processing.

Paul and Gilkerson remind us that the Hart and Risley research shows professional parents talk more to their children than welfare or working class parents, with children in homes with professional parents having high vocabulary. It is important to note that there was variation within the family categories studied (e.g., mothers who did not complete high school and those who graduated from college). This conveys that the amount of talk is not strictly an SES issue.

With turn count proving the most valuable metric related to achievement, Paul and Gilkerson suggest that this measures an aspect of communication that reflects social relationships, social engagement, emotional connections, and knowledge of discourse processes. While book reading research studies have largely looked at the dialogic aspects of communication, they also represent a "close physical contact" or rapport and social skills of "engagement" and overall effective communication between parent and child.

Recommendations are made for improving the quantity of talk and turn taking between parent and child and there is discussion that feedback with instructions can be most helpful in increasing parent talk. Paul and Gilkerson's *Spotlight Recommendation* also calls for book reading and reducing attention to television/screen time. Another important recommendation is that parents should respond to the "communicative cues" and talk initiated by the child/infant—more important than getting the baby to simply respond to adult talk/cues. There are several types of intervention centers suggested as options for building talk, but most important is that the talk gap must be addressed at the start of a child's life if there is to be a reduction of the achievement gap. Thus, they say, "A focus on improving words and turns, shared book reading, and turning off electronic media is the best way to close the talk gap, and may also be an efficient way to improve the social and emotional environment" (pp. 164).

One factor worth emphasizing is that today's children in low-income families do not come from a home where there is both a mother and father to whom they can turn. Many children are in single-parent households. Further, the family may consist of extended members such as a grandparent, or uncle or adult sibling, so talk may be in a first language with this adult—not English. We have yet to learn about how cultural backgrounds, intergenerational teachings and learning, and community lifestyles and practices are represented in these family dialogues and influence language development, learning to read proficiently, and knowledge for higher literacy.

Motivation: Reading Can Be Propelled by Curiosity, Self-Sustained Intrigue, and by Creating Attention and Interest

Reading researchers have studied cognitive and meta-cognitive strategies in reading for the last half of the 20th century. We have taken a turn to the social, affective factors of communication that are shown to be valuable in creating and sustaining interest and reading growth. The reading of mammoth Dostoevsky Russian novels is pursued by youth and adults when there is high motivation and interest for this type of Russian literature that incorporates intergenerational family stories.

Teachers set the stage for motivating students to read by designing curriculum, reading tasks, or situations that encourage curiosity, intrigue with text content, self-sustained questioning, and ultimately interest in learning. Students must develop intrinsic motivation that fires up the learner and keeps one moving forward. Guthrie and McRae's research identifies some of the factors that contribute to the learner's achievement in reading. These motivational factors may reduce the achievement gap for African American populations or other ethnic groups as well. Students who develop curiosity are their own leaders, as they become intrigued with a topic or seek to ask or answer long-held questions, developing a solid passion for the search for information. This human passion, an internal drive coupled with controlled behavior, carries the student forward with a persisting kind of inquiry that sustains itself and recycles attention (Lowenstein, 1994). The challenge is to ignite this process.

Guthrie and McRae identify three specific forms of *engagement*: (a) *cognitive engagement, thinking deeply*, (b) *motivational engagement* such as interest or aversion toward a subject, and (c) *active, behavioral engagement*—concentrating and focusing attention on class and school at-large attendance. Guthrie and McRae cite studies that show that behavioral engagements, *student effort, time*, and *persistence*, on a task help students sustain cognitive involvement with text and, in turn, succeed at reading and grow in achievement. The school behaviors that are counterproductive in schoolwork are not attending, skipping classes, being late, cheating on tests, and being sent to the principal's office. Interestingly, classroom participation was highly correlated with grades in school for African American males and high participators "… had solid expectations for future education." What is worth noting is that Guthrie and McRae argue signs of behavioral engagement are related to achievement, even surpassing the variables of vocabulary knowledge or mother's education, highlighted by several researchers in this volume. Completion of homework by African Americans correlated significantly with reading achievement and grades. Research by Frontera and Horowitz on student homework completion as it relates to grades, by Hispanics, suggests the completion of homework may be an index of acceptance of school requirements and goals and an important variable across cultural groups. Guthrie and McRae believe and, we concur, that we can teach these engagement acts.

Guthrie and McRae's chapter and research shows that the value of education is lower for adolescent African Americans than white European Americans. But how do students come to value education? Appreciation for education, for one, comes from parent discourse about the importance of education; from extended family members, siblings, grandparents, and peer groups; and ultimately from a "buy in" about the importance of reading to ignite or accomplish educational and work-related tasks. It may also emerge through spiritual and religious instruction, as was the case for founders of America, who emphasized Bible reading. A student's own creation of firm goals and dreams propel reading. Imagining oneself as an accomplished architect, pianist, or doctor on the border may be influential in completing reading assignments. We need to talk about these goals with our children and youth, a dialogue that used to regularly occur in the home.

The emotional component in learning has been neglected for too long in the research literature on motivation, yet Ainley and Hidi (2014) as well as Renninger and Hidi (2016) indicate that it is a powerful construct in sustaining attention and interest in school learning. Their research provides avenues for revisiting motivation in short-term and long-term achievements.

Guthrie and McRae argue, "It was the behavioral engagement, rather than demographic characteristics of learners that most markedly impacted reading achievement" (p. 63). The African Americans Guthrie and McRae studied had "solid expectations for future education and were substantially higher achievers than students with less participation or lower expectations" (pp. 63). So it is *student expectations and aspirations* that may overpower teacher expectations, the latter to which we gave high profile in the 60s and 70s. But we are reminded in the chapter by Guthrie and McRae that literate behaviors and motivation must be sustained over time with controlled effort and persistence. Further, African American students often disengage from school agendas as a "self-protective measure" due to low self-esteem and fear of failure. What is interesting is that the research presented in their chapter shows that African American behavioral engagement may operate differently than that of the European Americans studied and can be developed. Based on our collective teaching experiences, Samuels and Horowitz found African American adolescent students valued low-achievers in their community based on clothes or sports; however, Guthrie and McRae find in elementary grades African Americans valued high achievers, but this changed as they entered adolescence and secondary grades. Finally, they argue that for African Americans, the neglect of reading has more "deleterious effects" than it has for European American adolescent students, a matter elementary teachers need to recognize. Dedication, exemplified by time, effort, and persistence, they note, is highly valued and rewarded by teachers and results in high grades, which also increases motivation and the learner's persistence.

As students pursue secondary education and acquire expertise in content fields, high volumes of time and disciplined practice are essential requirements. Guthrie and McRae evoke the violinist, the baseball player, and chess masters, who spend large amounts of concentrated time at their practices as they acquire expertise (a theme S. Jay Samuels has lectured on for years). In Chapter 8, reference is made to the Chinese mother's demands for sustained study and homework completion, all of which may be a training ground for dedication and persistence in developing expertise in secondary school disciplines. Guthrie and McRae argue that valuing reading results in dedication and increases reading comprehension, and so is most important over what might be strictly one-time motivations.

Finally, Guthrie and McRae introduce an intervention method called *Concept-Oriented Reading Instruction* (CORI) for third through seventh graders, which requires the teacher to incorporate (a) relevant, hands-on activities, (b) choice among options, (c) potentially successful reading, (d) peer collaboration, (e) thematic units based on big ideas, and (f) added "importance" or "value rational" used with college students. They argue that this type of reading instruction increased valuing reading for students at several levels of poverty. CORI proved to be effective in increasing dedication for both African Americans and European Americans, but it decreased avoidance to reading more so for African Americans. If we can move African American students—and all others—who devalue reading to a valuing of reading, we will have set them up for effective reading practice, growing self-esteem about reading, and ultimately achievement.

Learners must be able to evaluate their ability to perform specific tasks, monitor self confidence, and determine means for self-regulation as they read. Students must constantly make psychological judgments about their ability to read a story, textbook, and expository information in a content field and to perform on related speaking and writing activities. This ability to judge one's skill will contribute to reading interest, practice, and ultimately achievement. Researchers Denissen, Zarrett, and Eccles (2007) stress the importance of one's personal perception of sense of ability and success at reading, and Ainley and Hidi (2014) show the role of interest and enjoyment in motivation are vital. In order to continue reading in a given area, students will need to experience genuine curiosity before reading and bursts of joy during or after the reading. Guthrie and McRae argue that individual resilience is more powerful an approach than cultural historical factors. This may appear to contradict Jiménez and colleagues, who call for emphasizing cultural factors in reading instruction, but on the other hand it may also complement their teacher cultural response approach to reading. Other scholars, specifically addressing secondary school populations, have argued that peer pressure is a powerful variable in reducing reading interests and goals particularly for middle and high school students. The CORI intervention decreased African American middle grade students devaluing of informational books and reading comprehension. Finally, the research reported is evidence that behavioral engagement of time, effort, and persistence influences African American learners more so than European American learners when European American learners who are studied are a more motivated group than African Americans studied in the research.

In their *Spotlight Recommendations*, sociological variables, such as income, housing, health, are said to correlate with literacy as noted by other contributors to this volume, but we are alerted that there is no evidence that development of strategic social programs will influence literacy. These sociological variables, thus, may just be worth scientific research and federal and state funding. The focus of this chapter is on the learner, the cognitive shift in the valuing of reading and its influence on reading, and the strategies for learning in the classroom, and there is attention to scientific inquiry that will make a difference—all meritorious goals.

Conceptualizing and Measuring Achievement in Reading is Complex

Michael Harwell states that statistical measures used are instrumental in understanding gaps. They can play a role in how we conceptualize gaps in reading between and within groups and are indicative of a gap between Black and White subjects. Usually mean differences between racial groups are the focus of quantitative measures of groups and standard deviations. Harwell's *Spotlight Recommendation* is that study of *variability* in reading performance within Black and White groups can provide valuable information about the antecedents/precursors of gaps, the value of particular approaches for policy and practice implementations to reduce reading achievement gaps, and also the nature and meaning of the gaps. As noted by researchers addressing policy implementations, the methods for developing policy need to be given our serious attention and addressed by way of the research methods employed (McDonnell & Weatherford, 2016).

How to best measure reading achievement performance, gaps, and successes has also been of concern in reviews of international comparative reports. Rosalind Horowitz presents in Chapter 8 what is depicted as an International Brain War. Adolescent reading proficiency, performance, and achievement have been presented from a competitive global perspective with sometimes the tone of marketing a business model. This competition strategy is used to juxtapose differences in performance in reading assessments, also used prematurely or inappropriately for policy reform. It is not clear what generates different levels of performance within populations or across nations. The international reports provide little background or cultural information. Furthermore, the reforms acted upon in particular nations or neighborhoods need analysis and reconnecting to the reading performance and achievement measures and findings. As in many reforms, sufficient time must be invested in determining whether the new efforts have been effectively exercised and take hold.

Time and Place: Variables That Influence Achievement and Human Development

Reading researchers are consistently vehement that time allocated for reading is a significant factor in the equation which leads to reading achievement. Schools have, of late, reduced playtime to increase reading and math time. While reading time may be too often limited within schools, outside of schools, many adolescents, and children alike, are rarely reading extended discourse, argumentation, or opinion-type book length sources, and other printed volumes outside of schools.

Richard Allington and Anne McGill-Franzen identify studies in Chapter 10 that show that low-income children can and do gain as much as middle- and high-income children in reading achievement during the school year. However, the rub is in the summer months. During the summer, high income children may have rich opportunities to read through attendance at a camp—including reading and writing camps, art, music, and sports camps, and religious camps. Moreover, the financially able family travels, whether nationally or internationally, during the summer, increasing talk time in cars, on airplanes, or on trains. Overall, this oral expression expands the prior knowledge that children will bring to the act of reading and increases access to the kinds of printed resources and books to which children have been exposed. Thus, Allington and McGill-Franzen agree with Berliner that the reading gap is *not* due to ineffective teaching of the poor but rather due to what we heard 30 years ago, that summer reading loss was the major cause of the poor/rich reading gap! It is between second and sixth grade over four summers that we see significant differences in reading achievement that are never regained.

Further, it must be clear that it is the children of the more financially able who attend preschool—not the poor.

What is important to note is that the poor child is less likely to read a book during the summer, or go to a library or bookstore. Over 40 years ago, poor and rich alike did go to libraries during the summer. It was not an unusual time to see mothers in major cities like Minneapolis, Boston, and Chicago help their children find books and in some cities for mothers and children to haul a pile of books as they walked home for reading time. Today, with single-parent families, and parents working more jobs, attention to bringing books home from the library is not a common summer priority or occurrence. In some cities and states, there are not many libraries. Further, schools may be closed and restrict the reading over the summer and the number of books children may check out. Thus, with few computer resources for use in reading, the gap widens during the summer. Allington and McGill-Franzen stress that the federal government has paid little attention to summer loss, although the issue has been addressed by scholars for more than a century. An important matter to note is what Horowitz and Samuels strive to highlight in this volume, that the summer loss factor is one that is not unique to a given city, as the studies that are reported in Chapter 10 reveal the same phenomenon occurs in many cities throughout the country. Also of note is that the present chapter argues that the summer loss of reading is due to less family involvement and community resources and methods available to support reading.

The *Spotlight Recommendation* proposed by Allington and McGill-Franzen is straightforward and simple to implement. They find that intervention which gives the poor an opportunity to self-select books is essential. When children choose what they want to read they are investing in the choice and it is a personal one. Allowing children to hold and keep the books is a sign of ownership and would also allow for rereading, common when the book is treasured. They allowed poor children to select 12 to 15 books for summer reading and they recommend this number for the three-month period. Their second suggestion, that we open school libraries for a portion of the week, over the summer, is a reasonable request. A third recommendation, which is to distribute three or four self-selected books on the final day of school, makes sense, with a scheduled return date to swap books. The fourth recommendation to schedule bus trips to neighborhoods with books that can be selected is valuable. Thus, the proposals here are for bringing more books to the children or children to the books and giving them genuine choice.

Federal and state funding for these alternatives are needed.

Attention to the 21st Century and Advancing Reading Achievement

Not only Allington, but The American Educational Research Association (AERA) *Knowledge Forum, Research Fact Sheet* concurs the gaps for many students are equivalent to three to four years of schooling (Kim, 2016). In high schools, we have found teenage writers may be performing at a second-grade level, due to lack of writing experience and low motivation. Unfortunately, writing has been given little attention or funding but is a powerful influence on reading.

This volume has focused on African American, Hispanic, and Indigenous populations. But we wish to recognize that there are many groups that the research literature has neglected who encounter substantial struggles in achieving proficiency in reading that will lead to a quality life. These include the growing number of youth who are homeless and have no set location for reading at home and could but choose not to read. There are the border crossers who travel regularly across Mexico and the United States, code switching, but not reading proficiently in either of the two languages. There are the new immigrants from China, Malaysia, or Africa and India. There are the males whose affiliations are with gangs. There are the poor who lack books in their homes or computers for processing text and writing tools. There are the disabled and physically abused. There are regions in the United States that have been neglected such as Appalachia, vicinities in the South, border regions, desert-like areas in the West, or northern regions.

What We Have Learned from Past Reforms

We began this book in Chapter 1 with a brief historical reference to national reforms. As noted, the emphasis on standards, testing, and comparing of scores has *not* yielded a higher level of reading achievement in the United States. The contributors to this volume suggest ways of building commitment to reading growth in teacher cultural responses, reading engagement behaviors, preschool practices, dialogue, and sustained summer reading or after-school programs.

Richard Long and Alan Farstrup's review in Chapter 11 of federal reforms intended to close achievement gaps, dating back to the 1964 *War on Poverty*, do show efforts to bring "fairness and equity" to the American way of life. These efforts, we are reminded, included attention to schools but also factors external to the school—housing, voting, and health, the latter discussed in several locations in the present book. What started out as federal funding for reading evolved into standards, requirements, and reporting procedures whereby the joys of individual reading and cultural group achievements were lost.

Long and Farstrup begin their discussion in 1965 with the *Elementary and Secondary Education Act* (ESEA), and Title I. In this first trend, it was believed that more funds were required for school programs in order to reduce the achievement gap. The states and districts determined the assessment of educational quality. A second trend was focus on federally financed reading programs and hopes that research-based information would bring success. In the 1970-1980s the Center for the Study of Reading produced research reports with results that were widely circulated, but their influence on practice may have been minimal. In the 1990s there was more explicit focus on scientific-based reading research and a focus on beginning reading and equity instruction. Access to good information on reading was viewed as the key to achievement in student reading. However, National Assessment of Education (NAEP) scores failed to show programs that eliminated the achievement gap.

A third trend was focus on the culture of poverty. Long and Farstrup report that in 1990s school-wide models were needed and since funding was used state by state, in a variety of ways, consistency across states was needed to avoid a child's education being determined by residency. The fourth trend is associated with *No Child Left Behind*, amazingly an eighth revision of ESEA! Long and Farstrup note a realization that equity in access to achievement was insufficient and that proficiency in reading meant applying thinking to more complex information, which became the hallmark in 2012. There was also the new *Response to Intervention* (RTI), with reading performance screening and monitoring, and evidence-based instructional methods. Long and Farstrup make the important point that at this time there is a realization that "behavior and mental health" can have a significant influence on learning and reading, a concern that may still warrant our attention. A fifth trend, President Obama's policy initiative, included attention to the lowest performing schools and *Race to the Top*. Their chapter pinpoints flexibility in state efforts and relief from the *No Child Left Behind* controls. Interestingly, the *Promise Neighborhoods Grants* that came about have a greater community focus on achievement, a matter Ralph Tyler called for in the 1990s and before.

Recently noteworthy in new trends and reforms is that federal and state attention have shifted to high school students and academic success, with efforts to facilitate the transition to college and work. The focus has been on moving Hispanics, African Americans, and Native American students rapidly into and through higher education (see Crisp, Taggart, & Nora, 2015; Selingo, 2016)

This 50-year track record of federal policies and reforms is revealing. Efforts have been focused on teachers, children, and school systems but are not at all comprehensive or interconnected in vision. The knowledge of teachers and other school personnel has not been properly exercised and as Long and Farstrup note there has not been sufficient time for reforms to take hold before a new reform is operationalized. To what extent have educational researchers been included in decision-making processes? The tide has shifted, but without long-range planning and without solid demographic, cultural, and research-based knowledge as guideposts about the future of the American and American society (Ravitch, 2010).

Cross-Discipline and Cross-Leadership Approaches are Needed for Reading Achievement by All

This volume suggests that schools cannot go it alone. Family, social groups, and cultural factors outside of schools play a substantial role in reading achievement, but less is known about these out-of-school sociocultural factors: parents, community services, neighborhood forces and centers, health resources, political institutions, and spiritual resources. But at the same time there is evidence and concern by prominent researchers that we must build a student's internal motivations for reading so they value the possibilities reading offers toward structuring goals in life. This is emphasized by Gordon and Heincke. Suggestions are posed by Guthrie and McRae that are internal to the student and by Blanchard and Atwill that are external to the student, and Jimenez and colleagues highlight the importance of teacher knowledge and responses to the culture of the student.

This book offers perspectives by notable scholars. These perspectives offer possible approaches for bringing reading achievement to all. The perspectives offered do not need to operate in competition with one another, but rather can complement one another through collaboration among diverse researchers, administrators, leadership, and teachers. Professional organizations and education and government officials and administrators must bring together a variety of experts to work toward overcoming the obstructions and narrow perspectives that have yet to be re-conceptualized and operationalized.

Recognizing the Complexity: Commonalities versus Contradictions in Educational Research and Planning

Jerome Bruner has recognized the complexity of educational aims (1996) and referred to the contradictions that we face in designing educational aims. This is also true for establishing goals for academic achievements in reading.

> As in most revolutionary times, our times are caught up in contradictions.... Indeed, contradictions in such times often turn out to be antinomies— *pairs of large truths, which ... contradict each other.* Antinomies provide fruitful grounds not only for strife, but also for reflection. For they remind us that truth does not exist independently of the perspectives of those who hold them to be so.
>
> Educational truths in revolutionary times are also afflicted by antinomies.... The first antinomy is this: on the one hand, it is unquestionably the function of education to enable people, individual human beings, to operate to their fullest potentials, to equip them with the tools and the sense of opportunity to use their wits, skills, passions to the fullest. The ... counterpart to this is that the function of education is to reproduce the culture that supports it—not only reproduce it, but further its economic, political, and cultural ends.
>
> But can schooling be construed both as the instrument of individual realization and at the same time as reproductive technique for maintaining or furthering culture [or cultures]? (pp. 66–67, *italics ours*)

Bruner goes on to say that it is it is through collaborations with teachers that children have access to the symbol systems and the technology of the culture. "And it is the right of every child to have equal access to these resources" (p. 68). Activating the right to access literacy will inaugurate possibilities for perpetuation the American dream and forge hope for full lives of all of the children in the United States.

References

Ainley, M. & Hidi, S. (2014). Interest and enjoyment. In R. Peckrun & L. Linnenbrink-Garcia (Eds.), *The international handbook of emotions in education* (pp. 205–227). New York: Taylor & Francis.

Berliner, D. C. & Glass, G.V. (2014). *50 myths and lies that threaten America's public schools: The real crisis in education*. New York: Teachers College Press.

Bruner, J. (1996). *The culture of education*. Cambridge, MA and London, England: Harvard University Press.

Crisp, G., Taggart, A., & Nora, A. (2015, June). Undergraduate Latino/a students: A systematic review of research identifying factors contributing to academic success outcomes. *Review of Educational Research.* 85(2), 249–274.

Denissen, J. H., Zarrett, N. R. & Eccles, J. S. (2007). "I like to do it, I am able, and I know I am": Longitudinal couplings between domain-specific achievement, self-concept, and interest. *Child Development,* 78(2), 430–447.

Guthrie, J. (2016). *The achievement gap in reading.* Presentation at the American Educational Research Association Conference. Washington, DC.

Hart, B. & Risley, T. (1995). *Meaningful differences in the everyday experience of young American children.* Baltimore, MD: Brookes.

Horner, B. & Olson, D. R. (1999). Literacy and children's conception of words. *Written Language & Literacy,* 2, 1 (28), 113–140.

Horowitz, R. & Samuels, S. J. (1985). Reading and listening to expository text. *Journal of Reading Behavior,* 17(3), 185–198.

Horowitz, R. (Ed.) (2007). *Talking texts: How speech and writing interact in school learning.* London and New York: Routledge/Taylor & Francis.

Horowitz, R. (2015). Oral language: The genesis and development of literacy for schooling and everyday life. In P. D. Pearson & E. H. Hiebert (Eds.), *Research-based practices for teaching common core literacy* (pp. 57–75). New York: Teachers College Press and Newark, Delaware: International Literacy Association.

Kim, Y. -S. (2015). Language and cognitive predictors of text comprehension: Evidence from multivariate analysis. *Child Development,* 86(1), 128–144.

Kim, Y. -S. (2016). Language as an entry point for improving literacy skills. AERA *Knowledge Forum. Research Fact Sheet.*

Lowenstein, G. (1994). The psychology of curiosity: A review and reinterpretation. *Psychology Bulletin.* 116(1), 75–98.

Mathis, W. J. & Trujillo, T. M. (Eds.). (2016). *Learning from the federal market-based reforms: Lessons for ESSA.* Charlotte, NC: Information Age Publishing.

McDonnell, L. M. & Weatherford, M. S. (2016). Recognizing the political in implementation research. *Educational Researcher,* 45, 233–242.

Moore, R. (2013). *Basil Bernstein: The thinker and the field.* New York and London: Routledge/Taylor & Francis.

Nell, V. (1988). *Lost in a book: The psychology of reading for pleasure.* New Haven, CT: Yale University Press.

Noguera, P. & Wing, J. Yonemura (Eds.). (2006). *Unfinished business: Closing the achievement gap in our schools*. San Francisco, CA: Jossey-Bass.

Ortar, G. (1966). Classification of speech directed at children by mothers of different levels of education and cultural background. Proceedings of the XVIII International Congress of Psychology Symposium. 31, Moscow: Nauka, 6, 22-25.

Ortar, G. (1971, March). *An experiment to improve disadvantaged mothers' speech directed at their small children*. Research Report to the Ford Foundation, Jerusalem: The Hebrew University.

Ravitch, D. (2010). *The life and death of the American school system: How testing and choice are undermining education*. New York: Basic Books.

Reardon, S. F. (2013). The widening income achievement gap. *Phi Delta Kappan*, 70(8), 10–16.

Renninger, K. A. & Hidi, S. E. (2016). *The power of interest for motivation and engagement*. New York: Routledge.

Searle, J. R. (1975). Indirect speech acts. In P. Cole & J. L. Morgan (Eds.). *Syntax and semantics*. Volume 3, *Speech acts*. New York: Academic Press.

Selingo, J. (2016). *2026, the decade ahead: The seismic shifts transforming the future of higher education*. Washington, DC: The Chronicle of Higher Education.

Spiro, R. & Tirre, W. C. (1980). Individual differences in schema utilization during discourse processing. *Journal of Educational Psychology*, 72(2), 204–208.

Stanovich, K. (1986). Matthew effects in reading: Some consequences of individual differences in the acquisition of literacy. *Reading Research Quarterly*, 21, 360–407.

Weisleder, A. & Fernald, A. (2013). Talking to children matters. *Psychological Science*, 24(11), 2143–2152.

AUTHOR INDEX

SUBJECT INDEX